User-Centered Design for First-Year Library Instruction Programs

USER-CENTERED DESIGN FOR FIRST-YEAR LIBRARY INSTRUCTION PROGRAMS

Cinthya M. Ippoliti and Rachel W. Gammons

Foreword by Joan Kaplowitz

 LIBRARIES
UNLIMITED™

An Imprint of ABC-CLIO, LLC

Santa Barbara, California • Denver, Colorado

Library of Congress Cataloging-in-Publication Data

Names: Ippoliti, Cinthya M. | Gammons, Rachel W.
Title: User-centered design for first-year library instruction programs /
    Cinthya M. Ippoliti and Rachel W. Gammons ; foreword by Joan Kaplowitz
Description: Santa Barbara, California : Libraries Unlimited, 2017. | Includes
    bibliographical references and index.
Identifiers: LCCN 2016032797 | ISBN 9781440838521 (paperback : alk. paper) |
    ISBN 9781440838538 (eBook)
Subjects: LCSH: Information literacy—Study and teaching (Higher).
Classification: LCC ZA3075 .I67 2017 | DDC 028.7071/1—dc23
LC record available at https://lccn.loc.gov/2016032797

ISBN: 978-1-4408-3852-1
EISBN: 978-1-4408-3853-8

21 20 19 18 17   1 2 3 4 5

This book is also available as an eBook.

Libraries Unlimited
An Imprint of ABC-CLIO, LLC

ABC-CLIO, LLC
130 Cremona Drive, P.O. Box 1911
Santa Barbara, California 93116-1911
www.abc-clio.com

This book is printed on acid-free paper ∞

Manufactured in the United States of America

CONTENTS

Contents

FOREWORD

It is often said that what we learn in school becomes obsolete almost as soon as we learn it. And that fact seems more true today than ever before. Think of all the changes that have occurred over the last five years in the ways in which we access, gather, and disseminate information. Now think about what you were sharing with your learners in your information literacy (IL) instruction offerings before all these changes occurred. Did you really prepare your learners from five years ago to deal with today's world? And did you consider the fact that learners' information needs become more sophisticated as they move through their academic careers and out into the world? Did your IL instruction enable your learners to deal with these changing needs and to cope with an ever-evolving information world? And is it even possible to do so?

The digital age has presented both challenges and opportunities, and once again librarians have stepped in to address these issues. As the world becomes more complex and information more plentiful, successfully navigating this information-rich landscape can become a frustrating and difficult endeavor. Information literacy instruction can supply the means by which our learners can survive and thrive in the current milieu. It can also prepare them for whatever is around the corner or down the block. If we have done our jobs well, our learners will embrace the new, secure in the knowledge that they are equipped to deal with whatever comes their way.

Teaching how to find information and critically evaluate what is found is still crucial to IL instruction. But now we must also address issues related to learners becoming creators and disseminators of information of their own making. Learners need to know how to be both researchers looking for others' ideas as well as information creators in their own right. The truly educated person of today is not someone who merely absorbs and regurgitates information on cue. He or she also wishes to create new information and then contribute that information to the knowledge base for all to use. Social media has provided us with an environment geared to sharing our ideas and experiences. It is only natural that our learners see little difference between social sharing and the sharing of their own thoughts, ideas, and research discoveries. But this creates even more challenges for the instruction librarian.

Does your current information literacy instruction address all of these complex issues and challenges? Furthermore, how do the individual elements of your IL instruction endeavors fit together? Do the individual parts mesh into a coherent whole? Will learners who are exposed to your instruction leave your care as truly information-literate individuals? To answer these questions, you must take a step back and examine the overall impact of your instruction. In other words, you need to look at your instruction from the programmatic perspective.

But time is a precious commodity. While we all agree that programmatic planning is important, when can we make room in our already busy schedules to do all the work program planning requires? However, if we do not address this bigger picture, we are doing our learners a disservice. No matter how good each individual class, workshop, or course might be, if we are only addressing learners' current needs without also preparing them to grow into more competent and sophisticated information consumers and creators, we are not doing the best job we can do. We must make sure our instruction is contributing to our learners' continual development as information-literate individuals. We must get them ready to cope with both current and future information needs. And we must ensure we are preparing them for all the inevitable changes in the information landscape that are sure to come.

To truly adopt this broader view, IL instruction must also evolve. As a response to this changing information landscape, the Association of College and Research Libraries (ACRL) has developed their new *Framework for Information Literacy for Higher Education*. Perhaps you followed its evolution; you might even have been involved in its creation by submitting reactions and comments during the process. But now that it has been released, you might be wondering how the *Framework* impacts you and your instruction programs. You might be worried that its adoption means a complete revamping of the ways in which you approach information literacy instruction. And you would be quite right to be concerned. The *Framework* does represent a new and different way of viewing information literacy. If you wish to continue to offer the best possible type of IL instruction (and I know you do), you are obliged to examine the impact this document has on your own practice.

Are you beginning to feel overwhelmed and anxious? I assure you that you are not alone. Instruction librarians everywhere are struggling with the same pressures you are, trying to find the energy and the time to both examine their current IL instruction practices and also explore ways to align those practices with those outlined in and recommended by ACRL's *Framework*.

The *Framework* starts from the premise that what learners need to know keeps getting more complex and sophisticated in our ever-changing and evolving information-rich and information-dependent world. Its overall aim is to help us support our learners' current needs and to supply them with the means to cope with whatever might come their way in the future. A laudable goal, but now what? How do we as instruction librarians respond to this new document? How do we go about continually expanding and refocusing our instruction given the still-prevalent constrictions under which most instruction librarians continue to operate? It seems like a daunting and maybe impossible task. But books like the one you are currently holding can help. The authors, Ippoliti and Gammons, have not only acknowledged the problems faced by instruction librarians today but have graciously chosen to share their ideas with you, the reader.

Based on their own experiences and expertise, Ippoliti and Gammons offer practical tips, techniques, and examples of good information literacy instruction practices in the *Framework* era. They provide realistic guidance on how to align your instruction with current trends and conversations in both information literacy and higher education in order to ensure your instruction remains relevant in an ever-evolving information landscape. The topics covered may not be new (needs assessment, active learning, outreach to and partnering with faculty, etc.), but they are examined through the lens provided by ACRL's *Framework*.

Being well aware that it is often difficult or even impossible to "do it all," the authors suggest ways to help you identify where you need to concentrate your efforts. They urge you to reflect on all your current IL instruction practices and identify what you need to change, modify, or adapt in order to help your learners develop into information-literate individuals who can succeed not only in their academic pursuits but also throughout their lives. So do not despair. And do not give up. Use the advice offered in this book to help you on your journey. Start small if necessary, and do what you can. Make changes and then build on those changes. You may not be able to do everything overnight. Be realistic, but remain optimistic. It might take a while, but you will reach your goal if you stay focused and dedicated to creating the best information literacy instruction possible for your learners. And isn't that what we are all aiming for?

Joan Kaplowitz, PhD, MLIS
UCLA Librarian Emerita
Transform Your Teaching
Joankaplowitz.com
joan@joankaplowitz.com

INTRODUCTION

What separates an "instruction librarian" from a librarian who participates in instruction? The "program." Instruction programs focus on general education courses that involve large numbers of students and standardized curriculums and are frequently taught by graduate student instructors or adjunct faculty. Depending on the institution, an instruction program could run the entire two-year or four-year curriculum, or it could begin and end with the core first-year courses. But it is always larger, more complex, and less discrete than the work of a specific department or campus unit. Instruction librarians are the kind of people who build mountains out of air. With limited staff and resources, we create programs for hundreds (sometimes thousands) of students, while carrying large instruction and reference loads. The work is hard and often, too often, thankless.

As authors, each of us has gone through the process of building or maintaining an instruction program: both alone and as part of a team, under budgetary strain and with limited resources. We understand the struggle. This book is intended to offer the insight and support that can be difficult to find in a single institution. What do you do when you are the only instruction person at an institution, the head of a department, or part of a large instructional team? How do you collaborate with colleagues? How do you develop assessments and teaching outlines? How do you keep the big picture in mind when you are mired in the daily details of the program? We hope the discussions in this book will help with the practical tools you need to get started or make changes.

STRUCTURE OF THE BOOK

We have divided our discussion into six parts: Curriculum, Assessment, Teaching, Outreach, Staffing, and Spaces. Each of these is a lens through which you can view an instruction program. Rather than serving as discrete stages, these lenses are intended to operate not only as individual perspectives but also as unified and important discussions about the nature of instructional planning in a time of budgetary and personnel strain. We hope that these perspectives offer a way to break down the enormous work of programmatic development and oversight into discrete concepts, allowing you to simplify and compartmentalize.

Part 1: Design

- Curriculum: This means thinking programmatically about information literacy instruction—in other words, approaching a series of disparate instruction sessions and outreach efforts as a complete and thoughtful sequence. This is the basis of any instruction program.
- Assessment: Assessment is often tacked on at the end of instructional design as a way to evaluate success. Our discussion will approach assessment as an integral part of development and design. We argue that ongoing assessment improves an instruction program by creating a continuous feedback loop that encourages innovation and growth.

Part 2: Implementation

- Teaching: This is the crux of the instruction program, including scaffolding content and professional development. Teaching activities will set the tone of the program and tie all of the elements together into a cohesive vision for student learning.
- Outreach: Librarians are increasingly called to collaborate with colleagues (in and out of the library) to create programs and further services. Outreach explores not only the work it takes to keep an instructional program up and running but also how to continue growing and improving your practice.

Part 3: Administration

- Staffing: Here we discuss the personnel side of instruction programs—the labor, time, organization, and administration of programmatic oversight.
- Spaces: Instructional programs are inevitably shaped by the spaces in which they take place (be that online or in person). Spaces explores the impact of space on pedagogy, but also the management and administration of classroom spaces, which often fall to instruction librarians.

CASE STUDIES

At the end of each chapter, we have included one or more case studies contributed by practicing librarians from academic libraries both big and small. These short, reflective sections demonstrate how the ideas inherent in the lenses manifest themselves in our day-to-day work. While the chapters speak in generalizations, the case studies explore tangible aspects of an instructional program, from staffing shortages to curricular challenges, community colleges to research institutions, the case study authors have graciously shared their experiences. Their stories are familiar while also maintaining their individuality. We hope that they give you an opportunity to reflect, either as an individual or with your colleagues. To that end, we have provided a reflection question at the end of each case study. Use these as a launching point to (what we hope will be) a meaningful discussion. We hope you find as much joy in reading them as we have had collecting them.

USER-CENTERED DESIGN

The second goal of our book is to frame the process of programmatic develop-ment within the context of user-centered design (UCD). Like programmatic design, UCD is cyclical and evolutionary, involving the repeated interrogation and improvement of a system. We have kept a user-centered or learner-centered focus at the heart of each of our lenses, embedding each with a focus not only on us—as designers, librarians, and administrators—but also our users, as the ultimate goal and purpose for the programs.

UCD has its roots firmly planted in the world of usability testing and has tra-ditionally stemmed from a web design perspective, but in recent times this has expanded to include the entire user experience, which doesn't always occur in an online environment but can run the gamut of everything from interactions at a service point to using the website to place an interlibrary loan request.

User-centered design keeps the needs of users at the forefront by incorporating various mechanisms of soliciting needs and feedback. To implement it, we follow similar steps to those used in instructional service design: identifying the user base, maintaining an awareness of requirements, designing creative solutions, and con-tinuously evaluating and updating the product. If this sounds familiar, it should!

Moving into the realm of designing an instructional program, each of these con-cepts are broken into several components:

- In order to think about users, or in this case learners, you must first identify the problem you want to solve. Are you hoping to increase their understanding of how to use the library, or how to become better researchers? If you don't know why you're helping students and what you're helping them do, your program won't be very useful for either side, and you could find yourself being left out of instruction requests and feeling disconnected from the very groups (e.g., writing, composition) that you're trying to collaborate with and support.

- Once that crucial initial element is in place, you can follow the basic progression mentioned above of designing the solutions to help you address the problem or learning challenge, implementing and testing them, and evaluating them. These are the building blocks of curricular design, and they will allow you to step back from your current perspective to think holistically about what you are doing, why you are doing it, and how you can do it better.

- Building from the user experience side of UCD, you would typically specify what the goals are for improving a website as you undergo the creation process. For example, you might say that one goal is to increase the visibility of your website. If we switch over to our instructional context, those very same goals serve as your learning outcomes. Just as you would specify that one measure of increased visibility is higher traffic to the site, so you would develop your assessment strategy for measuring the effectiveness of a specific component or even the overall success of your program.

- Finally, you will want to think carefully about your content strategy (curriculum, pedagogy, assessment) as well as your capital strategy (staff, workflow, policies). Ask yourself what content you need to successfully meet your core learning outcomes and how this content will be organized, prioritized, and delivered. Similarly, how will your capital strategies support the life cycle of your program through the logistical details of effectuating your plan? And how will you relate the goals and activities of your program to that of the larger institutional context in which they reside?

Throughout each of the conversations, we have interwoven the state of the higher education and information literacy landscape, including the ongoing transition from the Association of College and Research Libraries *Information Literacy Competency Standards* to the *Framework for Information Literacy*. As librarians, the environment in which we operate inherently informs our work. Our instruction programs are intellectual embodiments of the professional conversation surrounding research and learning. We hope to enter into that conversation not as experts but as fellow librarians, doing our best to make it work with what we've got.

Part I

DESIGN

We begin with the logistics of creating the content of your program. This section details the decisions you will have to make regarding what to cover and how to determine its effectiveness. As part of this process, you will answer the "how" portion of the design process, thinking through the scope, scale, and assessment processes your program will contain. This is also a good time to think globally about the entire program and how it will fit in with broader national conversations and your own library and institutional efforts.

Chapter 1

CURRICULUM

CHAPTER OBJECTIVES

- Explore strategies for engaging in the curriculum development process (goals, content, scope, format, and scalability).
- Analyze both the theoretical and practical elements of curriculum design.
- Transition the approach to information literacy from a concept covered in class to a design methodology.

INTRODUCTION

While Bibliographic Instruction has been a mission of the academic library since the early 20th century, it was not until the introduction of information literacy (IL) in the 1960s and 1970s that librarians began to consider the integration of library skills into the academic curriculum (Ariew, 2014). Susan Ariew describes this as the movement from the collections-focused academic library to a teaching library. "The teaching library described in 1979 . . . embraced a stronger teaching role than was mentioned in any of the prior discussions . . . this role included evaluation of instructional programs and activities, as well as recommendations for curriculum analysis to determine where bibliographic instruction would be most needed" (212). Although the instruction programs of the 1970s and 1980s emphasized IL concepts, such as lifelong learning, it was not until the 1990s that IL came into its own (Bawden, 2001). Through the early 1990s to the 2000s, IL continued to grow in popularity and was eventually concretized in 2000 with the introduction of the Association of College and Research Libraries (ACRL) *Information Literacy Competency Standards for Higher Education*. Intended to support the development of the skills needed to "find, retrieve, analyze, and use information," the IL standards prioritized access over the creation of information and focused on the ability to negotiate a complex information ecosystem to achieve a desired result rather than on the interactions with that environment.

Although the importance of IL within the profession has continued to develop, the concept in itself has remained a "moving target" (Ariew, 2014). In addition to spanning the depth and breadth of an evolving information economy, IL is being pulled into the larger conversation about the purpose of higher education. As a result of these changing expectations, IL is also experiencing a shift within higher education. In addition to preparing students to effectively navigate a particular library system, IL is becoming part of a larger context that strives to provide students with all the necessary skills and knowledge to become successful in their academic work as well as their future career paths. Today, library instruction and IL programs are often the linchpins of library connections to student success. Featuring not only sophisticated instructional techniques but also a wide variety of technologies, approaches, and formats, instruction programs guide students through information, meta, and digital literacy concepts.

Within the information profession, this is best illustrated in the recent release of the ACRL *Framework for Information Literacy for Higher Education* (2015). In addition to presenting a more robust definition of IL, the *Framework* focuses on students' personal relationship with IL, effectively dissolving the notion of IL as a discrete set of skills and embracing it as an iterative and lifelong journey. Although currently the *Framework* exists in tandem with the standards, it is expected to eventually replace the document to become the overarching guidelines for IL in academic libraries.

While the foundations of library instruction continue to evolve, institutional environments are also calling for agility, adaptability, and innovation on a scale never seen before. Gone are the days of pointing to the standards as the guiding mantra for both pedagogy and assessment and counting on administrators and faculty to accept them as de facto indicators of excellence. Academic librarians can no longer rely on the idea that teaching students something, *anything*, is better than nothing at all. Current best practices seek to broaden and redefine the research experience for students by supporting them along the entire duration of their journey: from identifying their initial need to the creation of the final product of their work, whether it is a paper, presentation, or other form of output. If the profession is to truly engage in the scholarly conversation, it needs to be attuned to the changing landscape of the scholarly environment, especially where students are now faced with new forms of authorship as they curate, repurpose, and share digital information. This poses new challenges in helping them develop the skills to engage in digital inquiry by selecting and analyzing reliable digital tools and seeking out mentors and experts. By initiating and expanding upon these opportunities, librarians and administrators are able to meet students' increasingly complex and changing needs in a proactive and informed manner. If leveraged appropriately, this transition will allow for a shift in thinking and greater opportunities to provide students with academic experiences that will prepare them to meet their future goals.

Although the conversations around IL in higher education continue to evolve, for librarians on the ground floor, the lofty intentions of the *Framework* do not always translate into a concise working strategy, particularly for those who coordinate first-year programming. Unlike traditional subject specialists or liaisons, first-year librarians deal with a much larger and more varied incoming class. First-year students are often undecided in their majors, sharing few academic or personal commonalities beyond their moment of entry. Equipping these students to become responsible information producers and consumers is a tall order for even the most prepared of institutions, let alone those that are struggling with staffing and resources, as most are. Having a solid content strategy is imperative to building a robust program that can serve the needs of hundreds to thousands of incoming students while also sustaining a realistic understanding of how the program functions.

You will have to consider how to transition from IL as a concept that's taught in a class to designing a methodology that underpins your entire program. This runs counter to our usual approach, which includes trying to squeeze everything into one session. You will now have to think in the opposite way and stretch out the various outcomes and skills involved across time and groups of learners in order to take advantage of that programmatic point of view. In addition, you will begin to think of IL as an undercurrent rather than the star attraction so that you can mold it into what you want it to be as opposed to letting it dictate what's covered, when, and how. Librarians often work so hard to make a perfect home for all those threshold concepts when they'd be better off determining what can be jettisoned and if it really makes sense to cover something at that particular time (regardless of what the faculty member thinks is best simply because it's always been done that way). These are difficult conversations and require listening to that often ignored, but very knowledgeable, voice inside of you that knows what to do.

DEVELOPING AN IL CURRICULUM

For the purposes of this book, a "program" is an interconnected series of one-shot class offerings and online learning objects, as opposed to a single, or small series, of one-shot session(s). In other words, we are thinking *programmatically* at a level that encompasses all of the students within a given cohort. In addition, the content and methods described will assume application to a large number of students, making their structure designed to work on a broad scale, not a one-time subject-specific course. For the purposes of this chapter, we are using freshman composition as our primary example. These courses are often required for many, if not all, incoming students and have multiple sections per semester.

We also wish to contextualize our definition of curriculum design. The goal of this section is to enable you to step back and think through your motivations for developing or refining your IL program. Go back to the basics of what curriculum design is and consider how you can apply the concepts of design within your own institutional context. When thinking about your IL program, you must take into consideration several factors of design, discussed in the following sections.

Program Rationale

Before you start planning your program, take a moment to ask yourself *why* you are creating the program. While this might sound obvious, this important question is frequently overlooked. Many times, you skip over the "why" and move straight to the "what." *What* do you want students to know at the end of our cutting-edge, innovative, and amazing instruction program? For those with experience teaching one-shot sessions, this is second nature. However, when you move from a single session to a comprehensive program, those measurable and discrete outcomes become less focused. While a one-shot session might empower students to effectively integrate sources into their writing, a program looks at the curriculum as a congruous set of events. Rather than preparing students for an assignment, a program *equips students for a lifetime of IL*. To grapple with such a large and ambiguous outcome, you have to have a plan. Be prepared to articulate everything, from the goals to how and when the instruction itself will be delivered, how learning is assessed, and what that means for the library and the university as a whole. But before you can begin any of that, you have to understand why.

Needs Assessment

The first step toward identifying the "why" is to conduct a needs assessment on campus. Although needs assessments are often used in service-based models, such as resource access and sharing, it can be a helpful tool for any type of program design. In their research on scholarly communication, Megan Bresnahan and Andrew Johnson (2013) describe their needs-based assessment of faculty members as "a way for the individuals who will participate in training to influence the design of the prioritization process." As an instructional designer, gathering the input of your community allows you to base the "why" of your program on data rather than conjecture.

Needs assessment for IL instruction can take many forms: informal conversations with library faculty and staff, focus groups with campus partners, or qualitative surveys distributed to stakeholders. The important thing is that at the end of your assessment, you (1) have a better understanding of what your student population needs to be successful, and (2) are able to effectively demonstrate that need to your administrators.

If you already have an IL program in place, a needs assessment gives you an opportunity to reassess the effectiveness of your program. It will allow you to realign any portions that have fallen out of sync with changes in other programs' curricula, vision, and even staffing. A new director or faculty member can often make a world of difference in how a department approaches things, which might mean that you will have to adapt as well. If you don't have a program in place yet, the needs assessment will provide a much-needed reality check and prevent you from making wrong assumptions. While reading the literature and seeing what other institutions are doing is a great way to find ideas, they might not always work for your environment. For example, if a small college has a required English course in which students must complete a research project, it might be fairly easy for you to become a critical part of that course due to the close working relationship you can establish with faculty and perhaps the discrete number of sections you to work with. At larger institutions, however, this might prove more challenging as you grapple with tens of adjuncts and hundreds of sections, and you might not be able to achieve the same individualized approach. But you won't know any of these things until you talk with the program coordinators and determine what they need and what they think the students need.

Assessment? Who's Got Time for Assessment?

You have an entire IL program to build or rebuild. Take it from two people who learned it the hard way: this is the part where you need to slow down. You can build the most amazing program with the most innovative instructional tools, but if it doesn't solve a problem or fill a gap on your campus, chances are it will not be as successful.

Your needs assessment will be specific to your campus community and will depend entirely on how much time and support you have to conduct it. Think about what you need to know to build your program, the amount and type of data that you can realistically tackle, and what the hot-button issues are on your campus. Then, create an assessment that will yield the type of data that administrators will respect. Does your administration value informal feedback, or are they numbers driven? In what format will administrators be most receptive to the information—a report or a presentation? It might feel premature to consider the final format of your results, but if your needs assessment does not give you what you need to be successful, what's the point?

Here are some things to consider as you plan your assessment:

- One size might not fit all. Rather than attempting to tackle the entire faculty population in one survey, consider creating smaller assessments for target areas. While 10-question surveys might work well for the English 101 instructors, it could be that 20 minutes in a department meeting with the communications faculty will yield more useful information.

- Your call for participation in a survey, questionnaire, or focus group will carry more weight if it comes from someone that the faculty knows and respects. Whenever possible, try to get a department chair, program director, head of a department, or anyone whose title includes the word "dean" to distribute the assessment on your behalf.

- When dealing with academic faculty, gentle subterfuge is encouraged. If you receive less than stellar responses, consider reframing your message or offering a small prize. You could also send personalized messages to those from whom you most hope to hear as a way to indicate that you really, really, want them to respond without actually saying that. You'd be amazed how much weight the term "very important person" carries when applied in this context. If all else fails, think about switching your methods and opt for a meeting, interview, or simply going out for lunch.

If the data you are collecting will enable you to lobby effectively for the budget, space, staff, and time that your program needs, go forth and conquer. If not, consider what might make your curriculum plan "sticky," meaning that it will have traction and garner some attention. Target the type of data that will be the most impactful for your stakeholders, and then perform the minimum necessary to gather the information that you need in the format that will get your program to the place it needs to be. If you are organizing first-year programming at your library, you do not have lots of time. You are most likely overworked and understaffed and attempting to serve hundreds or thousands of students, probably by yourself. Stay targeted. Stay concise. Stay purposeful.

PROGRAM COMPONENTS

Once you have your rationale in place, you will need to clearly articulate your vision for the program, which is comprised of the elements discussed below.

Anticipated Skills and Abilities

Essentially, this is a list of your learning outcomes. Why is it important to have this list? First, it shows your colleagues and students what the program values and measures. It is a tangible representation of what you hope to accomplish and ultimately what you would like the students to accomplish as well.

It also provides a roadmap for students to self-assess. Too often librarians think of outcomes as a secret not to be shared with anyone. When you include students in the learning process by telling them why you are teaching them the concepts and skills covered, they will give you more buy-in and support. They can then better monitor their own progress and identify when they need assistance.

The list of anticipated skills and abilities helps focus and organize your teaching. Keeping your end goal in mind can help ground your activities and structure the learning so that you can support students along the entire journey. You can now build a roadmap that not only details where you are headed with your program but will also show you how to get there and what the benchmarks are along the way.

Target learners and skill levels—if you are to concentrate on the learner, then knowing what that learner already knows is a crucial step to achieving a well-rounded IL program. This information will help you determine several things: what to include in your program, at what point during the students' first year it should be offered, and how to present it. It will also allow you to set goals for what you want students to know when they are finished with the program—whether it comes at the end of a particular semester or year or at the end of their academic journey within the institution itself. In addition, it's important to have a clear vision of what you want students to achieve. If you don't know how you can improve student learning and to what end, what's the point and value of your program? Develop a clear and well-articulated idea that you can use to market and forge partnerships.

Scope (Range of Content to Be Covered)

This is another element of curriculum design that is very institution specific. A good way to think about how much content needs to be covered at each step is to create a curriculum map that visualizes all of the instructional touch points students might experience as they complete their degrees. What are the courses in which students are likely to receive instruction? Are there specific research-based courses that students often encounter later in their studies? Are there general education courses that have a high student enrollment? Rather than focusing on the courses where your library has already successfully integrated instruction, try to focus on the moments where it makes sense objectively. Are there opportunities that you haven't leveraged? Are there redundancies that should be scaled back? From there, where do your responsibilities begin and end? Should a first-year instruction program include an introductory speech course that includes both freshmen and sophomores? These questions will be specific to your institution and library. It will depend on your staffing, your student population, and your ability to force your colleagues into participating in your programming (just kidding, kind of).

Thinking through these concepts will help you to assess the progression you want the students to experience, and it will help you decide where your program ends and more discipline-specific instruction takes over. For example, you might want first-year students to be able to appreciate that new information and data are constantly being produced and that there is always more to learn. As they move into their third year, students might recognize a need for information and data to achieve a specific end and define limits to the information need. Finally, as seniors, they might understand the scale of the world of published and unpublished information and data. So you can see that it doesn't always make sense to cover the dissemination of information at a first-year level, because it is outside your scope of responsibilities within the program you are creating. It might fit in very well, however, within a more advanced capstone or research methods course where seniors and graduate students are learning about how the research they conduct will be shared in a scholarly context.

Scaffolding

Scaffolding is the order in which content is covered and how the skills are addressed at each level of the program. Scaffolding is not a new idea, but it can be a difficult concept nonetheless. There are two levels of scaffolding that need to be taken into account: (1) within the program itself, and (2) in the way the first-year program relates to the upper-level or subject-specific instruction that follows.

Scaffolding within the program

Even if you are teaching a one-time session and never plan to see the students again, there is some element of scaffolding involved, even at the consultation level. This is even more important if there are any follow-up sessions or online content built into the proposed program. Scaffolding is not about piling on as much content as you can; it is about strategically determining the progression a student will take through the program and what the learning goals are at each stop. Scaffolding forces us, as designers, to think through each of the basic elements of the program and decide when they should occur and how the next level will be reached.

If you are lucky enough to be working with a standardized syllabus for a large-scale course, such as English 101, making a roadmap that is literally mapped onto the course syllabus is a great way to start. Knowing when students have each assignment and what the requirements are at each step will help you develop your own curriculum. So how can you tell? Again, this is largely dependent on your institutional context. Is your program limited to one-shot sessions, where you won't have the opportunity to see students again? This is the worst-case scenario, but there are still a couple of scaffolding options:

- Use online content as much as possible, keeping in mind that the goal is not to substitute quantity for quality. Focus on what students need to know before and after your session, knowing that they might never contact you. The scaffolded online content has to serve two separate purposes—both introduction and assessment—and still be able to stand on its own, book-ending your face-to-face session. You can also build in assessment to see how much students absorbed and applied this layered knowledge you've provided.
- Rely on the faculty member to scaffold the content for you. Most classes build on the content as they go along. Seldom do first-year students have a big paper due at the end of the semester without additional smaller assignments in between designed to get them to that final project. Working with the faculty member to reinforce the concepts you covered and perhaps introduce more advanced searching techniques or tools might make for a better approach than nothing at all. Scaffolding does not have to be all within the context of your instruction and can evolve organically within the course itself. In fact, having this content embedded as part of each assignment is better than several ill-timed sessions that don't connect to what the students are working on for class.

If you are lucky enough to be in a position to provide more than one session to students, your task has become much easier. One way to tackle scaffolding in this version is to provide a pre/post assessment for students and have some type of homework in between. How does this accomplish your scaffolding goals? First, the assessment allows you to get a benchmark of your starting point, which will help you determine where to begin. Students already know about Boolean operators? Great! Give them something more advanced in class (hence the scaffolding). Students have never heard of Boolean operators? Time to slow down and begin with the basics. Having something in the middle of the program is also useful because it lets you gauge where students are on the path you set forth for them. If you think they are ready to move on to advanced searching techniques, why not confirm this by assigning a brief exercise they can turn in before the next session? If most of them got it, you might just want to provide feedback for those who didn't. If most of them didn't, it might be that they are not yet ready to build on what you covered and repetition is necessary. This method requires some degree of flexibility, which is needed as the program grows and develops.

Because you are working with a learner-centric model, you might have to adapt to things midstream or make unanticipated changes. Be sure to leave room for ambiguity, trial and error, and even failure within your program. Chart out several "what if" scenarios so that you are prepared to implement them depending on how things go. You can always add or take away elements without compromising the program structure if you plan ahead to do so. Don't make assessment or activities so rigid that one change will destroy all of the other efforts. Think of your approach as an organic process that can be adapted if needed. For example, if students are struggling with a survey question, rewrite it and resubmit the assessment. If no one understood how Boolean operators work, you might have to cut out the section in class where you show them three databases and just focus on one, taking the time to cover their questions instead. Scaffolding is not about creating a perfect program or class outline; it's largely about being able to work within the natural progression of how students learn and change throughout the program.

Scaffolding beyond the program

Scaffolding beyond the first-year program becomes even more challenging because pedagogical control is no longer within the purview of first-year programs as instruction moves into upper level and subject specific areas and therefore out of your immediate reach. It is important to have a conversation with those teaching more advanced classes to determine how this scaffolding might work. Curriculum mapping can help the group ascertain at what points and to what degree students are being exposed to IL concepts so that efforts can be combined and presented cohesively. It might also make sense to look at each discipline separately with the first-year program as the starting point for all students and then determine where they encounter these concepts as they progress through their various discipline-specific courses. Or perhaps it makes sense to look at students collectively as a cohort and try to identify what skills they need at what points in their academic career regardless of their discipline. This is more challenging for a variety of reasons: Not all students begin and finish their degree at the same time; therefore, you are dealing with a variable that will never be stabilized. Retention and graduation rates are a focus of higher education efforts at the moment, and this might be a way to increase those numbers and actually understand how research skills and IL can help keep students on the right course. At this stage, consider having a conversation with your institutional effectiveness office and entities such as a graduate college or other similar organizations on campus to determine how you could chart and embed these competencies at key points of students' academic path, regardless of what school or college they are part of. Perhaps you can simply target a specific group, such as teaching assistants, or work this part into something like a dissertation/thesis process where all students who want to graduate must fulfill some requirements that can be more easily controlled and managed.

A way to tackle this progression is to think more broadly than face-to-face sessions and perhaps discuss the possibility of a credit-bearing course, tutorial, or other method of delivering content independent of discipline. However, it could be that you decide, especially at the university level, that in-depth subject-specific instruction is still needed. Within this model, you can still provide enough flexibility so that the general concepts that are becoming more advanced work in parallel with course- or subject-specific instruction. Ask yourself what do all students need to know at x point in their academic development and determine how to best answer that question with a combination of general and more discipline-specific instruction.

Curriculum mapping is the tool of choice for this activity. Curriculum mapping refers to a process where you can identify at what points in a student's career within your institution IL should be integrated. One way to begin this analysis is to determine where it is already included, if it is. This will help you fill in the gaps and decide where to go next. This process largely operates on a perfect-world level, knowing that you might not be able to embed IL into every course at every level, but it can give you a place to start having conversations with those departments on campus where the courses might fall. In addition, curriculum mapping can help you chart the progression students would ideally go through in terms of acquiring skills at key points in their scholarly development and what those skills are.

A final or capstone course might also assist with this effort and can draw a comparison between assessments that are done at the first-year level with those completed at this end point. For reliability and validity of data, ensure you have a steady cohort of students and that the same students are going through this assessment. This is difficult, but it can provide important information about how students are getting exposed to IL, to what degree concepts are retained and applied along this continuum, and how students are doing in their classes as a result. This is obviously a much longer-term and larger-scale project to undertake, but it might be worthwhile to provide a complete picture of student success and the library's role in contributing to that success.

Here are some additional challenges and decision factors you might wish to take into consideration:

- *Articulation with the other program(s) with which you are working.* For example, most, if not all, universities have English or some other type of introductory-level course that intersects with your IL program. In this case, it makes sense to ensure your program is aligned with the goals and outcomes of the course. For example, if a goal of the course is for students to understand how to cite properly, but you do not cover that as part of your instruction, program faculty will wonder what the library can offer that the department itself cannot. By making sure that you are on the same page as the program or course, you can not only demonstrate the value of library instruction but also your program can grow and develop alongside the one you are partnering with.
- *Level of faculty buy-in.* Faculty buy-in affects the level of engagement within the program. It won't help for you to have a perfect model of instruction that requires three in-person sessions and additional homework if the faculty teaching the course only wants to give up one class session. Some faculty might not even be

aware that any approach other than that "typical" 50- or 75-minute brain dump is available, so starting small, building trust, and showing results might be more helpful than trying to convince someone that design thinking is the best thing since sliced bread (even if it is). Other chapters will address how to overcome this issue and will provide some ideas for effectively reaching out to faculty and gaining their cooperation.

- *Internal resources and staffing levels as well as opportunities for external support.* You must know ahead of time who is available to assist and what, if any, funding or additional resources you have at your disposal. On the one hand, if you are the only librarian teaching first-year instruction, that will greatly affect how you structure the program as you will not be able to teach hundreds of sections or see students individually. If, on the other hand, you have several librarians and student assistants, the possibility to provide more in-depth support will shape how you approach your curriculum.

In addition, you must think about the benchmarks of success for your learners. In other words, how will you assess that students have mastered the learning outcomes of the program? You must evaluate both the overall structure of the program itself as well as the learners within it.

Scalability

Scalability presents another seemingly insurmountable challenge. The purpose of creating a student-centered program is that it will give each student as much individual attention as possible. Multiply that by 500 or 1,000 or 4,000, and you are suddenly faced with a nearly impossible task. Did your multiplication include an influx of staff members? If not, you are not alone. The luckiest of us are blessed with a small team of librarians or staff members. If you are attempting to accomplish this Herculean task by yourself, fear not. Here are a few strategies to help you cope:

Don't be afraid to start out small. Piloting a new program or approach is the best way to see if something will work out. You might have an easier time convincing faculty to participate and administrators to support a cheap, small project that only involves you and another person as opposed to something that requires the entire IT department to write a new program or buy an expensive tool or resource. If you don't have the cooperation of your fellow librarians, don't sweat it. Pilot something you can manage yourself and use your success to demand support.

Fail quickly. For the sake of argument, let's say that out of the five sections of English 101 that piloted your new approach, none of your students demonstrated an improved understanding of how authority is contextual. Buck up, cowgirl. That's a lot better than launching your program full scale and having none of the students in 100 sections of ENG 101 understand the concept. You now have the opportunity to improve your approach and target your content.

Failure is success delayed. After your pilot, you will be armed with knowledge— knowledge about the clarity and effectiveness of your approach and the insight to know what is not going to work. Don't be afraid to report these failures and how you recovered. Thoughtful failure and recovery shows that you are aware of the limitations of the program as much as its benefits.

Build a coalition for success. Not every faculty member who teaches a freshman composition course has to be part of your pilot. Identify who the early adopters might be and get them excited about the idea. Working with a smaller group is often more manageable, not only because there are fewer of you who have to agree but also because it gives you opportunities to try multiple ideas and get feedback from a body of individuals who have a vested interest in your success. Use these innovators as your ambassadors, so when the time comes to have a broader conversation, they can help you explain how well the model worked for them and why it should be expanded.

Celebrate small victories. Friend, you are traveling a lonely trail. Be kind to yourself and to your ideas. If the majority of the students did not complete the amazing assignment you handed out in class, don't let the haters get you down. Focus on the students that did complete the assignment. Focus on the information learned. Use those results to convince your faculty champions to assign extra credit next time. Above all, do not be ashamed at a less-than-perfect outcome. You are one person. Share your small sample with your stakeholders and focus on what you can prove, the changes that you are able to make.

But what happens if you tried doing all of these things and at the end of the day you still do not have enough resources to implement your program on a large scale? First, appreciate that this is not a problem that you alone are facing. It is endemic among academic libraries of all shapes and sizes. Take a moment for self-pity. Honestly, this cannot be underrated. Buy yourself a deeply unhealthy latte from the library coffee shop that has subsumed the entire identity of your library in the eyes of your undergraduates. Take a few long minutes and just indulge in feeling sorry for yourself. Then, channel your inner Tim Gunn and make it work.

Here are a few things to think about.

Train the faculty themselves. Putting aside any judgment about how this might undermine the complexity of what librarians do, let's just all agree upfront that training the faculty is not an ideal solution. In a perfect world, you would have a team of enthusiastic and willing librarians who had the time to devote to teaching each aspect of your programming. If you are enjoying the spoils of a perfect world, this might be a viable option. However, keep in mind that academic faculty might not be open to this revolutionary idea. They are busy managing constantly expanding class sizes. They have also spent many years training themselves in how to conduct research in their field and might be resistant to the idea that they should be retrained in how to teach IL to first-year students. Again, start small, recruit a few champions, and go from there.

If you are working with a population of adjunct instructors, training them might be an option worth pursuing. These members often teach heavier loads than traditional academic faculty. They rarely receive the type of orientation to campus that permanent faculty do. Sometimes they are graduate students who are navigating the complexities of doctoral research in conjunction with teaching first-year students about scholarly research and would benefit from learning about your library resource and services. Next steps would include: (1) identifying the target skills or concepts that the faculty-trainees need to be successful, (2) creating a programmatic approach to the training, and (3) identifying how the trainees can help you assess the effectiveness of this approach, be it through reflection on their own experiences or examples of student work that shows an improvement in quality. This approach does require that you relinquish some control over how this will work in the classroom. Critics might contend that this de-emphasizes the role of the librarian in the student learning process. Agreed. But perhaps creating a robust training for faculty will enable you to devote more time to developing strong partnerships and might improve your chances of having a stronger voice in assignment creation and evaluation and ultimately curricular design.

Think about the most relevant elements of the program and focus on developing those areas. If you do not have enough library support to make sense of thousands of points of qualitative data, a quantitative survey might be the smarter option. If you really want to integrate a for-credit assignment into the curriculum but don't have the faculty support, it might make more sense to focus on a shorter, in-session activity. Three in-person sessions would be ideal, but what if two of those sessions were conducted asynchronously online and robustly assessed? Your challenges will vary based on your institution. They might appear early in your program or wait in silence until you try to implement your ideas on a large scale. Try to keep perspective on your side. First-year programs are not meant to give students all of the tools they will use for the rest of their academic careers and beyond. They are the foundation.

Think about what needs to be covered in person versus online. Online tools give you the ability to present content independently of staffing or resources. There are many free tools that can help with content delivery, assessment, and interactivity. The ratio of face-to-face and online components will also vary by institution and will be dictated not only by the size of your first-year program but also by such factors as access to course management systems, web-based tools and their costs, and access to adequate support. If your IT department cannot assist you, you will obviously be limited to the tools you can use and maintain on your own. The most important question still remains, however: Does this concept have to be covered in person? If the answer is no, you know where you can begin to make cuts.

Partner with anyone who can help, and offer experience as the benefit as opposed to pay. On the simpler side, recruit students to participate in a training program so that at the end of their tenure they will have earned marketable skills, and consider offering a digital badge as evidence of these skills. If your institution has a library school, that is a natural partnership in the making. If it does not, think of what majors might be interested, such as education, instructional design, or even career services. This training program will have to be holistic and might require you to create something like a non-credit course that all those teaching first-year students will have to take. Be clear about what the teaching program offers participants, especially if these benefits are in lieu of a salary. Having a clear goal and message and a good marketing plan will help sell it outside the library. Some things to think about include the goals of the program, how to train students who might never have taught before, what content is important, and how you will assess the effectiveness of the program. In addition, having students shadow librarians and team teach before they go out on their own might also be helpful. An end-of-semester/year evaluation and feedback discussion about what went well, what didn't, and what can be improved should assist in creating a strong and effective training program for future students. Corporate sponsors might either donate their time or help support your efforts financially. Finally, getting support from grants, awards, and other means might also open the door so that you can sustain the program without having to worry about hiring for new positions.

Quantity of Content

Librarians have a tendency to try and cram as much information into each session as possible. This is in part because they often only have a single interaction in which to teach students everything they need to know about research at this basic stage of their academic and professional careers. And in some ways, that makes perfect sense. But in others, a one-time session can hardly be a substitute for a process that takes repetition, feedback, and even failure before it can be successfully mastered. So you have to really think about what it is you want your first-year students to get out of their session with you. Ideally, set one or two goals that are achievable and that will not leave them confused after a 75-minute lecture filled with database names, unfamiliar terms, and probably more detail than is needed at this stage. If you have the ability to see students more than once and/or add some online content to supplement your session, all the better. But what if you don't? Stick with just a few of the basics, and make sure students are clear on what to do next by inviting them to contact you and providing a concise handout with additional information. If there was absolutely no way to see these students again, the focus should be on the following items:

- Who to contact for assistance
- The most basic way to come up with a workable research question
- The simplest way to search *any* resource (and knowing when to use Google) regardless of vendor platform
- The basics of determining what makes a source credible

Anything beyond these elements is add-on information that might be useful but is not necessary. If the assignment calls for something specific, you will have to decide what can be cut and what you need to cover in order for students to successfully conduct the research. But thinking that you need to point out the specific search features of all the general databases in the library's subscription profile is not the solution. Instead, ask yourself if you were a student in this class, what would you really need to know to find the information you need for the assignment? Less is often more, and just because you don't spend the majority of your time going over details that will likely be forgotten does not mean you are providing any less quality instruction for the students. In fact, it might be an interesting exercise to compare assessment data from classes where you employ these different approaches and see what works best. The results might surprise you.

THE FRAMEWORK FOR INFORMATION LITERACY AND OTHER MODELS OF DESIGN

Framework for Information Literacy

Again, how you apply the *Framework* depends largely on your institutional context and how it relates to the first-year courses within which it is embedded. Because of the way the *Framework* is constructed, the threshold concepts are intended to be abstract. Some, like the way in which information is disseminated within a particular discipline, are also too advanced for students who are struggling with the basics of defining a topic for a general paper. More useful might be to examine the various knowledge practices or abilities that follow and determine based on those how they might apply. For example, the ability to identify markers of authority when engaging with information is something that can be transformed into a learning outcome, taught, and measured. Following is an example of how to engage students in this activity:

Outcome: Students will determine what criteria make a source authoritative.

Activity: Have a class discussion about what makes something authoritative and generate a list. For example, items might include author credentials, inclusion of citations, and statistics. Then break the class into small groups. Give each group the same two sources and ask them to determine which is the more authoritative based on the criteria they generated. Alternatively, they can also find their own sources based on these criteria as another way to get them to think critically about them.

Assessment: By discussing why they believe one source is more authoritative than the other, you can determine to what degree students have mastered the concept of authority as it applies to their sources. If you have the ability to follow up with the class, a possible homework assignment would be to have students include an explanation of why the sources they included in their paper were authoritative.

Instructional Design Concepts

We recognize there is a plethora of information on how to engage students in the classroom using active learning techniques, online tools, and a myriad of other approaches. However, if you look to the literature coming out of the instructional design field, there might be other approaches that will work just as well and can propel your program in a completely new direction. As with everything else, you will need to decide what model will work best for you. Below are just a few examples so that you can get a feel for how these models might be applied to your efforts.

1. Backwards design

This model starts with the ending, really. It's about what you want students to *know* and, more importantly, *do* by the time you're done with your instruction. From there, you will have to determine what evidence (in our case, assessment) would demonstrate that those skills have been acquired, which will dictate what instructional interventions you will put into place.

This model also allows you to distinguish between concepts and skills that are crucial versus those that would be nice to know even within a specific threshold concept. This will help you set pedagogical and programmatic priorities to ensure you accomplish the core goals first. If there is room for the rest, great, but if not, you've at least covered the most significant aspects. This is especially important if you know you will only have a one-time session with a class; it will force you to make the dreaded decision of what to include versus what to let go. And you will have to let go of some things no matter what you do, because in most cases you will simply not have an unlimited amount of time with students, even in the most perfect scenario.

For example, if you use the threshold concept that authority is constructed and contextual, your most important goal might be for students to be able to generate criteria for markers of authority for a particular subject, and you will focus your instruction and assessment to make sure that after they attend your class, they will be able to generate that list. While it's wonderful for students to think about the broader environment of information and how authorities interact across time, you might not be able to come up with meaningful evidence of understanding of this concept (especially if you are talking about freshmen); a multiple-choice question on a survey will provide you with only a very superficial confirmation of learning. Using the backwards design model, you would likely choose not to jam this element into your already-full class or make a generalized statement about it that might be more confusing than helpful; instead, you might eliminate that idea and focus on criteria for authority, which is more useful for students' upcoming papers where they will need to explain why the sources they chose were credible.

2. Design thinking

Design thinking is a creative process wherein one generates ideas about an often abstract and messy concept, keeping in mind the end user's wants and needs. An example of a design thinking process could have several stages: *define, research, prototype, implement,* and *learn* or *assess.* This process was conceptualized by IDEO CEO Tim Brown and is currently in practice at the Stanford d.school (Stanford Design Program).

Using these steps, problems can be reframed, questions can be asked, more ideas can be created, and the best actions can be chosen. The steps aren't linear; they can occur simultaneously and be repeated. There is also a strong element of experimentation involved, and "failure" is seen as an opportunity to learn rather than something to be avoided. Design research also emphasizes the need for interventions based on the identification of the problem and a subsequent evaluation of the success of these measures.

Design thinking can be applied in two ways. The first application can work as a methodology for you to think differently about your instructional challenges. It requires broad conversations, brainstorming, and taking some risks, but it can really help you see a problem in a new light, and you can then begin to approach it from a different perspective. The "Design Thinking for Educators Toolkit" kit cited at the end of this chapter goes into great detail about how you can apply this approach to your planning work and include the feedback from your stakeholders and colleagues as you go through each step.

The second application can work as a tool to help students think through their paper as a "product" of sorts, and you will see that the research and design thinking processes are quite similar in nature, making them perfect partners. To take this idea further, several framing questions can be generated to assist with this process.

Discovery (understand the challenge/topic and prepare research):
- What do students know and need to find out about this challenge?
- How can you narrow or broaden the challenge to frame the topic?
- Sketch out goals—What do students need to do in order to complete the assignment?
- What are their constraints?

Interpretation (search for meaning and frame opportunities):
- Identify themes within the challenge.
- Group themes together in patterns.
- Look for links between themes and highlight ones of importance.
- Identify patterns by finding "headlines" and turning them into statements).
- Summarize each idea in one sentence (think of paragraph headings).

Ideation or prototype (generate ideas and refine them):
- Develop research questions for each of these main ideas.
- Uncover Insights (So what? How does this help the topic? How might students . . . ?)
- Support ideas with research and brainstorming keywords and where to look.
- Dig deeper; what is the relevance of this information for this assignment?

Experimentation (make the prototype or draft and get feedback):
- Create a storyboard/diagram/model
- Decide what the students should get feedback on. Ask what is the best thing about their paper and what is one thing to change or improve, or just provide general impressions and identify patterns in the feedback.

Evolution and analysis (track learning, what worked/didn't work, and move forward):
- What changes do students need to make as a result of the feedback they received?
- What else do they need to do that they might have missed? What are the gaps?

Applying design thinking to IL makes sense because the various steps mirror the research process students would engage with, especially as the new framework allows for even greater ambiguity and fluidity than before. This process allows for a more organic flow of discovery and a shift away from the traditional tool-based approach to IL. So you would essentially be guiding students through their own process of discovery and iteration, which weaves process and content, so that by the end of their semester they will have gone through an iterative and messy process that incorporates the framework's threshold concepts with your instruction and their own methods for integrating the feedback they receive from their instructor into what has hopefully become a much richer final paper or project.

3. *ADDIE*

ADDIE (stands for *analysis, design, development, implementation, evaluation*) is a more generalized model of instruction that follows a similar process to design thinking. Whereas design thinking focuses on determining user needs as a springboard for planning, ADDIE is more of an introspective model that instructors might apply to their own instructional development process to reflect on the methodology of instruction as much as on the content.

This method can still be useful because even if you don't have the ability to interview faculty and students before you begin to plan your instruction, going through some steps that oblige you to think through what you are doing and why you are doing it still has great value. Perhaps it's easier for you to go through this process first, then determine that you really need to talk to your stakeholders. In this way, you will be much better prepared to ask those good questions so that your planning is more effective and useful for you and for them.

You can almost think of ADDIE and design thinking as nesting dolls for your overall process, while backwards design can assist you with that second step of the progression so that you synthesize both the *how* and the *what* as you plan and make changes based on feedback and your own observations.

Format and Delivery Modes

What structure will the program have? Only you can answer this question, and here are a few more just to complicate things. Do you envision that a one-time session will be enough for students to gain all the necessary information in order to successfully complete the assignment and ultimately succeed in the course, or would multiple sessions work better? Is the program a stand-alone experience that might lead to further instruction along the road, or is it highly interconnected with the fabric of upper-level and subject-specific instruction? Will students have homework in between sessions, and if so, how will it be scored and counted? Will the students access materials ahead of time or after the fact, and how will you determine if they have actually done this? At what point(s) in the semester will all of these elements be introduced? Will it be slowly incorporated along the way or delivered all at once (most likely sometime in the beginning), and are you hoping that all of the information presented will somehow stick with the students throughout the rest of the course? How will you know? Are faculty willing to give students grades or extra credit points for library-related assignments and activities, or are you relegated to the role of "guest speaker" for the day? Are faculty willing to let you assist with the design of the assignment itself, or are you working within the constraints of the three-to-five scholarly resources wheel of doom where the definition of "scholarly" is so impossibly narrow that it is rendered almost useless?

All of these elements will influence how the program functions, how and when it is introduced, and how it will progress. Knowing the "ideal" model ahead of time will help you sell your vision as opposed to letting others dictate what it might be. Of course there will have to be some compromise around the way assignments are given and timed as well as their format, but it is still up to you to determine how to best work within the constraints instead of letting them limit you to the point of compromising your goals.

The eternal question of providing face-to-face or online instruction—or perhaps both—continues to pose a challenge for large-scale courses such as these. Here are a few things to consider, some of which harken back to the goals of the program. Which concepts should be covered online? This is a difficult question to answer. Typically, how-to concepts can be covered in a video or tutorial. For example, there are several videos that describe (in sometimes painful detail) the search mechanics of Academic Search Premier. This does not have to be covered in person. Understanding the subject headings in the database, however, might. Typically, if it's a point-and-click function, leave it online. If you need further engagement or perhaps expect students to work together, such as when narrowing a topic and coming up with a research question, those concepts might be better served by conducting a short activity in class and walking students through what that really entails, since watching a video on the same content will most likely not lead to a greater understanding of how to actually do this.

Do you have the ability to purchase tools or subscriptions? If so, you are well on your way to using something that's already been created for this purpose. Instructional design websites often have great information and approach each tool from its instructional purpose rather than featuring the latest and greatest in terms of technology. Do you have IT support? If so, they might be able to help you design or tweak something that you have found. If not, it would be best to rely on a tool that you can configure, troubleshoot, and maintain on your own, and to stick with something simpler. How easy will it be to maintain and update this tool or video? For example, Camtasia is a popular tool used to make videos of database navigation techniques. But writing, recording, and editing your script will take up much more time than is necessary. In addition, every time the database interface changes, you will have to reshoot your video. It might be best to link to videos already created by the vendor in this case.

Will you design something that is embedded into a course management system (CMS) or portal, or is this meant to be a stand-alone tool? CMSs have several built-in tools that might serve your purposes, and you will have support from central IT if you want to add it as a course component or as its own module that anyone can access.

What would students gain by interacting with the content online as opposed to face to face or not at all? If the answer is nothing, leave it out entirely. Simply because something is online does not automatically make it better or more relevant. Think carefully about what you'd like students to gain by interacting with the content in this manner as opposed to in class or not at all. You might be surprised at what you leave out.

How will you determine if this approach is successful or not? Online assessment tools are also varied. Some are built in to the online tools you are using—Camtasia, for example, allows for the creation of quizzes within the video itself. Others require you to look at students' written content and decide if they have succeeded in mastering the outcome. Others still are completely stand-alone tools, such as Qualtrics, which allows you to design surveys that can be linked from anywhere. There is also a difference between measuring what the students actually learned and how they used the tool itself. If they had difficulty with it, that will affect their scores and could even impede them from completing the activity altogether.

FINAL TAKEAWAYS

1. Curriculum design is about the overall vision, shape, and arc of your program and less about what you are going to cover in an individual session.

2. Before you create something or make drastic changes to an existing structure, make sure you have a clear understanding (through activities such as needs assessments) about how the goals for your program fit in with the programs with which you hope to collaborate (such as composition or writing).

3. If you find it helpful, you can use one of the many theories of design to provide the theoretical underpinning of your program as you transition from theory to practice and begin to create the actual program components.

4. Information literacy should not be relegated to one portion of a class; it should permeate both your design and the pedagogical choices that follow.

Case Study: A General Education Mandate Inspires New Information Literacy Strategy

Susan M. Anderson, Indiana University–Purdue University Fort Wayne
Beth Boatright, Indiana University–Purdue University Fort Wayne

Brief Abstract: When Indiana's Commission for Higher Education mandated the adoption of statewide general education learning outcomes, the librarians at Indiana University–Purdue University Fort Wayne took action. By analyzing information literacy concepts in the mandated outcomes, mapping associated courses, and exploring new teaching methods, our librarians developed a new strategy for integrating information literacy throughout the curriculum.

INSTITUTIONAL BACKGROUND

Indiana University–Purdue University Fort Wayne (IPFW) is a multisystem metropolitan university in Fort Wayne, Indiana. The campus offers undergraduate and graduate degrees from both Indiana University and Purdue University. Our student population of almost 13,000 students hails primarily from northeast Indiana and northwest Ohio; 51 percent of our students are first-generation college students.

IPFW's Helmke Library has a team of nine liaison librarians, all responsible for developing information literacy outreach and outcomes in their liaison departments. For the last several years, the department has delivered focused information literacy instruction to upper-level classes, relying primarily on a train-the-trainer model to reach introductory undergraduate classes.

DESCRIPTION OF PROGRAM, PROJECT OR SPACE

A General Education Challenge

In 2012, Indiana's Commission for Higher Education mandated that all state colleges and universities adopt a Statewide Transfer General Education Core. Under the General Education Core, students must take a series of classes that teach specified statewide learning outcomes. These standardized outcomes make the credits easily transferable between state universities. IPFW's implementation of the requirements involves an approval process in which existing and new general education courses must identify which of the 41 required outcomes the class will address and describe how the instructor will assess student learning.

The librarians at Helmke Library realized that many of the General Education Core learning outcomes overlap with ACRL's Information Literacy standards. Interested librarians mapped these commonalities, producing a detailed overview of information literacy–related outcomes in general education classes. For example, Learning Outcome 2.4 involves the same skill set as ACRL Standard 4, and Learning Outcome 4.2 is a subject-specific application of ACRL Standard 3 (see Table 1.1).

Table 1.1.
Indiana Statewide Competencies

Indiana Statewide Transfer General Education Core	ACRL Information Literacy Standards for Higher Education
Learning Outcome 2.4 Advance an oral argument using logical reasoning.	Standard 4
Learning Outcome 4.2 Distinguish between scientific and unscientific evidence and explanations.	Standard 3

Note: Full text of standards can be found at www.in.gov/che/files/STGEC_BW _Binder_Final_5.19.15.pdf (Indiana Statewide Transfer General Education Core); www.ala.org/acrl/standards/informationliteracycompetency#stan (ACRL Information Literacy Standards for Higher Education.

This mapping exercise identified a few core outcomes that were related to all five ACRL standards. For example, Learning Outcome 1.7 requires that students "demonstrate proficiency in reading, evaluating, analyzing, and using material collected from electronic sources (such as visual, electronic, library databases, Internet sources, other official databases, federal government databases, reputable blogs, wikis, etc.)." Our librarians designated objectives with significant information literacy overlap as "library focus areas." As courses with these outcomes were approved on the IPFW campus, we were able to easily identify them.

The clear link between general education learning outcomes and information literacy provided an entrée for discussions with faculty members about library involvement in their classrooms. These conversations were particularly fruitful with the coordinators of our foundational writing courses, who identified areas of the curriculum where instructors could benefit from additional librarian support. It was clear that librarians could teach and assess information literacy–related general education learning outcomes, but instructor buy-in would be necessary. If we could deliver this content online, faculty members would be able to integrate library instruction into their classes without significantly impacting their existing teaching plans. A suite of online modules could provide complete coverage of state-mandated outcomes while remaining flexible for instructors who might prefer to incorporate just one or two targeted lessons. Either way, this strategy would assist instructors in meeting the learning outcomes while enhancing the library's reach.

In 2014, the library piloted a small series of online modules and an embedded quiz, testing the concept of modular online instruction in several sections of introductory writing classes on campus. Based on the input of writing instructors, we chose to pilot modules about selecting a topic, identifying popular and scholarly sources, using Academic Search Premier, evaluating sources with the CRAAP test, and using citations. Rather than create new instructional content for the pilot, we curated and combined existing instructional resources into our online modules. Each module included an introduction, an instructional video, links to additional resources, and application exercises. A machine-graded multiple-choice quiz was included for assessment purposes. Although the pilot did not include sufficient content to meet an entire state-mandated learning outcome, the lessons laid the foundation for future growth of this information literacy strategy.

Our pilot efforts reached students more effectively than our earlier train-the-trainer model and provided preliminary assessment of student learning through the online quiz. It also made the writing faculty more aware of library-provided options for meeting general education learning outcomes related to information literacy.

TACKLING THE LENS

A New Curricular Approach

The work on scalable, assessable information literacy modules for online delivery progressed in tandem with an analysis of general education course enrollment figures. Librarians identified classes with both information literacy–related objectives and consistently high enrollment, enabling our small team of librarians to target and scale our efforts efficiently. With this data, our pilot experience, and an awareness of the university's goals related to retention, the librarians reimagined IPFW's entire information literacy curriculum.

Our first change was to the foundation of the library's curriculum. Although the library had been successfully using the ACRL Information Literacy standards as the core of our instruction program, we chose to adopt the Association of American Colleges & Universities' (AAC&U) Information Literacy VALUE Rubric as the new foundation of our academic program. Although we still engage with ACRL's Information Literacy standards and the *Framework*, the AAC&U rubric offers several benefits. The rubric acknowledges that information literacy is complex and should be developed as student needs and abilities grow. The outcomes define clear and assessable stages of understanding that provide a strong foundation for scaffolding information literacy across campus curricula. Since the AAC&U is a well-respected authority for higher education in Indiana and the Indiana General Education Transfer Core was based on AAC&U learning outcomes, using the AAC&U rubric lends legitimacy and relevance to the library's information literacy efforts. Aligning with the AAC&U also ensures that our efforts are in sync with the priorities of university administration.

Our new information literacy curriculum has a three-point strategy. First, the entire team of librarians works together to deliver in-person and online instruction to the largest introductory courses on campus. These classes, two introductory writing courses and a communication course, include general education outcomes identified as library focus areas. Our goal is that students will reach the third level of the AAC&U rubric by the time they have taken all three of these courses. We have assigned different aspects of information literacy to each class. Based on the positive reception of our initial pilot, we are developing new online modules for each course to allow for flexibility and scalability in implementation. We hope to have our information literacy lessons included as a required element of these classes in the future.

In the second part of our new strategy, librarians incorporate information literacy into other general education classes based on both the needs of instructors and the information literacy principles reflected in the statewide outcomes for each course. In classes at the 100 and 200 level, we focus on basic skills. This includes reiterating the principles we teach in the targeted introductory courses, emphasizing the relevance of information literacy in every area of study, and helping students develop understanding in line with the third level of the AAC&U rubric. Upper-level information literacy integrations build on these basics and move students toward expertise. Ideally, this scaffolding will allow our librarians to provide instruction that is targeted to the students' capabilities and needs.

Finally, each librarian is developing an upper-level curricular integration plan to ensure that our graduates leave with strong information literacy skills in their major subject area. These plans vary by discipline, librarian, and the willingness of subject-area faculty to collaborate with the library, but they generally involve analyzing course content and sequencing in each major and identifying opportunities for information literacy integration. When these plans are fully developed, we expect that librarians will teach and assess information literacy at the fourth level of the AAC&U rubric by the time our students graduate.

LESSONS LEARNED

Ongoing Efforts and Lessons Learned

We are working with faculty to develop support for our vision of librarians' contributions to general education requirements on campus. As always, our goal is to form productive partnerships with faculty to develop and embed information literacy learning outcomes into curricula, courses, and assignments, assuring relevant, scalable, and assessable information literacy education experiences.

We have learned that our success will depend on librarians adopting the best pedagogical practices in classroom teaching, online tutorial design, and other educational interactions. This includes integration into online learning environments like the campus CMS, where we hope to improve delivery of online library resources and services closely tied to student assignments and course learning outcomes. We are also emphasizing meeting students at in-person and virtual points of need, including through social media. Although these are not traditional areas of strength for our team, our librarians are pursuing professional development opportunities to enhance their expertise in these areas, and we have instituted a voluntary peer review of teaching process in the department. We are also beginning to incorporate elements of the ACRL *Framework for Information Literacy* into our instruction, ensuring that our approach emphasizes the rich connections between information literacy and other academic and social learning experiences on our campus.

We hope that our new approach to information literacy in the curriculum will enhance student learning and the library's integration in the academic life of IPFW.

Table 1.2.
National and Statewide Standards

Title of Document/Material	Description
AAC&U Information Literacy Value Rubric	www.aacu.org/value/rubrics /information-literacy
ACRL Information Literacy Standards and Framework for Information Literacy	www.ala.org/acrl/standards /ilframework www.ala.org/acrl/standards /informationliteracycompetency
Indiana Statewide Transfer General Education Core	www.in.gov/che/files/STGEC _Guidance_13May22.pdf

Case Study: Strategies and Tools for Academic Research: Using the STAR Project to Build Curricular Coherence

Danielle Rowland, University of Washington Bothell and Cascadia College Campus Library

Brief Abstract: The primary problem the library was trying to solve with our curricular intervention in the introductory first-year (FY) class was a lack of consistency in what and how first-year students were being taught about information literacy. The goals of the project (which we have been meeting for a few years now) are to:

- Introduce all FY students to library research in a manner that enables librarians to help them build on that information literacy learning in future classes targeted by our instruction program, and
- Integrate library instruction with class assignments, themes, and discussions in a developmentally appropriate manner (providing instructors with an example of "guided" research).

INSTITUTIONAL BACKGROUND

The Campus Library sits at the center of a campus shared by University of Washington Bothell and Cascadia College, serving the students, staff, and faculty of both. Cascadia has been a two-year community college until this year (2015), when it added a small four-year degree program. It has been enrolling about 2,600 Full Time Equivalent (FTE) each year for the last several years. UW Bothell has been growing rapidly for the last 10 years since its lower-division program was added in 2006. This year, the FTE is expected to be about 5,000, up from about 1,900 when I started in 2008.

This case study focuses on the first-year curriculum at UW Bothell, which rests on the foundation of the Discovery Core (DC) sequence of courses. This is a three-quarter program of study that all entering first-year students are expected to take. The first-quarter course is the DCI: an interdisciplinary class designed to give incoming freshmen common experiences, expose students to campus resources, and build learning communities. It is also one of two courses the library strategically targets for information literacy instruction in the lower division.

DESCRIPTION OF PROGRAM, PROJECT, OR SPACE

The primary problem the library was trying to solve with our curricular intervention in the DCI class was a lack of consistency in what and how first-year students were being taught about information literacy. We scaffold our information literacy learning goals across courses, reaching students with information literacy learning objectives at several points of development. The library's learning goals in the 100-level research writing course build on learning goals we have for students in the DCI. In order for library instruction in the research writing course to be effective, it's important that the basic introduction students experience in the DCI covers roughly the same content across sections.

When I stepped into the library's new First Year Experience (FYE) coordinator position in 2010, the library already had a strong relationship with leadership of the first-year program, then in its fourth year. However, the majority of Discovery Core courses were taught primarily by lecturers with short-term contracts, which created a challenge for the library. Our library instruction plan is based on integrated sessions in targeted courses, which require a high degree of collaboration with instructors in those courses. The inconsistency librarians created with DCI instruction developed as a result of our strong commitment to "teaching to the assignment" in collaborations with faculty.

Our librarians have a robust history of collaboration with faculty in UW Bothell's upper division, where faculty have longer-term appointments. The curricular foundation on which individual partnerships are built in the upper division has been maintained through meeting and communication structures that facilitate institutional knowledge over time. As an additional challenge, these communication structures were mostly absent from the lower division until very recently (for several reasons, including rapid growth, budget issues, etc.). As a result, librarians did not have regular venues through which to build consistency with faculty in the way we offered integrated instruction in the first year.

My first year in the FYE coordinator role, I wanted to find some way to help our students more reliably meet our information literacy learning objectives for the DCI. The STAR Project (Strategies and Tools for Academic Research), conceived then and adapted yearly since, is the way that we have been trying to do that. The goals of the project are to:

- Introduce all FY students to library research in a manner that enables librarians to help them build on that information literacy learning in future classes targeted by our instruction program
- Integrate library instruction with class assignments, themes, and discussions in a developmentally appropriate manner (providing instructors with an example of "guided" research)
- Sustain scalable librarian collaboration with the FY program, allowing us to take on more sections as we grow but to maintain or even reduce classroom teaching and preparation time

Components of the project include:

- A web guide customized for each section
- A short welcome video embedded in the guide, covering basic information about the library
- A STAR worksheet that librarians customize in collaboration with faculty. A limited number of topics are suggested based on class themes and the course assignment for which the project is assigned. Then the librarian working with the section runs searches related to the topics in the databases featured in the project and recommends keywords for students to try for each topic.

TACKLING THE LENS

The first-year DC curriculum was developed by founding faculty and representatives from student support units on campus (e.g., the Writing Center). They designed a sequencing table outlining broad learning goals in six major categories, one of which is information literacy. Materials provided in Table 1.3 show the progression of skills and concepts taught across the DCI II and III courses and has been a useful starting place for librarians when negotiating with faculty new to the Discovery Core (consistently a majority of the DCI instructors) about the nature of information literacy activities in the sequence. However, the dearth of faculty development venues in the first-year program meant that there were few opportunities to build a shared understanding of how to interpret the sequencing table's broad guidelines.

The STAR Project offers much more specificity when librarians attempt to convey to new instructors the library's learning objectives for students in their courses. It helps model for new faculty, with whom we may have little face-to-face time, what we mean by "guided research." Many of our DC faculty are new to teaching FY students, and the project can help them calibrate their expectations of student performance with regard to library research. For example, on the STAR worksheet, librarians provide suggested keywords for suggested topics. This facilitates the conversation about FY student inexperience with databases and academic vocabulary. Essentially, the project allows us to still "teach to the assignment" that DCI instructors use, but librarians now have a greater influence on what that assignment will look like, since the project requires them to be collaboratively involved in its design.

The library's priority with the STAR Project was to increase consistency for students, but not at the cost of librarians building strong collaborative relationships with first-year faculty. There have always been some faculty who return to teach DCIs more than once, and that number has increased over the past five years. In some cases, fostering partnerships with returning instructors is more important than forcing them to adapt their syllabi to the library's, or even the first-year program's, curricular design. For that reason, we have made participation in the STAR Project voluntary (though still strongly encouraged) for DCI instructors, while collaboration with a librarian on integrating information literacy in the DCI in some capacity is still required for all. In the minority of cases where a DCI does not use the STAR Project, we are usually able to ensure that library learning goals are met in other ways.

LESSONS LEARNED

The first two goals (described above) continue to be mostly met through the project. These are the goals that relate to building developmentally appropriate consistency into the library's DC instruction. Progress on the third goal, related to sustainable scalability, is more questionable. In particular, librarian preparation time does not seem to have been reduced in the way that was originally hoped, except in cases where instructors return to repeat the same DCI course with the same librarian (a minority of DCIs). The consultation and negotiation that has historically been required with first-year librarian and instructor collaborations has remained a time-consuming priority.

At the same time, however, some benefits we considered but didn't prioritize at the time of development have increased in importance. When the project was designed, library classroom space had not yet reached the high premium it holds now, especially during our busy fall quarters. Taking most of the DCI instruction out of the library classrooms has proven very helpful for scheduling other targeted classes in the fall quarter. Another less-expected benefit has been increased student engagement. Since the project is roughly pedagogically equivalent to moving a classroom assignment online, when we transitioned out of the classroom to an online environment, I didn't expect an increase in engagement. Our learning objectives for the course hadn't changed, and the activities involved were ones that several librarians had been doing in the classroom. However, based on students' reflections, the autonomy given to students with the online assignment appears to help them synthesize the STAR Project experience with their previous knowledge in a deeper way.

Overall, our annual evaluations have indicated that the project continues to be seen as valuable. Previously, the worksheet component of the project has been a downloadable Word document that students fill out. This year, however, we're piloting a module that is more tightly integrated with Canvas, our local learning management system. We will continue to engage such adaptations as needed and may switch to another method of trying to meet first-year student learning objectives if that need becomes clear over time.

Table 1.3.
Handouts and Worksheets

Title of Document/Material	Description
STAR worksheet	STAR worksheet sample, http://guides.lib.uw.edu/bothell/dcil/star
DC STAR Guide for Faculty	http://guides.lib.uw.edu/bothell/dcil/star
DC Faculty Handbook (2014)	DC Sequencing Table http://guides.lib.uw.edu/c.php?g=345768&p=2330573

Case Study: Reframing Freshmen Orientation to Include an Information Literacy Component

Jeremiah Paschke-Wood, University of Louisiana at Lafayette

Brief Abstract: With changes to the University of Louisiana at Lafayette's UNIV 100 freshmen orientation program, librarians at Edith Garland Dupré also needed to revamp a relatively stale, staid library assignment to not only encourage active learning among students but also to include a stronger information literacy component. This case study describes the thought process behind the changes and the successes and pitfalls of making such changes on the fly.

INSTITUTIONAL BACKGROUND

The University of Louisiana at Lafayette is a large land-grant university with a full-time enrollment of just under 20,000 students. From its beginnings as a small regional university, it's grown into a large national university—in the last 20 years particularly. The university's UNIV 100 program was founded in 2009 as a way to help incoming freshmen—particularly those from rural areas—more easily acclimate to college life. For the fall 2015 semester, it was decided the class would instead focus on a more thematic approach as opposed to the traditional "this is what a college campus looks like" orientation class focusing on issues like time management, athletics schedules, and study skills—though many of those elements are still introduced in some way.

DESCRIPTION OF PROGRAM, PROJECT, OR SPACE

Initially, the library's role in the UNIV 100 class was to provide support for a comprehensive test measuring knowledge of library resources. The test, primarily a multiple-choice exam focused on usage of the databases and online catalog, was typically preceded by a one-shot library session covering use of the databases and catalog and a short tour. In some cases, the classes came in for two sessions, one a tour and one an instruction session. In 2014, the test was adapted to focus on five particular learning outcomes, but information literacy was not one of them. For the new thematic approach, the library portion of the class is expected to be incorporated into the students' projects over the course of the semester, and information literacy is now a key component.

TACKLING THE CURRICULUM DEVELOPMENT LENS

The initial library test was multiple choice and focused on mostly rote library research activities. The questions contained detailed explanations of the path to follow for the answers but seldom left the students using the skills they'd learned and applying them to actual research. Also problematic was that the university's freshmen English courses (English 101 and 102) often come to the library for instruction sessions focusing on mostly rote research skills (although classes are not required to have a library session). So with a library assignment largely focused on basic database usage and finding books in the collection, it was possible, and even likely, that a large percentage of students would receive similar library instruction multiple times due to the requirements of the UNIV 100 assignment. With a new director in the Office of First-Year Experience, it was decided (with help from the library's Instructional Services Department) that the class would be made thematic to not only challenge the students but also be more appealing. A library portion was constructed that would focus less on usage of library resources and include more on information literacy skills. The goal was to convince instructors, typically adjuncts and other UL Lafayette staff, to integrate information literacy into the students' thematic projects as opposed to having a stand-alone library session that would have little to do with the rest of the class.

This plan would put less significance on knowledge of using library resources but would also not require the instructors to be as well-versed in library research such that they'd be expected to ask students to think critically about the resources they would use for their projects—then if they needed assistance with their search, they could come to the library for that instruction. The library conducted two "Teaching Information Literacy" workshops aimed at university faculty (particularly those in UNIV 100), with more planned. Librarians work with instructors (and remain embedded in their Moodle pages for the classes) in constructing activities that require not only practicing information literacy skills but also require students to use library resources in order to finish their projects for class.

Also, instead of having one standard library instruction session across a variety of themes and concepts, each individual class (or group of thematic courses) will have specific library session planning and activities built around the themes of the class and their individual projects—if a library session is requested. This could reduce the strain on library resources while providing research and instruction help that students enjoy and find useful in conducting their research. Active learning sessions were drawn up that allowed students to both gain experience conducting searches to find library resources and also to find resources that were appropriate to their specific discipline and needs as researchers, as opposed to the first results they received after conducting searches. With the activities, the students were also asked to justify why they picked certain results and what their process was in finding those sources.

LESSONS LEARNED

Though these changes are still in the testing phase, there have been several lessons learned already. For one thing, a change like this requires a lot of upfront time. Given the changes, a lot of the instructors need help not only in creating information literacy projects for the students but often just understanding the concept of information literacy. This upfront time takes the place of actual class time but still requires librarians to be available. As the program moves forward, there will be less requirement timewise. Also, many instructors will still want to have the librarians teach instruction sessions because of their lack of comfort with the topic of information literacy (or library research in general), so providing the instruction without returning to staid, old methods of lecture-based lessons is a challenge. Unfortunately, with a program like this, it's also difficult to debut new ideas early to see how they work—particularly if the program doesn't try a test run in the summer (which wasn't possible). Theoretically, as instructors become more familiar with this program, that will change.

Regarding the design of the sessions, I have learned that I have to be willing to be flexible and be prepared for constant revision. When creating instruction sessions, particularly those with assessment components, you have to be prepared to evaluate yourself and the session after each class. Every class is a new experience, and students will often interpret content and information differently than an instructor. Understand that at times the process and the experience may be challenging, but meaningful and gratifying instruction is possible.

Case Study: Try, Try Again: Designing Library Instruction Sessions for a Freshman Writing Program

Jennifer Jackson, University of New Orleans

Brief Abstract: Designing sustainable one-shot library instructional sessions for first-year writing courses can be a seemingly daunting task, particularly when attempts have been made in the past with no success. This case study explores the process taken to develop meaningful and lasting instruction sessions for the Freshman Writing Program at the University of New Orleans.

INSTITUTIONAL BACKGROUND

The University of New Orleans is a small institution with approximately 8,800 students. As a state institution, the student populations come from different backgrounds. Many students are commuter, transfer, or international. The university offers a range of degrees from bachelor's to doctoral.

Earl K. Long Library is located at the heart of the campus, open approximately 80 hours a week, with a variety of services designed to meet the needs of the students, staff, and faculty. Services and spaces include the Learning Commons, Circulation, Government Documents, Louisiana and Special Collections, computing and printing, as well as four floors of study space (group and individual). Aside from the undergraduate and graduate students, the library also assists public researchers who come from across the country to access our archives and government document depository.

Earl K. Long Library employs 20 full-time employees (12 staff and 8 librarians), who serve in different capacities and often work in multiple departments within the library. Six of the librarians serve as subject liaisons and provide library instruction, research consultations, and collection development to those departments.

DESCRIPTION OF PROGRAM, PROJECT, OR SPACE

Upon my arrival in 2012, Earl K. Long Library had gone through numerous instruction librarians and had been unable to create a sustainable instruction program at the first-year level. It was the library administration's hope that a sustainable, engaging, and creative program could be designed to meet the needs of the Freshman Writing Program. In order to create a program, I knew that I needed to have an understanding of the specific outcomes and goals of the Freshman Writing Program. In the first year of my tenure, I worked diligently to meet with the director of the Freshman Writing Program as well as the dean of the library. After meeting with the director of the Freshman Writing Program, the following outcomes for that program were incorporated into the instruction program:

- Summarize, analyze, evaluate, and respond to the ideas of others.
- Incorporate the ideas and texts of others.
- Use library and nonlibrary research methods.
- Evaluate sources.
- Document sources in MLA style.

The initial implementation for the program began in the spring of 2013. That year was an experimental year with regard to my research for designing a sustainable program. I read numerous articles related to first-year writing, active learning, and classroom assessment techniques. During this time, I had the opportunity to try different methods of instruction. Also during that year I was provided the opportunity to attend ACRL's Teacher Track Immersion Program. Attending immersion was truly a transformational experience as an instructor. I learned how to refine the scope of my instruction sessions and focus specifically on individual outcomes, honing in on the idea of quality of information rather than quantity of information. After seeing how librarians from different regions created options for instruction, I decided to create a menu of instruction sessions. It was my hope that this menu would give Freshman Writing course instructors more flexibility in choosing what could be taught while helping me communicate information literacy.

By the summer of 2014, I had developed the three unique sessions that are currently used. These three sessions directly address the outcomes listed above as well as our outcomes needed for accreditation. These three sessions are:

- **Popular versus Scholarly: What's the Difference?** In this session students will develop the skills needed to identify the contextual differences and similarities of a variety of informational sources in order to evaluate purpose, audience, and authority.

- **Get Excited to Cite (and Impress Your Professors).** Too often first-year students lack the skills needed to properly incorporate research into their writing. This can have unfortunate results when a student is approached for plagiarism. This session will teach students how to effectively apply the ideas and text of others while using their writing voice and how to recognize issues related to academic integrity and plagiarism.

- **Finding the Right Balance: Successful Steps to Topic Development**. When it comes to choosing a topic, sometimes the student's topic is either too broad or too narrow, and this can make finding and choosing the appropriate sources challenging. This session will focus on asking the right questions by exposing the students to different research methods in order to refine paper topics and develop keywords.

By the fall of 2014, I shared the sessions with the Freshman Writing Program. I sent a mass email to all course instructors of the Freshman Writing Program with the session descriptions, the guidelines for requesting an instruction session, as well as a discussion of the intent and purpose of the new format. In the year since debuting the program, feedback has been overwhelmingly positive. From an observational standpoint, instructors were pleased because they knew what would be covered. It also provided a framework and reinforcement of ideas previously covered within the course. From a library instruction standpoint, it provided a foundation that could be built upon. With each session there was a PowerPoint presentation, supplemental handouts, and an assessment quiz. The quiz was particularly helpful in determining what the student gained from the session and where I may need to make changes in the design or my approach.

TACKLING THE LENS

A large problem I experienced was the competing interests of those involved. Initially, the Freshman Writing Program instructors envisioned library instruction differently than what the library was hoping to accomplish. You want to meet the needs of the instructor, but you also have to incorporate or address the information literacy needs of the students. Another problem was my limited access to mentorship. While the dean of the library is well-regarded within the area of information literacy, there was only so much time she could spend guiding my efforts. As a result, I spent a lot of time doing independent research on curriculum design and increasing my level of understanding of what would be best suited to first-year students. I also had to focus on what would work best for one-shot instruction sessions, since most of the classes that I encountered would only get library instruction once that semester.

A priority for me in designing these sessions was that they incorporated active learning and that they could be assessed within a 50-minute period. I also wanted to provide variety to the content that I taught and covered, so it was important that three unique sessions were designed, the hope being that three different sessions would encourage the instructors to seek multiple instruction sessions per class in a semester.

LESSONS LEARNED

The biggest lesson I learned was to ask questions. It's important to ask questions in order to make an evaluation of the subject matter you're going to teach or focus on but also to understand your subject and what information literacy principles you need to get across. It is also important to be proactive about your own learning process and level of engagement. This means being willing to listen to different ideas and potentially move away from old classroom practices or methods. Being actively involved means accepting responsibility for your growth and development as an instructor. Go to conferences, read the literature, join listservs, speak to other teaching librarians in your area, and network with other librarians at conferences or online. There are other teaching librarians also struggling with the same issues that you are: incorporating information literacy principles, making the class engaging, and communicating with faculty or even other librarians at their institution.

Popular vs. Scholarly Session Handout

Popular vs. Scholarly Sources: What's the Difference?

Directions: Based on your topic find two sources. The first source should be a popular source, and the second source should be a scholarly source. Provide your selection/evaluation criteria for the formats selected (using the CRAAP Test). Compare and contrast the type of information found in each format. For each source write the MLA citation.

Selection Criteria for Selected Articles

_____
_____
_____
_____
_____
_____

MLA Citation #1 Popular Source

_____
_____
_____

MLA Citation #2 Scholarly Source

_____
_____
_____

Compare & Contrast

Similarities	Differences
_____	_____
_____	_____
_____	_____
_____	_____
_____	_____
_____	_____
_____	_____

JMJ 10/14

POPULAR VS. SCHOLARLY QUIZ

THE UNIVERSITY *of* NEW ORLEANS

Please take a few minutes to fill out this quiz to help us improve the quality of library instruction for Earl K. Long Library. Data collected from this survey will be used for statistical purposes. For more information about this survey contact our Instruction Librarian at jmjacks9@uno.edu.

Instructor : _____

Course Name and Number (Example: MANG 4211): _____

Prior to this class have you been to the library before?

Yes   No
○   ○

If yes, please indicate why you visited the library. (Select all that apply.)

Printing/Computing   Studying   Privateer Enrollment Center   Research
○   ○   ○   ○

Other: _____

Directions: Choose the most appropriate answer

1) A scholarly source is defined as. . .
- A) Information that is for a specific audience with knowledge or expertise in a particular field
- B) Information that is written by those in academics, scholars in a specific field
- C) Information that is often footnoted and a list of references is provided
- D) All of the above

2) All of the following would be considered primary sources except:
- A) Original documents
- B) Creative works
- C) Literary criticism

3) All of the following would be considered secondary sources except:
- A) Textbooks
- B) Magazine article
- C) Diary entry
- D) Encyclopedia

4) A popular sources is defined as . . .
- A) Information that is intended for general audiences
- B) The information is not peer-reviewed
- C) The information provides general information or a brief overview
- D) All of the above

5) The selecting or evaluating sources you should consider the following except:
- A) Currency
- B) Relevance
- C) Affluence
- D) Accuracy
- E) Purpose

List at least one thing that you learned in this session that you did not know before:

_____

_____

JMJ RE:1 1/1 1/14

Get Excited To Cite! (And Impress Your Professors)

Directions: The following is the format example of what your citation should look like when citing a website.

> Last name, First name. "Article Title." *Website Title*. Publisher of Website, Day Month Year article was published. Medium of publication. Day Month Year article was accessed.

This is the title for an article recently featured in the New York Times online: ***Changing Tactics, Apple Promotes Watch as a Luxury Item by Brian X. Chen***

Without using a citation generator what is the correct citation for this website?

Please Note: Remember to use *n.p.* if no publisher name is available and *n.d.* if no publishing date is given.

_____

_____

_____

_____

_____

_____

_____

Directions: Using a citation generator of your choice or the citation feature of a library database provide the citation for 2 sources related or connected to your paper topic

MLA Citation #1 from a library database

_____

_____

_____

MLA Citation #2 for an internet source (blog, website, wiki, etc.)

_____

_____

_____

JMJ RE:11/13/14

Get Excited to Cite Quiz

GET EXCITED TO CITE QUIZ   THE UNIVERSITY *of* NEW ORLEANS

Please take a few minutes to fill out this quiz to help us improve the quality of library instruction for Earl K. Long Library. Data collected from this survey will be used for statistical purposes. For more information about this survey contact our Instruction Librarian at jmjacks9@uno.edu.

Instructor : _____

Course Name and Number (Example: MANG 4211): _____

Prior to this class have you been to the library before?

          Yes   No
          O   O

If yes, please indicate why you visited the library. (Select all that apply.)

Printing/Computing	Studying	Privateer Enrollment Center	Research
O	O	O	O

Other: _____

Directions: Choose the most appropriate answer

1) **A MLA citation for a book will include the following information except**
   - A) Title
   - B) Date of publication
   - C) Author's date of birth
   - D) Publisher

2) **The University of New Orleans has an Academic Dishonesty policy**
   - A) True
   - B) False

3) **The following is an example of plagiarism**
   - A) Copying and pasting information without crediting the original author
   - B) Paraphrasing without crediting the original author
   - C) Using entire original works and crediting them as your own
   - D) All of the above

4) **Citation generators are helpful when creating and saving your work but you should always do what before submitting your references**
   - A) Get 8 hours of sleep
   - B) Check the references with alternative source before submitting
   - C) Eat a balanced breakfast
   - D) Watch a YouTube video

5) **The following resources can be used to verify your citation is in the correct style and format**
   - A) Your textbook
   - B) Purdue's Online Writing Lab (OWL)
   - C) The MLA Handbook for Writer's of Research Papers
   - D) Your professor
   - E) All of the above

List at least one thing that you learned in this session that you did not know before:

_____

_____

JMJ RE:11/11/14

Finding the Right Balance Session Handout

FINDING THE RIGHT BALANCE

Search Strategy

Write your research topic here:

_____

_____

List the 2-3 keywords (search terms) for your topic in the table below:

Keyword 1	Keyword 2	Keyword 3

Think of at least two synonyms (like or similar words) for each keyword write those search terms in the first two rows. For the last row, look at OneSearch for the keyword, and view the subject words list on the article page. Write down the best match.

	Keyword 1	Keyword 2	Keyword 3
Synonym or similar words			
Synonym or similar words			
OneSearch Subject Terns			

Database Exercise

Use the keywords and synonyms for your topic in OneSearch. Your goal is to get at least 100 results.
Write the citation in MLA format of at least two sources from OneSearch that you found that you might use for the topic in the space below:

Source #1:

_____

_____

Source #2: *(For your second source, if you are able to identify a book title list that as your second source)*

_____

_____

JMJ 04/14

Finding the Right Balance Quiz

FINDING THE RIGHT BALANCE QUIZ   THE UNIVERSITY *of* NEW ORLEANS

Please take a few minutes to fill out this quiz to help us improve the quality of library instruction for Earl K. Long Library. Data collected from this survey will be used for statistical purposes. For more information about this survey contact our Instruction Librarian at jmjacks9@uno.edu.

Instructor : _____

Course Name and Number (Example: MANG 4211): _____

Prior to this class have you been to the library before?

       Yes   No
       O   O

If yes, please indicate why you visited the library. (Select all that apply.)

Printing/Computing	Studying	Privateer Enrollment Center	Research
O	O	O	O

Other: _____

---

1) **When identifying and finding keywords you can use the following to assist you (Select all that apply)**
    a) Topic or thesis statement
    b) Subject headings from database
    c) Synonyms related to topic

2) **What is the best way to focus your topic?**
    a) Think about the discipline you are researching
    b) Tailor your topic to the requirements of the assignment
    c) Discuss with your professor or librarian about the resources that are available on your topic
    d) All of the above

3) **If your keywords provide too many results, which of the following options would narrow your results? (Select all that apply)**
    a) Limit your search by date, document type or language
    b) Remove a synonym or alternate search term
    c) Add another search term or keyword using AND
    d) Use phrase searching when appropriate

4) **If your keywords provide too few results, which of the following options would narrow your results? (Select all that apply) Information that is intended for general audiences**
    a) Check for spelling mistakes or other errors of your specific search terms
    b) Add a search term using AND
    c) Add a synonym or alternate search term using OR
    d) All of the above

5) **The following question(s) can be utilized to assist you in investigating your topic? (Select all that apply)**
    a) Who?
    b) Where?
    c) Whatever?
    f) How?

List at least one thing that you learned in this session that you did not know before:

_____

_____

JMJ 09/17/14

CASE STUDY REFLECTION QUESTION

How can you leverage the various elements of curriculum design discussed in the chapter and in the case studies to make a meaningful change to your IL program or design a new one?

FURTHER READING

Ariew, Susan. "A Historical Look at the Academic Teaching Library and the Role of the Teaching Librarian." *Communications in Information Literacy 8*, no. 2 (2014): 208–224.

Bawden, David. "Information and Digital Literacies: A Review of Concepts." *Journal of Documentation 57*, no. 2 (2001): 218–259.

Beetham, Helen, and Rhona Sharpe. *Rethinking Pedagogy for a Digital Age: Designing for 21st Century Learning.* New York: Routledge, 2013.

Booth, Char. *Reflective Teaching, Effective Learning: Instructional Literacy for Library Educators.* Chicago: American Library Association, 2011.

Bresnahan, Megan and Andrew Johnson. "Assessing Scholarly Communication and Research Data Training Needs." *Reference Services Review 41*, no. 3 (2013): 413–433.

IDEO. "Design Thinking for Educators Toolkit." 2012. Accessed December 10, 2015. https://www.ideo.com/by-ideo/design-thinking-for-educators.

Secker, Jane, and Emma Coonan. *A New Curriculum for Information Literacy* (pp. 4–39). 2011. Arcadia Project. https://newcurriculum.wordpress.com.

Shell, Leslee, Steven Crawford, and Patricia Harris. "Aided and Embedded: The Team Approach to Instructional Design." *Journal of Library & Information Services in Distance Learning 7*, no. 1–2 (2013): 143–155.

Spencer, David, Matthew Riddle, and Bernadette Knewstubb. "Curriculum Mapping to Embed Graduate Capabilities." *Higher Education Research & Development* 31, no. 2 (2012): 217–231.

Chapter 2

ASSESSMENT

CHAPTER OBJECTIVES

- Examine the data points you want to measure as part of your program.
- Develop strategies for collaborating with colleagues and faculty and handling both logistical and methodological issues.
- Decide how to collect data, including timing and format (survey vs. rubric), and how much technology to incorporate.
- Determine how to structure your approach so that it aligns with broader campus-wide strategic goals and initiatives. This includes:
  - Gathering additional campus data you may need
  - Defining outcomes and success indicators
  - Finding additional supporters and collaborators
  - Deciding how to best report the data you gather

INTRODUCTION

Assessing a program is different from assessing a one-shot session. This chapter will focus on how to look at assessment programmatically—in other words, how to focus on the big picture. This chapter is *not* about helping you design effective learning outcomes or valid assessment methodologies, but suggested readings are included at the end of the chapter to help with those tasks.

Assessment can be challenging for many reasons. There are many barriers to conducting assessment on a large scale, such as infrastructure or political issues, time on your part or that of your colleagues and even administration, and finally simple buy-in from everyone around you! Use this chapter as a blueprint to get the momentum started or help you keep it going.

Definition of Assessment

What is meant by "assessment"? Assessing student learning is not the same thing as reporting on your instruction program. Instruction program statistics, such as number of sessions taught, are important to help you situate your assessment efforts within a larger context. Following are some of the things to think about as you begin to track your program and build your assessment model.

Keeping track of what you teach is one part of the equation. You will need to know what information you need ahead of time and that you are able to capture that information. For example, information regarding students' final grades in the class for which you taught an extensive IL component might be much harder to come by than a simple count of how many students were in the class.

You will also have to decide what information is most meaningful. Too often librarians have a tendency to count everything down to the last detail. While that might be useful data, you need to think about answering that ever-nagging question, "Who cares?" Knowing the number of students in each class might not mean anything to library and/or campus administration; you will have to explain why that number matters. Are you trying to say your program is successful and that is one of the ways you define success? Are you trying to show that you are sorely understaffed and ask for additional resources? Depending on your purpose, some data might not need to be collected. You need to think carefully ahead of time about what you are collecting and, more importantly, why. It will save you a lot of time in the long run if you focus on the most important elements and forget about the rest.

Typically, these are the data points you will want to think about. Depending on your context, there may be others:

- *Number of sessions (discrete, repeat, etc.)*. This is pretty self-explanatory, but you will want to note how many sessions were one-time sessions, multiples, and even which were new ones. You want to show that your program is growing and that you are getting requests to come back as much as possible. Even if your program is not growing, having this information will provide you with the evidence you need to either make a case for growth or for keeping things as they are, but it's always a good idea to have a sense of your baseline figures and mark your starting point. This will also improve your argument that your program is an integral part of learning at the institution. The more you can demonstrate your program's impact through added contact with students the better.

- *Number of students in each session*. Also fairly obvious, but again it's an important marker of context. No matter what the size of your institution, finding the ratio of students who go through your program in relation to the total number of students in the institution will give you a good idea of where you stand and provide some benchmarks for where you want to eventually end up. Saying that you want to have 100 percent participation is noble, but in some cases it's just plain impossible.

- *Learning outcomes assessed*. This is hard to do, and again you must fight the urge to include a laundry list. This is where curriculum mapping will come in handy (yes, again) because you will have to determine what outcomes should be assessed at what point of students' academic path and focus only on those one at a time. Each set will have its own personality and require different approaches, so trying to squeeze 10 of them into one will not work. Not only is it impossible to effectively assess, it's not realistic that you will cover all of the outcomes in a one-shot class no matter how awesome of an instructor you are. And you're far more awesome than you realize!

- *Assessment methodology.* Specific methods are talked about later in this chapter, but you have to think of the logistics as much as the processes. It would be lovely if you could assess all the students' papers in your 100+ section of English Composition and get an amazing snapshot of their mastery. But if you're a one-person shop, that may not work. Similarly, having a multiple-choice survey might seem like a great time saver, but is having student answers about which Boolean operators they would choose given a search string the most appropriate way to determine if they know about search strategies?

- *Timing is important too.* Giving an assessment at the end of class is not really assessment, it's measuring students' ability to remember what you just covered—that's really more evaluation. If there's nothing you can do, and getting this information at the end of each session is your only strategy, try to assess as you go along rather than at the end so that you can gauge how students are doing and if they really understand a concept rather than regurgitate it at the end. Try to do a little pre-test and then a post-test to see if there's any meaningful change (there should be). But it's really optimal for you to give the assessment toward the end of the semester because you want to measure true learning, not simply retention. This will require collaboration with faculty members to (1) provide students with incentives to complete something when they might not even remember that they had a session with you, and (2) incorporate the assessment as part of the overall course structure so that it's meaningful and integrated as opposed to an add-on. More on this later!

- *Assessment tool (if any).* But do you really need to use Qualtrics if a well-designed one-minute paper might do the trick? Technology and assessment work best when you have large amounts of data to digest. Otherwise you might waste more time trying to figure out how that tool works rather than focusing on synthesizing the results. If available, working with an instructional designer or your IT department might help shed some light on this.

- *Results (that make sense).* Whatever data you end up collecting, make sure it's as clear as possible. Remember, most of the folks reading your report will most likely be outside the library and will not understand how your outcome for "scholarship is a conversation" relates to student learning. Explain what you collected, how you collected it, and why it's important. If you can tie it into broader campus efforts for recruitment and retention, so much the better. But don't stretch out the data to accommodate an argument no matter how tempting that might be. If the results show you need to improve how you teach certain concepts, don't be afraid to say so and explain how you would do that. Not everything has to be perfect or show improvement every single time.

- *Dealing with data.* Make sure you are really clear on what you need before you release the data into the wild, so to speak. Do you need to decide on collective benchmarks? Are you simply reporting the data as it comes in? Do you need to create a cohesive picture of the program as a whole and situate it within a larger context? To what extent will you need to connect the results to any general education or other strategic campus outcomes? These questions will drive not only how you collect the information but how you actually organize it.

- *Getting data from others.* To make things more difficult, it's easy to collect and organize this information when you are the only one in control, but what happens if you have to collect data from your colleagues and compile it all into one (ideally) cohesive report? For starters, set some expectations. Hopefully someone in administration is backing you up so that you can (gently) set some deadlines for when you expect the data to be reported, if you are the lucky one who's compiling everything into a nice, neat report. Knowing when things are due and how you will structure everything ahead of time will save you and everyone else a ton of aggravation down the road.

- *Consistency in reporting.* Design a uniform way to collect the data. Using an online form or other mechanized data-collection method is helpful because it forces everyone to include the same type of information. Collecting qualitative data is very challenging because it will be up to you to synthesize it and make it meaningful. You can also choose to gather this information for certain classes and not others if it means maintaining uniformity and coherence. It's very difficult to be able to speak to various courses each with different outcomes and results and have that data look like anything but a jumble of numbers. If there's a way you can work with colleagues to standardize what they measure, choose from a few assessment methods, and report the data in the same way, it will only help. If you can't, do your best to look for patterns and determine what administration would be most interested to hear about as opposed to reporting every single response.

Assessing Your Own Program

Only assess what you plan to change. Don't build an assessment to prove what you are doing is right; create an assessment to improve your program. You must continually do this. Looking at how the program is working is as important as looking at what students are learning, as you cannot have a structurally flawed program that yields great results (or not typically anyway). This means that you will have to make some decisions about what it is you really want to know in terms of student learning and also how good of a job your program is doing in terms of achieving those goals. You may have to let go of some data, as you will not be able to measure every student interaction, and conversely, you might have to think of some elements that you were not planning on including. For example, it could be that your classroom space is not just a source of frustration due to its inflexible setup but that it could actually be a factor that leads to decreased learning. In that case, you would have to collect data on how this is happening and think about ways you would combat that in light of the fact that you might not have the luxury of building a brand-new space.

Just as you set benchmarks for student learning outcomes, you will need to create benchmarks for what a "successful" program looks like at your institution. The Association for College and Research Library's (ACRL) Characteristics of

Programs of Information Literacy that Illustrate Best Practices is a good model to get you started thinking of what elements you want to use as your criteria. You can also use this document to help you make your case with library and perhaps even campus administration. That's not saying you need every single item in order to have the best program, but going through the checklist can help you identify areas of weakness that you can correct as much as areas of strength that you can build upon. If students are consistently scoring low in certain areas, you might want to examine your curriculum. If you are stretched too thin trying to cover classes each semester, you might need additional help and ask for added staffing support. Try to map out the learning outcomes with your assets so that you can make a direct correlation between what success would look like in each outcome with the resources that are in place to make it so and what you would need if they are not. This is kind of like an internal curriculum map of sorts, but instead of looking outward to what courses your library instruction is a part of, you look inward at how your program is directly meeting the learning outcomes that you have designated. Then you can begin to map it to the strategic plan or direction the campus is following and start to make those connections, but not until this self-evaluation is complete.

Before You Assess: What Can You Do to Set the Stage for Success?

Next you will need to choose an assessment method: qualitative, quantitative, or critical. This is a tough one, and again, it really depends on several things. Qualitative methods such as rubrics or student artifacts are best if you really want to get at what students learned. It's a lot more time consuming to norm rubrics and sift through essays or paragraph-type answers, but this is the most authentic way to determine what students actually know. Surveys are great if you need a quick snapshot of student skills ahead of time or if you just want to get a broad feel for how a group scores overall. But there are so many more variables involved. First, you have to make sure that the questions are asked in such a way that they actually solicit the information you need and are not too leading. Not too much is covered about survey design here, but if you can test out the survey ahead of time, this will help you identify those tricky questions.

In addition, you will want to make your survey as "natural" as possible and avoid rote questions where students select the "correct" Boolean phrase out of four or five choices. Why is this important? This type of question, albeit useful in determining if students understand the mechanics of searching, doesn't really get at the broader conceptual framework. This assessment would be great if you are teaching the "point and click" method of searching databases. It's not so wonderful if you really want to know if and to what extent students understand that different types of sources provide varying types of information and that each one requires a slightly different search technique.

The new *Framework for Information Literacy* moves away from having us teach mechanics, which are easily covered in a video, and stresses that the assessment must match the instruction. It would be counterproductive to teach students all about different types of sources and their purposes then turn around and ask them how to search a database. This is also a good time to ask yourself if you are simply teaching them a bunch of database search strategies or if you are really moving on to more advanced critical thinking concepts. You may discover that you think you're doing one thing, but in reality your assessment uncovers that the opposite is true. So take a moment to examine exactly what you're covering in class (and online), and make sure the assessment is really measuring what you think it is.

The timing of assessments is also important. Giving any type of assessment at the end of a session is more about evaluation and short-term retention than about assessing what students learned. One of the pros of doing this is that you are guaranteed a high response rate and you eliminate variables that might affect answers later on. For example, if students were to do some added homework on their research topic that would help them understand Boolean operators, they might score a lot higher than peers in the same class who did not do added work, thereby skewing the results. But if you are really interested in longitudinal knowledge, you have to wait until the end of the semester or even a particular year to measure true synthesis. Just as you cannot expect students to understand and apply everything in a one-shot session, so you cannot assess their learning immediately, remembering that these skills take time to master and that the framework is built for learning across time. So you will have to think of what assessment should be given to students and when and what the best format for that would be. This will require close collaboration with program directors and even campus committees and groups as this goes beyond what you are covering in class.

Collaboration is a recurring pattern, but one that is becoming increasingly important as you look outside of our concentrated efforts during library instruction. Yes, this is much harder and requires significantly more outreach and partnering, but the time is gone when you can rely on only what you're doing within your own one-shot model, because it's neither sustainable nor really accurate in terms of measuring student learning and connecting it to broader efforts on campus. If you are serious about your instruction program making an impact on student recruitment and retention, you cannot do so within your library bubble; you will have to expand your work to include these other element.

Consider the amount of time you have to dedicate to building an assessment instrument. This is where surveys look so tempting. A few multiple-choice questions and you're done, right? Not really. If you don't have time in a semester to build your assessment strategy and your tools, think about expanding that to the entire year. Yes, this will require that you be patient and that you set aside dedicated time to work on it. But it will certainly result in a better tool. If you have strict deadlines to follow, see if you can report on part of the data or a sampling or a smaller subset of the entire pool. Much like pilots and prototypes, thinking on a smaller scale will help you design something more quickly and test it out before you commit. Break your work into chunks so that you can see exactly what you need to do as you go along. It's far more daunting to think you need to create an entire set of rubrics and collect hundreds of student artifacts than just saying you will create one rubric for one outcome and test it out with one section of a course. If you absolutely need to have the entire project ready, enlist some help from colleagues and students. Sometimes it really might just be a matter of having more than one person working on a piece of the larger project in order to get it done.

What is your budget? What can you afford? As will be mentioned in the teaching section, you may not be able to afford the latest version of Qualtrics or a really fancy statistical package to help you measure deviations. And that's OK, but make sure your assessment fits in with what you can do. Rubrics are great because other than requiring some type of student artifact and time, they are really low tech. Even survey software provides free versions of tools online that you can use. If you want to do something more complicated like create some type of tutorial, you will have to think through how you will collect and store the data. Typically, this requires a database that can be queried, unless you use something like Google Forms, which, while free, does have its limitations. If you can't work with a programmer to build an application, this will obviously limit what you can do. But don't think that if you don't have the latest technology you can't create a meaningful assessment method for your classes, because you can. It might just take a little extra work. Remember to reach out to IT and instructional design colleagues. They would at a minimum be able to tell you what campus tools are available and help you select something appropriate if not offer to partner with you to help you design and implement your assessment. It never hurts to ask, and you'd be surprised at how many people will say yes.

Building a Culture of Assessment

Bottom line: it's hard, especially if there isn't a history of assessment or evidence-based decision-making at your institution. Creating a culture of assessment in your library and on campus takes a long time, especially if your library has not done assessment on a strategic level before. This could be the case for various reasons, but there are some things you can do to help change that.

Working with Library and Campus Administration

Nothing is more discouraging then feeling like library administration doesn't understand, or worse, support your assessment efforts. This is where those outreach techniques can really work. Have a meeting with the appropriate administrators and talk with them about your goals. Chances are they simply don't understand what you are trying to do. In addition, go to them with solutions, not problems. Craft a proposal so that you have something to send them ahead of time that outlines everything in your plan. Especially if something requires funding, show them that you've thought through all of the issues.

If you can come up with a way to either save or deflect the costs involved, there's really no reason why they should say no. Making the case for piloting something or using student assistance can go a long way toward alleviating concerns about resources in times of budgetary constraints. Make sure they know you are willing to do the work and that all you need is for colleagues to help you collect the data, which is a minimal investment of their time. If you really need money for your program, make the strongest case possible, and if you have evidence to back it up, so much the better. Do be prepared, however, that the answer might still be no, in which case you should have a backup plan that you can ask to be supported instead so that you can still do something and not lose momentum. Any support you can garner is better than none, and you just need that push in the right direction to help you get started and build on your success. That is why it's always better to start small, succeed, then build on that instead of having a huge plan that you want to implement all at once that goes nowhere. It's OK to have your larger goal in mind, but think of the steps you need to take to get there. Just as you can't build an instruction program overnight, so you cannot create an assessment model overnight. You will need time to see what works and what doesn't before you dream big. It's OK, your amazing plan will still be there even if you have to create a few smaller plans along the way. Patience is key, especially if you're building something from scratch or trying to update something that's been done a certain way for a long time.

Tips for Integrating Your Program into General Education Efforts at the Campus Level

It can be done! In some instances, it might be harder than in others, but based on our recent success in making this happen, you can do it! First and foremost, make sure you have a clear idea about what you are asking. For example, it's one thing to ask if you can report your data at a campus-wide level, it's quite another to ask for a general education designation to be passed. Knowing ahead of time what you would like to see happen will help you sell the idea to the appropriate folks on campus.

That brings us to the second point: Pick some champions! Sometimes the argument is easy because the library already has a presence at the general education table, and you are simply asking for a modification or update of a certain element. Other times, you are trying to get to the table in the first place, which will require some work. Find out who is the administrator responsible for general education and assessment. Meet with that person first to make sure he or she understands what you want to do and can help you navigate the sometimes choppy political waters on your campus. If the appropriate administrator doesn't support you, you might not be able to convince anyone else either. Next, determine who else on campus you need on your side—perhaps there is an assessment office or several committees where this will need to be approved. Find out who the stakeholders are and engage them in conversations to get a feel for their level of support. Based on how that goes, you can then decide what the next step might be and if it would be worth pressing the issue or waiting a little longer, or if there are any intermittent, smaller (and less politically charged) steps you can take on the way to achieving your final goal.

If you do get the green light, have a clear strategy for talking about this issue at any meetings or presentations that you hold as a result of these discussions. Have a handout or a short presentation that outlines the basics as well as the logistics of what your program would look like. Offering to do the actual assessment work itself will go a long way toward alleviating the perennial faculty complaint that they don't have time for one more thing. Don't assume faculty members know what IL is (even if they schedule library instruction) or that they are aware of the importance of assessment at a broad level. Be as clear and concise as possible.

Once an action gets approved, be ready to act. You need to show that this was an important endeavor for your program and that you are serious about doing these activities. If your efforts don't work the first time around, try again. Sometimes a change in committee membership or administration is all you need to get the ball rolling again, and assessment data that shows the strength of your program can always be shared, even if it's not part of any formal efforts (yet!). No one will penalize you for sharing information, even if they don't ask for it, and in fact it might prompt conversations and awareness to surface simply because you took that proactive step and gave administration something they didn't even know they needed.

Partnering with Groups on Campus (Writing Center, Career Center, etc.)

Partners outside the library, such as writing and career centers, can often be your biggest allies. They can help open doors where others can't, and they can also help build momentum and rally around your cause. It would be good to set up a separate meeting with each partner before you bring everyone together or attend that all-important campus meeting. This way, you can explain what you are doing and find out quickly if they are on board or not. If they aren't, you need to think strategically and decide if you really need their support. Sometimes you think you do and it turns out you really don't and vice versa. But you would be amazed at what you can find out by simply talking with people and asking them to collaborate. Chances are they are just as stretched and overworked as you, and any opportunity for assistance will be welcome.

Groups such as the campus assessment or institutional data office can be crucial to providing you with information about the way things are done, who you need to involve, and how they can help you. To give you an example, at one of the authors' institutions, the library had never been a part of general education assessment reporting on campus for various historically steeped reasons. When the library decided it was time to change that, a few librarians met with the university's assessment office before meeting with anyone else and found out that artifacts were already being collected for general education assessment and it would be simply a matter of applying an IL rubric, so it would really mean no extra work for anyone involved other than the library.

This information turned out to be the key element needed to sell the campus committees responsible for general education assessment on the merits of adding this rubric and measuring these outcomes because it required no changes in the existing structures and, in fact, it was seen as providing value-added data the institution did not currently have. This is to say that you need to do your homework and work with as many campus partners as possible because they can bring an added layer of support (and information!) to a process that can be fraught with politics and turf wars, and you might just be able to uncover something that can make this process a lot easier and ultimately successful.

Connecting assessment results with student learning and retention is a tough thing to do! Megan Oakleaf's work can help you through this; she has written and presented extensively on this topic. What follows is an attempt to summarize the main points to keep in mind when trying to connect your assessment data with larger campus efforts in student retention and recruitment.

Decide what data you want to collect (and more importantly report on) for this purpose. You must decide before you begin what data makes the most sense to collect so that it can be tied into institutional information later. Are you going to look at student grades in a course where you taught an IL component? Are you simply going to list the learning outcomes and how students did in each one and somehow extrapolate that to student retention scores, comparing those who had library instruction to those who didn't?

For this type of assessment, you will have to think of what institutional data is available and how *your* data can be connected. If campus data is quantitative in nature, yours might have to be too. If there is room for qualitative analysis, you will have to include that as well. It's one thing to think about how you will report this information for in-library or in-house purposes, such as changing how you cover topic selection, versus thinking of how this same information will be analyzed from a much broader perspective at a campus level and by people who may never have heard the term "information literacy" much less understand what it means (Oakleaf, "Are They," 67).

You may have to do a lot of defining of outcomes and methods used as well as determining how to align the information you collect with what campus is collecting so that the two types of data speak to each other and help support one another. This might make you change how you do assessment, and it may force you to try things that you normally would not. To some degree that's fine and you will have to adapt. You will also have to consider if you need a second set of assessment data for more internal purposes that conform more closely to the type of information you would want to gather. This will require a lot of flexibility and adaptability on your part, and in some instances it will feel duplicative. But you have to realize that the campus is not interested in how it can support your program with the data it collects but rather how you can prove your program supports campus initiatives. Leave the internal successes and instruction improvement to be just that, and focus on how you can maximize the power of your data even if it means having to assess in a way that seems counterintuitive or difficult at first (Oakleaf, "Are They," 70).

This means making sure you know what the strategic plan and/or directions for your institution are and that you connect your data with them. Just about every institution will have something related to student learning, and that's a broad umbrella that will allow you to sneak under there and make it appear as though you were planning this all along and, by the way, look at these amazing results! You have to make some mention of how your program fits into whatever general education or learning outcomes are out there, and if it doesn't you need to ask yourself why not. Is your program so removed from institutional activities that you cannot see any relationship? If that's the case, you need to go back to the drawing board and have those conversations with campus groups and library administration to see what you might be missing.

Decide how you want to measure impact and connect that to institutional goals and strategic priorities. Defining impact is going to take some work. Your definition might differ greatly from the one on campus, and you will want to make sure they match as closely as possible. That said, you will need to determine if you are talking about better grades, retention, completion, better job prospects, or something else. Each one of these areas will require a slightly different focus and type of data that you can request from your institutional effectiveness (or something similar) office on campus (Oakleaf, "Are They," 74–75).

You will also have to think about privacy issues, since you will likely be linking specific outcomes to specific student cohorts and classes. You will need to work with the appropriate entities on campus, such as your Institutional Review Board office, to determine what you will need to do if you want to make this data publicly available through a presentation or publication. Even if you don't, there might be other privacy issues you need to keep in mind if you are planning on keeping disaggregate data as opposed to making broader generalizations about student learning in general.

This is not going to be a quick process. You will not be able to demonstrate that students have a better chance of staying in school if they are successful researchers within the construct of a one-shot session. You will have to track your groups over time, and that might mean at least one semester, if not one or more academic years. This means you need to be patient and build your assessment from a summative perspective to demonstrate how learning occurs over time using the markers you choose (grades, etc.) as your targets toward the final goal (i.e., staying enrolled).

In addition, you might simply want to focus on a particular cohort instead of all students. That will help you manage that group better and extrapolate results to broader student populations. This is where your office of institutional effectiveness or similar entity can help you identify that cohort and decide how to track it and what data you want to collect for your long-range study. If there is no such group on your campus, you might have to ask administration to assist you in collecting this information, but most institutions have a way for you to work with a set of student records and gather information such as grade point average or other necessary data. You might also need to enlist the support of a statistics department or faculty to help you make these mathematical models work, as you undoubtedly need to think about the validity of the data, especially if you are extrapolating to large numbers of students or need to perform some type of statistical calculations.

It's important to make the distinction between correlation and causation. Megan Oakleaf is adamant in this regard. It's nearly impossible to prove or show that students have a higher grade in a particular class because of the direct intervention with you (causation). The reason for that is simple—there are too many other variables at play that you may not be aware of and therefore cannot account for. As an example, if a student receives additional help from a librarian or even a tutor, chances are he or she will do better in that class, but it might have nothing to do with your session on how to do research for the assignment in question. At best, you will be able to infer that as a result of contact with you and the library in general, students tend to do better or simply stay enrolled (correlation). In other words, do students who have library intervention generally do better, stay enrolled longer, or find a job faster than those who do not and to what degree? If you can answer that type of question, that's probably more meaningful and useful than trying to establish something more concrete (Oakleaf, "Measuring Value," 13–14).

Working with Faculty

Chances are you will need some assistance from the faculty whose students you want to assess, which is why you need to work with the people who will support you! The outreach chapter will help with specific tips and tricks on how to approach those pesky people who might not want to talk with you, but you simply cannot force those faculty members to help you who do not want to spend time outside of class on your stuff or those who don't see a value in what you're trying to do. If this means you have a smaller pool to draw from, so be it.

Collaboration with faculty members on assessment can take many forms. At a minimum, they can provide extra credit points for assessment completion. That gets back to the add-on concept mentioned earlier and is helpful in ensuring that you get results that you can report. A better approach would be to actually design the assessment together so that it fits in with the assignment, timing, and objectives for the course. If you can build the assessment as part of whatever project students are working on so that you can append the research piece, that approach will give you the most seamless and authentic experience possible.

You will need to talk with the faculty member about what type of assessment will work best for the class (pre/post, survey, rubric, observation, etc.). There are two ways to go about this. You can create something "external" to the course, whether a survey or additional assignments or exercises for students to complete, or you can integrate the research element into class assignments themselves, so they would be "internal."

In the case of the external pieces, they can either be assigned as homework or as extra credit elements, while some might be appropriate for in-class completion. In either case, you will want to specify in your analysis that this might not be representative of learning over time but rather a more formative type of assessment. Having faculty buy-in for grades and extra credit is crucial because students will simply not do your assignment if they aren't required to, no matter how easy you think it is. If you are planning on fully integrating your module into existing coursework, you will want to ensure that the same method for scoring the assignment itself will be used for the research component as well. For example, if you are using a research essay for this purpose, you will want to include the research component as part of the grading criteria listed by the faculty member. You can then decide if you want to develop a shared rubric and/or criteria and score everything together or keep your own.

Timing is of the essence! Especially if your assessment lies outside existing course assignments, you need to make sure they are given at the correct time in the overall course. This again relies on faculty who are willing to help you, as you cannot necessarily be there in person when this occurs. You can release something via a course management system or post something online or simply ask the faculty member to send it to students on your behalf. If you are piggybacking onto the existing assignment, this is much easier to do.

But wait, there's no way your faculty will go for that; they already complain that they can barely fit in your session to begin with, now you should do even more?! Yes, you heard us. Start small, with just a few courses, see what happens, and work with folks who are willing to take that risk. Surely there must be at least one intrepid soul who will want to work on this with you. If this is not an option for you at all, ask if the faculty member can apply the assessment for you (train the trainer) when he or she grades the assignment anyway. You will still have to collaborate even in this scenario, as you will literally have to train the faculty member on what to evaluate and you might even have to norm the rubric to ensure he or she doesn't either oversimplify or complicate the application of the rubric.

Finally, no matter what approach you take, you will have to send the results back to the faculty members with a plan for improvement for next time. They need to be a part of the entire process as much as the students do. Ideally, this will prompt conversations about how their assignments might need to change and how your role might become even stronger in their course as a result. Even if the results are stellar, you can always find something to improve or discuss. Do this even if you did not work with that faculty member because that might just open the door to a conversation you did not anticipate happening!

Work with colleagues and create tools to help coworkers be successful. This really depends on your role within the library's assessment structure. If you are required to collect and report assessment data, have a clear process in place and provide everyone with the right tools to help them give you what you need as easily (and quickly) as possible. This goes beyond the mechanics of data input, especially as you will most likely need buy-in from everyone in order to make this work. You can begin with some of the internal outreach efforts already discussed, but this is the time to also consider the creation of a group or taskforce that can assist you. This committee can provide structure and clarity for instruction-related activities and lend a hand in pushing a broader agenda.

This means developing any necessary training so that you are all on the same page in terms of how learning outcomes are measured and assessed, creating appropriate materials to accompany that training, and providing best-practice policies to govern overall assessment activities so that when the time comes to collect the needed information you are not getting questions about what this is and why you're doing it.

An assessment coordinator might already be appointed in the library. Depending on how your institution is structured, it might be best to have one person handling all things assessment, or a committee structure might be better. If the person in charge of assessment is not you, it goes without saying that you will need to cooperate with that person to make sure your efforts are not working at cross purposes and that there is support for what you're doing. That person can (ideally) help you develop whatever structures you need to make assessment a well-integrated portion of your instruction program. So what happens if he or she does not? Schedule a meeting to find out what his or her agenda is before you assume that the person will either be your best friend or your worst enemy.

As with your conversations with administration, if you can't achieve complete buy-in and the person is hemming and hawing about having you as a part of assessment work, see if he or she will let you at least contribute in a small way, however minor. That may seem like a loss to you, but in fact, it might actually give you the freedom to do what you need to do without stepping on toes. This might seem totally counterintuitive, but it's a way to ensure you can move forward with your work because the person has already been put on notice that this is what you intend to do and if he or she chooses not to cooperate, let that come from that person, not you. If you absolutely need the person's assistance in order to make your program work, the best solution might be to appeal to administration, as you will most likely have to come to some sort of consensus about your respective roles and responsibilities.

In addition, letting everyone know about your plan ahead of time is key. At this point, you may be thinking that this is madness—after all, you have a beautiful plan in mind, and if everyone knows about it, surely there will be strong opposition. That could happen, of course. But this can often help you work on your plan on the side without really raising any red flags. Because the information is out there ahead of time, those who have a problem can address it before you get too far down the road, while those who are supportive can continue to be so. Now if you are proposing an increased assessment workload for librarians, you would want to make sure you've cleared it with the appropriate administrators, and this message may even be better coming from them directly. But if you are simply asking to collect assessment data and need some basic collaboration from them, this should not pose any insurmountable obstacles if you've done the legwork ahead of time.

Know your limits. That being said, it definitely is *not* your job to do the work for your colleagues; they know their classes best and should take responsibility for assessing them. It's OK to say no to someone who wants you to create their survey for them. This is where having a repository of materials and examples can come in handy to allow people to adapt existing tools, or if you have a graduate assistant or student who can help, that might be a good alternative as well. Now there is a difference between doing the work for others and developing a centralized set of tools that they can use. Speaking of that data entry form, it will probably save you a lot of time and aggravation if you just design the thing yourself, how you want to (assuming you can do this without too much additional input), and then let everyone fill it out on their own. Only you can strike a balance between these various elements and decide where your involvement needs to end.

Share your work and explain what you did! Assessment can involve enormous invisible labor, and nobody will know that you're doing it if you don't share. This gets back to the whole outreach conversation. Make sure your results get included in annual campus reports, and distribute them to targeted departments, organizations, or anyone else who might need to see them. For one, you certainly want to brag about the great work that you're doing, and this is a subtle (yet effective) method for tooting your own horn without coming across like you're simply bragging. OK, you are, but pointing to student improvement and talking about how your program fits into that will allow your readers to make the connection without you having to spell it out for them.

Conversely, this information can be a great way to get a foot in the door. Going in armed with evidence might be just the thing you need to get a department chair's attention, and it can provide you with a very specific issue to discuss as opposed to simply saying that someone should work with the library because it's the right thing to do. That person doesn't know that, and sorry, it doesn't matter. But he or she might if you show that overall students benefit from library instruction and in fact scores went up by 20 percent for those who participated in your program. And don't forget to share the results with your colleagues! Letting them see how they contributed is vital to their continued buy-in and involvement—when people feel like all the time they put into filling out your really long form was worth it, they will likely do so again. Thank people—even if they don't deserve it (within limits). Show your colleagues that you appreciate their time as much as you expect them to appreciate yours, and who knows, they might even offer to help you next time!

Working with Yourself

Assessment takes longer than you think, so give yourself time. Set early deadlines so that if something goes wrong you're not late in turning in that data needed for a campus meeting or report. Don't wait until the last minute to collect information from your colleagues because chances are you (and they) will be frazzled and you will end up rushing things. Build in cushions of extra time, keeping in mind the ebb and flow of the semester and when colleagues are typically at their busiest. It doesn't make sense to collect data at the beginning of the semester when everyone is busy prepping for classes, getting to their departments, and gearing up for projects. Try to have a "start of the semester" meeting to set timelines and goals, then provide the tools needed to collect your data and set gentle reminders along the way.

This should allow you to stagger when information comes in and how you process it instead of pulling an all-nighter the day before the report is due. If you feel like in-person meetings are better for checking in, schedule them at set intervals before calendars get booked up. Map out how you see the entire semester and what your key deadlines are so that you can communicate that with everyone well ahead of time. Add stuff to their calendars if you don't think they can do it themselves—it sounds a bit intrusive, but it works! Automate a recurring meeting, add agenda items to the meeting description, and streamline the process so that all they have to do is show up!

Dedicate time in your schedule. Prioritize assessment as a separate part of your job (don't lump it in with general instruction duties). Sometimes all you can do is come up for air during any given semester. But if you can, try to block out, and yes, *really* block out, time on your calendar when you turn off your email, silence your phone, and analyze the data that everyone has turned in. Go to another room or office if you know you're likely to be interrupted, or simply close your door. This might be easier said than done, but you will need uninterrupted time to focus on the numbers to see if you can make sense of them and ask any follow-up questions that might arise.

Be kind to yourself; assessment doesn't happen in a day. Nor should it! Don't be frustrated if you feel like the entire semester has gone by and you still cannot make heads or tails of the heterogeneous data provided by your colleagues. Guess what? Assessment is not a perfect thing; you will never have all the answers, and you will be lucky if you can make any sense of the information you've been given, much less present it to anyone else in a way that can make a compelling case for anything.

Depressed yet? This should not make you feel hopeless, but you must let go of the notion that assessment comes in a perfect package that you can wrap with a neat little bow and deliver without any issues. At best, assessment can help you ascertain if all the hard work you've put into your program is actually paying off and to what degree. At worst, assessment is a jumble of meaningless information that might not be helpful. Ever. But that shouldn't stop you from trying and refining as you go along, even if you do feel like all you're doing is spinning around in circles. Chances are others feel the same way, and as long as you can point to some positive movement along whatever scale you decide to use, you're way ahead of everyone else.

FINAL TAKEAWAYS

1. Start small and work your way toward a full-scale programmatic assessment implementation. That way you can build on your successes and address any issues that arise before they get blown out of proportion.

2. Think about assessing the overall effectiveness of your program as much as its content and curriculum.

3. Give yourself time to work through any changes the assessment results reveal. Don't try to change everything all at once or from semester to semester. Let changes sink in for a while before adding new layers.

4. As with teaching and curriculum design, you will have to make some decisions about the timing and type of assessment you want to apply and what your ultimate goal is for that information as that will impact your methodology and design choices.

5. Working with colleagues can be tricky, especially if you are responsible for collecting their assessment information. Make things as simple on them (and yourself) as possible; stay organized and build consensus for logistics and processes as you go. Same goes for working with faculty.

6. Connect your assessment results to broad campus-wide initiatives, programs, and goals for maximum bang for your buck. More importantly, come up with your working definition of success and how you want to demonstrate that your results help to achieve those goals.

Case Study: Rethinking Indirect Measurement as a Means of Student Assessment

Todd J. Wiebe, Hope College

Brief Abstract: Instruction librarians are often required to assess the impact of their teaching on student learning. A simple, commonly used approach to accomplishing this is through surveys, asking students to self-assess their abilities on a select set of research and information literacy skills, both before and after receiving library and information literacy instruction. This case study describes the lessons learned by one library upon attempting this method of assessment, reflecting what the scholarly literature says about such indirect measurement. It concludes with an example of how "flipped citation analysis" can be used to directly assess student skill and perception of research at the onset of their college experience.

INSTITUTIONAL BACKGROUND

Located in Holland, Michigan, Hope College is a four-year, private, coeducational liberal arts institution consisting of approximately 3,300 baccalaureate students with a student-faculty ratio of 13:1. Over 90 majors are offered among its four academic divisions—Arts, Humanities, Natural and Applied Sciences, and Social Sciences. Van Wylen Library (winner of the 2004 ACRL Excellence in Academic Libraries Award, college category) primarily serves Hope students, faculty, and staff but has a resource-sharing agreement with neighboring Western Theological Seminary. Its personnel consist of the dean of libraries, nine faculty librarians/archivists, and 12 library associates/support staff.

DESCRIPTION OF PROGRAM, PROJECT, OR SPACE

Library and information literacy instruction is well integrated into a wide range of courses at Hope, from First Year Seminar to senior capstones. It has an especially strong, long-standing connection with English 113 (Expository Writing I), a general education course that has been flagged in the curriculum to include a library and information literacy component. This usually consists of two to three librarian-led sessions, often coplanned by librarians and classroom faculty. Sessions are routinely designed to align with each course section's unique writing/research assignments. Librarians do, however, have their own objectives that they strive to cover with all students enrolled in the course, regardless of section. In spring of 2013, the research and instruction librarians updated their IL objectives for English 113 (below) and shared them with the English Department.

- Defining and developing topics ("pre-search")
- Identifying appropriate information resources for various research purposes
- Implementing search terms/strategy
- Accessing different types of information
- Analyzing and evaluating results critically
- Expanding and refining Internet research
- Incorporating and citing sources

See http://www.hope.edu/library/help-services/faculty-services/class-sessions/english-113.html

These were reviewed at a departmental meeting and adopted as what the librarians would agree to teach in the English 113 IL sessions. Naturally, then, the next step was to develop an assessment plan to see if these goals and objectives were, in fact, being met.

TACKLING THE LENS

In the summer of 2013, the four members of the research and instruction team met several times to discuss how to assess the newly revised IL component of English 113. Considering that there are usually 18 to 20 sections of the course offered per semester, each with approximately 18 students, the assessment tool, we thought, needed to be something that could be implemented rather quickly and easily while providing us with a basic snapshot of our instruction's impact. Feeling some pressure to have a plan in place by the fall, for this first attempt we settled on the commonly used pre/post survey, asking students to rate their abilities on seven specific research/information literacy–related skills or concepts (strongly agree = 5, strongly disagree = 1). The pre survey was given during fall semester at the beginning of the first library session for each class. In most cases, this took place in late September. With almost all English 113 enrollees being first-year students, this timing marked a very early stage in the overall college experience—most of them were as green as they come. The intention, then, was to give the survey again at the end of the semester once all sections had completed the library/IL training. Pre and post results could then be compared, making it possible to quantify, or assess, the impact of the librarians' contribution to student learning. As it turned out, however, the most valuable data came not from the *post* survey as expected, but from the *pre*, where students reported overwhelming and seemingly improbable confidence in their library and information literacy aptitude and readiness to do college-level research. Over 70 percent of students, across all 19 course sections, selected "Agree" or "Highly agree" to all seven questions on the survey, which each led with the phrase "I am able to . . ." Although not ignorant of the fact that students often misperceive research to be a simple exercise in searching and finding information tidbits online, we thought that our questions were phrased in such a way that first-year students, especially, would stop and think about whether they really were capable of doing research at a level appropriate for college. Basically, we assumed that most students would acknowledge some level of inexperience, and therefore, unpreparedness for college-level research. With this newly acquired information pointing decisively to the contrary, assessment took a different turn. It was the *pre*-survey results, then, that became the primary data shared with English 113 instructors as a call to action, of sorts, with aims to alert them of their students' imagined research and IL prowess. Although students were not given an actual skills-based test, the anecdotal evidence observed by librarians, and feedback from faculty, was sufficient to hypothesize an incongruence between students' perceived and actual skills. The post test was eventually given, with results showing a modest increase in students' self-reported abilities, but at this point, we had already been provided with the most compelling piece of the assessment.

LESSONS LEARNED

The main lesson learned from this assessment initiative gone somewhat awry came after delving into the scholarly social and behavioral science literature in search of an explanation. In what is now a seminal work of competence theory, Kruger and Dunning (1999) assert that "the skills that engender competence in a particular domain are often the very same skills necessary to evaluate competence in that domain" (1121). In other words, people who "don't know what they don't know" are more prone to exuding confidence in abilities they do not possess. Studies in an array of disciplines have since delved further into this phenomenon, revealing fundamental problems in assessment measures based on student self-appraisals (e.g., Kennedy, Lawton, & Plumlee, 2002; Baxter & Norman, 2011; Heath, DeHoek, & Locatelli, 2012). Not surprisingly, the academic library literature has also explored this in relation to students' research and information literacy skills (Gross & Lantham, 2009, 2012; Gustavson & Nall, 2011). Heath, DeHoek, and Locatelli (2012) say it best: "Although indirect measures of participant learning or mastery might tell us something about the level of confidence of the participants, they probably tell us little about actual ability or knowledge" (1). Hinging an information literacy assessment initiative solely on such measures is therefore weak, at best, unless the objective is in fact to gauge students' perceived abilities rather than actual competency/comprehension.

Initially thought of as a failed assessment initiative, the unforeseen results have since become an effective talking point for librarians while working to embed information literacy education deeper into the curriculum. Telling other faculty that over 70 percent of English 113 students in the first month of their first semester of college reported confidence in their existing level of research and IL skills has never failed to elicit a response containing a mix of both amusement and dismay.

Flipped Citation Analysis: One Librarian's Take on Pre-assessment

One way for librarians to more directly assess students' library research/IL skills is through citation analysis, looking specifically at students' source choice and usage (Ursin, Blakesley Lindsay, & Johnson, 2004; Mohler, 2005; Watson, 2012). This practice is often done by examining works cited lists or bibliographies, as seen on students' completed papers/projects, looking at appropriateness of source types, accuracy of reference formatting, and so on. In the abovementioned English 113 course, especially, it is commonplace that classroom faculty send student topics to librarians prior to a session so that relevant examples can be used and demonstrated during the instruction. For two years (four semesters) now, I have been taking this practice to the next level by not only reviewing students' topic proposals but also students' first attempt at locating appropriate sources. Rather than waiting to see how they fare at the end of the semester or after a library session, this "flipped citation analysis" provides insight to students' first stab at conducting research on their topic prior to any form of intervention or instruction. As a prerequisite to the first session with me in the library, students are required to submit: (1) their topic, (2) their top two sources so far (in MLA format), and (3) brief commentary on how they found the sources and why they chose them as their top two. These are emailed directly to me in the week leading up to the session. With this information, I am able to not only prepare relevant examples, but more importantly, I'm able to enter the session with a clearer idea of what students in these particular classes consider to be among the best sources available for their topic.

Naturally, implementation of such an added component requires buy-in and cooperation from the faculty member teaching the course. It also adds a significant amount of librarian prep time in the days leading up to each session. In this case, I have been emailing each student back with a short, personalized response, commenting on their top two sources, and providing a mini explanation of what we will be doing in class and how there will be many new options presented to them for further consideration.

In light of how students self-assessed their level of IL in previous sections of the course, this flipped citation analysis has been a great way to see where first-year students actually are in terms of their research (especially source selection and evaluation) skills. With each iteration, I gain a better understanding of the information landscape as seen by students, and in most cases, can confirm that they are not even thinking about where the library plays a role. I have not yet rounded out the assessment by comparing students' "pre" citations with "post" (on their final paper), but this would indeed be a great way to see more tangibly the impact of my instruction sessions. Admittedly, this method cannot possibly assess all seven of the goals and objectives we have for IL in English 113. What it has done, however, is directly assess the most questionable revelation (i.e., student IL self-assuredness at the onset of college) from our attempt at indirect measurement.

REFERENCES AND SUGGESTED READINGS

Baxter, Pamela, and Geoff Norman. "Self-assessment or Self-deception? A Lack of Association between Nursing Students' Self-assessment and Performance." *Journal of Advanced Nursing* 67, no. 11 (2011): 2406–2413.

Gross, Melissa, and Don Latham. "Undergraduate Perceptions of Information Literacy: Defining, Attaining, and Self-assessing Skills." *College & Research Libraries* 70, no. 4 (2009): 336–350.

Gross, Melissa, and Don Latham. "What's Skill Got to Do with It?: Information Literacy Skills and Self-views of Ability among First-Year College Students." *Journal of the American Society for Information Science and Technology* 63, no. 3 (2012): 574–583.

Gustavson, Amy, and H. Clark Nall. "Freshman Overconfidence and Library Research Skills: A Troubling Relationship?" *College & Undergraduate Libraries* 18, no. 4 (2011): 291–306.

Heath, Linda, Adam DeHoek, and Sara House Locatelli. "Indirect Measures in Evaluation: On Not Knowing What We Don't Know." *Practical Assessment, Research & Evaluation* 17, no. 6 (2012): 1–6

.Kennedy, Ellen J., Leigh Lawton, and E. Leroy Plumlee. "Blissful Ignorance: The Problem of Unrecognized Incompetence and Academic Performance." *Journal of Marketing Education* 24, no. 3 (2002): 243–252.

Kruger, Justin, and David Dunning. "Unskilled and Unaware of It: How Difficulties in Recognizing One's Own Incompetence Lead to Inflated Self-assessments." *Journal of Personality and Social Psychology* 77, no. 6 (1999): 1121.

Mohler, Beth A. "Citation Analysis as an Assessment Tool." *Science & Technology Libraries* 25, no. 4 (2005): 57–64.

Ursin, Lara, Elizabeth Blakesley Lindsay, and Corey M. Johnson. "Assessing Library Instruction in the Freshman Seminar: A Citation Analysis Study." *Reference Services Review* 32, no. 3 (2004): 284–292.

Watson, Alex P. "Still a Mixed Bag: A Study of First-Year Composition Students' Internet Citations at the University of Mississippi." *Reference Services Review* 40, no. 1 (2012): 125–137.

Case Study: Implementing a Sustainable, Long-Term Student Learning Assessment Program

Leslie Hurst, University of Washington Bothell
Jackie Belanger, University of Washington Bothell

Brief Abstract: This case study offers a model and set of practical approaches to implementing a sustainable, long-term student learning assessment program. While many academic libraries assess student learning outcomes, and the literature offers a variety of techniques and models for doing so, librarians can still struggle to build this activity into an ongoing practice. The Campus Library at the University of Washington Bothell developed a multiyear program that aimed to make assessment routine, predictable, and manageable. Strategies for developing a flexible assessment plan, managing the process of creating student learning outcomes, writing rubrics, assessing outcomes collaboratively with librarians and faculty, and using assessment results to make changes to the information literacy curriculum are discussed.

INSTITUTIONAL BACKGROUND

The Campus Library is located at the University of Washington Bothell campus about 20 miles northwest of Seattle, Washington. The campus was established in 1990 and offers 40 undergraduate and graduate degree programs, 33 of which were added within the last five years alone. It is also the fastest-growing public university in the state, with 66 percent enrollment growth since 2010. With 4,588 full-time students, further growth in both the student body and number of degree programs is anticipated.

The UW Bothell is committed to providing access, opportunity, and innovation, and its student body is one of the most diverse amid Washington's public universities. Nearly 46 percent of students are students of color or the first in their families to attend college, and 71 percent of the student body is of traditional college age (17–25 years old).

The Campus Library is a part of the tri-campus University of Washington Libraries system and maintains an interdisciplinary, curriculum-focused collection of over 110,000 volumes and a multitude of electronic resources. The library has a robust information literacy instruction program that is highly valued and supported by faculty and library administration. Librarians from all subject areas partner with faculty to strategically integrate hands-on and online instruction into targeted courses within the undergraduate and graduate curricula.

DESCRIPTION OF PROGRAM, PROJECT, OR SPACE

In 2012, the Campus Library's head of teaching and learning and the assessment coordinator took steps to develop a formal student learning outcomes assessment program. While the library's instruction program was well established at this time, and individual librarians assessed classroom instruction at the course section level, a broader and more systemic assessment program had not been created. The need for this program was driven by a number of factors. The rapid growth in the number of new programs, courses, and students at the UW Bothell meant librarians needed to be able to look across multiple sections of core courses (often taught by different faculty/librarian teams) in order to assess whether students were reaching the same learning outcomes. This institutional growth was also accompanied by a campus-wide emphasis on accountability and the assessment of student learning.

In order to respond to these developments, the library began by establishing information literacy student learning outcomes and a formal plan for assessing them. The outcomes offer a broad vision for information literacy and research-related student learning at UW Bothell and describe what we hope our students will have learned and what they will be able to do at various stages of their academic careers. Finalized in 2012, the outcomes formed the basis for conducting the library's annual assessment of student learning process. Between 2012 and 2015, the library's assessment program became a key component of the overall information literacy program.

TACKLING THE LENS

The key priorities for the assessment program involve sustainability, collaboration, and a commitment to improving student learning. A challenge faced in establishing the program was how to build this activity into an ongoing, sustained practice. In response, the library's head of teaching and learning and the assessment coordinator developed a multiyear program that aimed to make assessment routine, predictable, and manageable for all librarians. Each year, the head of teaching and learning and the assessment librarian, in coordination with colleagues, select one degree program and focus assessment on the core course targeted for information literacy instruction within that area. The information literacy student learning outcomes most appropriate for the course are identified, and instruction and assignments are closely aligned with these outcomes. In collaboration with faculty, librarians then collect existing assignments or create new ones that provide evidence of student learning for the defined outcomes. At the end of the year, a rubric is created from the outcomes and student work is assessed by librarians, faculty, and other campus partners. The results of the assessment process are reported to faculty and librarians, and any changes to instruction or course assignments are tracked. Although there are multiple components to this approach, the predictable structure and manageable scope has enabled librarians to embrace this work enthusiastically.

Collaboration between faculty, librarians, and others (such as writing center staff) is key to this process. Faculty who teach the core courses for our selected focus area are approached early in the process to gain permission to use student work and create buy-in for the activity. Faculty are then invited to participate in the annual rubric assessment "retreat" day in which we assess student work. This creates both opportunities and challenges: while this approach facilitates rich discussions between librarians and faculty about student learning, differing expectations about student performance also often emerge during these discussions. These perspectives have to be reconciled during a rubric norming process to ensure all participants score student work in similar ways. In addition, student assignments often vary across different sections of the same course. Using the same outcomes and rubric for different assignments can be challenging, as the same criteria may often not apply. However, this has led to fruitful conversations among faculty and librarians about the possible need to ensure that the same outcomes are being addressed in all sections of a course.

Assessing just one curricular area per year is the key to sustaining the program and securing librarian buy-in. However, this can be a time-intensive process for the head of teaching and learning, the assessment coordinator, and the subject librarian whose curricular area is involved. While this is currently manageable, continued institutional growth and the need to manage librarian workloads may mean that we need to look more closely at how we can do this work in more effective ways.

LESSONS LEARNED

On the whole, the student learning outcomes assessment program has been a success. We have gained significant insight into information literacy student learning in a number of our core programs, made numerous improvements to our instruction and assignment design, and strengthened collaborative relationships within and beyond the Campus Library. However, each year we learn more about the assessment process and make changes accordingly. In 2013–2014, for example, we experimented with assessing student work from two very different programs: Business and Environmental Sciences. This approach necessitated two different rubrics, two different sets of faculty participants, and two different rubric norming sessions on the same day. Librarians and others involved in assessing student work found it challenging to come to grips with the different assignments in a short period of time. In 2014–2015, we returned to the practice of focusing on just one core course in one curricular area.

Having a single day-long "retreat" model in which all librarians (regardless of subject area) come together to assess student work has reduced the overall time commitment for librarians. It has helped gain buy-in from colleagues, as they know that they will only be committed to a single day out of the year. However, condensing the tasks of norming the rubric and scoring 50 samples of student work into a single day can be challenging (and sometimes exhausting). Based on librarians' feedback, in 2015 we reduced the amount of time spent on the day itself and instead gave librarians the option to finish assessing work over the course of the following week. Analysis of rubric results should reveal if this longer period has led to wider variations in scores.

The development and norming of the rubric is a time-intensive process, and most of the rubrics are not continuing to be used after the assessment process. Going forward, it will be worth considering how we can encourage our colleagues to continue using the rubrics for their assessment activities. While most of the librarians anecdotally report increased attention to assessment as a result of participating in the program, incorporating rubric assessment into their ongoing work remains a challenge. If we could go back and do things differently, we would build this into the process from the start by emphasizing that the rubrics are designed for long-term, ongoing use by individual librarians.

Table 2.1.

Links to University of Washington Outcomes and Assessment Pages

Title of Document/ Material	Description	
Campus Library Teaching and Learning program	Campus program information	http://libguides.uwb .edu/teaching
Campus Library Student Learning Assessment program	Campus assessment information	http://libguides.uwb .edu/assessment
Campus Library Information Literacy Student Learning Outcomes	Campus information literacy information	http://libguides.uwb .edu/learningoutcomes

CASE STUDY REFLECTION QUESTION

Based on the experiences you've read about in these case studies, what is one new practice or activity you could initiate at your institution to change the way in which you approach assessment from a programmatic perspective?

FURTHER READING

Hofer, Amy R. and Hanson, Margot, "Upstairs-Downstairs: Working with a Campus Assessment Coordinator and Other Allies for Effective Information Literacy Assessment" (2010). Library Faculty Publications and Presentations. Paper 106.http://pdxscholar.library.pdx .edu/ulib_fac/106.

Oakleaf, Megan. "Are They Learning? Are We? Learning Outcomes and the Academic Library." *The Library* 81, no. 1 (2011): 61–82.

Oakleaf, Megan. "Measuring Value Using Research Productivity and Learning Outcomes." *Information Outlook* 18, no. 2 (2014): 13–16.

Oakleaf, Megan. "A Roadmap for Assessing Student Learning Using the New Framework for Information Literacy for Higher Education." *The Journal of Academic Librarianship* 40, no. 5 (2014): 510–514.

Zoellner, Kate, Sue Samson, and Samantha Hines. "Continuing Assessment of Library Instruction to Undergraduates: A General Education Course Survey Research Project." *College & Research Libraries* 69, no. 4 (2008): 370–383.

Part II

IMPLEMENTATION

This section is all about the nuts and bolts of implementing the wonderful program you created. It covers the logistics of how to select the best teaching approaches for your content as well as how to work with both internal and external partners as you begin to craft an identity for your activities and look outward to spreading the word on campus.

Chapter 3

TEACHING

CHAPTER OBJECTIVES

- Explore strategies for making decisions about curricular content, teaching methods, and session formats (face to face vs. online).
- Develop strategies to work with all those who contribute to your instruction program, whether they are direct reports, colleagues, or faculty.
- Gather ideas for how to create an infrastructure to support those who are teaching in your program, ranging from training opportunities to shareable materials.

INTRODUCTION

It's no surprise that a book on creating a user-centered instruction program contains a section on teaching. Our aim with this chapter is not so much to give you a how-to for designing active learning techniques—because that is more than adequately covered by a multitude of other resources (some of which are cited at the end)—but to help you think strategically through the choices you make when creating the nuts and bolts of your program. So here goes!

USING THE *FRAMEWORK FOR INFORMATION LITERACY*

A new framework is being discussed and implemented at most, if not all, academic libraries. Everyone is struggling with this new model and trying to figure out how to best adapt it to their instructional programs. For some, this will only require minor tweaks here and there. For others, it will require a major overhaul of the entire program. Some institutions are further ahead of the curve, and we suspect by the time this text is published, these discussions will be more developed and even more progress will have been made.

The new framework can help you think about your teaching, but let's face it, it's yucky. Gone is the easy-to-follow outline that more or less tells you what you need to teach at each step. What you're left with is a bunch of really abstract concepts with some suggestions for how to approach them in the classroom, really generating more questions than answers. You could choose to tear out your hair and revert back to the old, prescriptive ways. Or you could look at the whole thing as an invitation to change your pedagogical process. You may already be doing this, but you need to start situating your program within the larger context of students' academic life. What does that mean? Instead of viewing your one-shot session as the only time students will ever be exposed to these concepts, make a map (visual or otherwise) of all the possible ways in which you can work with students both in and out of the classroom.

What that does is suddenly give you more breathing room and builds nicely upon that idea of scholarship as process. You simply cannot (nor should you try to!) cover all of the threshold concepts and derivative outcomes in one sitting. It simply cannot be done. But this is what many of us are used to doing, basing our work on the old model where it was much easier to go through a checklist of outcomes because we were much more focused on our teaching as opposed to the students' learning experiences. Again, many of you reading this may feel insulted or indignant because you did not approach your program or your instruction in this way. We contend, however, that many of us might have. Witness our typical way of teaching how to search. How many of us have not fallen into the trap of simply doing a point-and-click tour through the library's myriad of databases as students glazed over and fell asleep due to the sheer repetitiveness of the activity? If you have never done this, ever, we applaud you. But for the rest of us, it certainly was a tried-and-true approach for many years and, guess what, it still is. But what if we had a larger discussion with those students about what resources are most appropriate in what situation and depending on what subject is being searched? OK, sure, no brainer—we've been doing that! Really? Have we all been talking about Google Scholar as a better option than Academic Search Premier? Or a blog as being more appropriate than a peer-reviewed article? How many of us have been warned by faculty not to cover Wikipedia and only show students the "library resources"? That's what we thought. Now is the time to throw out our previous ways of thinking and embrace the yuckiness!

Sorry for that digression, but it needed to be said. Getting back to this idea of viewing the learning as occurring at different points in time—what if you were to offer consultations for students? What if you could see that class more than one time? And what if students were watching the videos and tutorials you so painstakingly created? That is great, because that's exactly what the new framework invites us to do. Take the *collective* set of experiences, skills, and knowledge that students gather and assign these outcomes to each of them as a progression and advancement to more complex concepts so that (ideally) by the time they graduate, they will have been through the entire framework. This means that you will have to figure out which of the concepts is in play at what point of these seemingly unrelated experiences and piece them together. In addition, you will have to work even more closely with faculty to decide how the rest of the course is contributing (or not) to the framework when you only control a miniscule portion of the curriculum. Undoubtedly, this is tricky. You certainly can't be present in every session of every class to see what threshold concepts are being covered and to what extent they are being retained and synthesized. But you can decide which ones are a priority for *your program* and figure out how to best introduce them, reinforce them, and yes, measure them.

Your assessment will also have to shift accordingly; simply looking at student citation pages may not be the best approach to this new method. You might have to come up with rubrics for assessing the impact of your consultations or determining if giving students a quiz at the end of a video used in a blended course or activity will provide you with enough evidence that a particular concept has not only been learned but mastered. More on that in the Assessment chapter. You simply cannot rely on the one-shot, one-time approach as the catch-all to IL problems and feel confident that students are getting everything they need in just that one instance.

BREAKING DOWN THE FRAMEWORK AND WHAT THAT MEANS FOR YOUR PROGRAM

Threshold Concepts versus Dispositions versus Knowledge Practices

But what does it all really mean? Well, the threshold concepts are meant to be broad and abstract and are representative of the themes they encompass. It's basically a very general roadmap to how students who master these large, hairy, and daunting concepts behave, what skills they possess, and how we as professionals can work with faculty to help them get there. Again, this is much more tangled, iterative, and messy than the previous standards because you cannot simply move from one concept to the next in a nice, linear fashion. Why? Well, these concepts are rooted into the larger context of student learning in which they now reside.

Scaffolding

As mentioned before, the framework now allows us to stretch the synthesis of these complex concepts across both time and discipline because we can look outside of the classroom at all the other elements that comprise this framework and enlist our faculty and other campus partners to help us complete the puzzle when we cannot be present to do so. So what does this mean? Your program is no longer a snapshot delivered at a certain point in time that may or may not be optimal for a student need that may or may not be met. Now is the time to think about how your program becomes part of the larger fabric of the entire first-year (or upper-level, etc.) experience. You might think that this is all well and good, but what if you don't have that option?

You have both internal and external opportunities to make this happen. Internally, you will need to have that conversation with your colleagues and identify what classes are being taught, at what level, and in which disciplines. If this sounds an awful lot like curriculum mapping, it is. This is more of an internal audit to determine which of the concepts, dispositions, and practices are currently being covered so that you can identify the gaps. If no one is teaching a capstone course in English, and students never get to explore the notion that they themselves can be "authorities" for a particular topic, that might be problematic. This conversation will then open up the field so you can do an external analysis to see what courses each department, college, major, and so on requires and where it makes the most sense for the library to fit in. You and your colleagues can meet with those departments where a library presence is lacking (and is genuinely needed) and begin the conversations to help expand your reach into these areas. Internal outreach is your ally here, and we deal with this issue in our Outreach chapter. But it is imperative that you and the rest of the librarians who provide instruction think about your program as both a continuum that has certain milestones and increasing complexity that mirrors students' academic paths and as a web that reaches beyond a certain linear approach to curricular embeddedness and seeks to become integrated both in and out of the classroom!

You will then need to figure out who else on campus is dealing with student learning at any level as part of a freshman experience, a graduate student boot camp, or any other type of learning opportunity and how your program can provide support and guidance. This is not easy to do, especially outside of the classroom environment where you know that for the most part students are required to attend, there is a specific assignment, and you have the faculty member as backup for your efforts.

But you can still identify what student cohorts exist and how your program fits into their work. This will also most likely require you to identify which of the threshold concepts need to be covered in these situations, how this will be done (f2f, online, etc.), and how you will assess and ensure the success of these efforts, knowing that you might not have that ideal, ready-made audience. How exactly does this happen? It's a similar process to designing a program that works with an existing freshman composition curriculum. It will really depend on the program—for example, if you have a freshman research scholar type program, there will most likely be an assignment or project where you can overlay the outcomes that need to be covered. From there, you would treat the instruction and assessment the same way as if you were part of a typical course and you can introduce the same.

If you simply have a freshman or first-year experience type program or class without a research component, it could be that those students would be better served by the framework once they do enroll in a composition or other class. Otherwise, you may want to see how to apply the framework to something like an introduction to the library type of activity or module that is designed as a precursor to research but can still have an academic element without the need to turn it into the dreaded scavenger hunt. One way to approach this would be to have this happen online coupled with a physical tour (which is strictly that) and have the assessment and the learning occur virtually. Another option would be to assign students a problem-based scenario or case study so that you are in essence providing both the assignment and the research instruction as part of the same component. Again, you and the program directors will have to determine if it's of benefit to the students at this stage or if they would be better served by having a "true" research component embedded later into their academic career. It's perfectly OK to say that! We often feel the need to be part of every effort on campus, and if that works for you, great! But if not, it's best to save your time and effort for where it will have the greatest impact.

Creators versus Absorbers

So this is where things get interesting. The framework now allows for the possibility of students creating their own content and meaning! This is wonderful and exciting and places them squarely in the middle of that scholarly conversation. What this means for us is that instead of acting like we have some knowledge they don't (OK, we still do), they can become our partners on this journey of discovery. Some of this entails you letting go of the notion that they need to know everything about research in 50 minutes or less. This can be hard, especially if you've done the brain dump lecture where you talk about as much stuff as you possibly can before passing out because you ran out of breath. And you may have to allow them to go down a path that you had not intended simply because the activity they just completed takes an unexpected turn when someone asks a question.

This also means allowing for ambiguity. Having a perfectly crafted lesson plan might not be an option if you're planning on having several activities because you simply don't know how well they will work. You might have to spend more time on some or cut others out altogether depending on how the class is responding. Alternatively, students themselves may not understand a concept or may not participate in the way that you were expecting. Allow for feedback as you go along, and forgive yourself for not checking every item on the list. You can then try to work with the faculty member, offer additional consultations, or try to see the class again to continue where you left off.

Finally, mistakes will be made! Students will get this wrong! And guess what? That's OK! And that's your perfect opportunity to step in and assist them. This is about as much what they learn as how they learn it—are we right? And the beauty of it is the framework anticipates for that with the notion of the iterative and cyclical nature of the research process. It's all right there for you. So perhaps instead of showing them Boolean operators, you can let them try out some searches their way and if they get it, move on! What? Did we just say that? But if there are corrections to be made, you can offer them some assistance and perhaps gently suggest using *and* in between the 50 words they typed into the search box. Bam, done. Process accomplished.

Turning the Framework into Learning Outcomes and Activities to Assess

Great examples are now being discussed and shared via webinars and listservs. It's not the threshold concepts per se that are the drivers of these discussions, but rather the dispositions and knowledge practices are the true indicators of learning. So if we take the first threshold concept as an example:

Authority is constructed and contextual; how would you know that the student understands this idea, as you cannot "see" it as you could a sample Boolean search to judge whether or not the student really understands how authority is defined for his or her specific discipline and the context of the assignment. But if you look at the dispositions and practices, they begin to break down this rather abstract notion into some of the things that students should be able to do—and that are therefore measurable. For example, if you look at "Use research tools and indicators of authority to determine the credibility of sources, understanding the elements that might temper this credibility," now you can begin to break down what those indicators are and how you would know if students have applied them. This would lend itself well in two separate areas: (1) in-class activities designed to help students generate and apply those indicators, and (2) in assessment, as we would look at the types of sources students chose for their assignments and why they felt they represented authority for their purpose at that time.

So, to continue this thread, this is really a conversion of the old "evaluate a website" portion of instruction that has spawned endless acronyms like CRAAP and equally endless versions of the same criteria repackaged on library websites. Of course, the focus here is no longer on websites alone; it is on the entire universe of potential resources that the student might use for the assignment. That's change number one. Change number two occurs when students generate their own criteria (with some help from you, of course) and then apply it to whatever sources they find or use or are given for the purpose of the session. This can take many forms, and we will not get into details about these activities, but you can see that simply adding the notion that there *are* certain criteria that define authority in a particular context can now lead you down a much more specific path than simply grappling with this nebulous feeling that surely different disciplines handle authority in different ways.

Similarly, you can now turn the statement into an actual outcome that you can then assess. Here is an example using a rubric that was designed by the coauthors. You can see how a fairly abstract outcome such as "explain" really becomes identify, list, and so on—all things that can be concretely measured by a narrative in a paper about why the sources chosen are authoritative or a section in a lab report detailing what sources that had similar experiments were consulted. This forces students to be explicit about their thought process, which is very difficult to capture otherwise. That's why analyses of works cited pages are often lacking, because they do not tell the entire story. Just because a resource appears "credible" does not guarantee students understand how it shapes their research.

While this approach may also be less than ideal, you can at least begin to understand what the student was thinking about when including that resource, and you can bring those previously hidden connections to the forefront to get a clearer picture as to what extent the student truly learned and where more work needs to happen. You would then cycle back to the faculty member, offer additional assistance or be able to intervene in another way so that the learning opportunity is not lost simply because you were not aware of the student's degree of comprehension. Think of how much more powerful this approach is compared to the typical method where once the assessment results are in, we simply chalk them up to circumstances outside of our control and don't think to return to the learning moment and try to refine it and shape it so that it really does become meaningful and useful.

Table 3.1.

Sample Rubric Applying the *ACRL Framework for Information Literacy*

Goal	Outcome	Levels	Benchmarks
Characterize scholarship as a conversation with sustained discourse within a community of scholars or thinkers, with new insights and discoveries occurring over time as a result of competing perspectives and interpretations.	Analyze and reconcile varied and sometimes conflicting perspectives.	0 (does not meet competency) = Finds resources showing only one point of view, is not able to effectively weave them into topic or argument 1 (meets competency) = Recognizes different perspectives and mentions them, but does not effectively weave them into topic or argument 2 (exceeds competency) = Incorporates different perspectives into analysis and explains/ demonstrates how they relate to the topic or argument	75% of students will score at least 1

ACTIVE LEARNING, TECHNOLOGY, AND THE ETERNAL STRUGGLE BETWEEN FACE TO FACE AND ONLINE

Now let's get down into the weeds and explore how teaching practices work with the framework and how you can make the most out of the many types of instructional methodologies you have available and have probably been using all along.

Everyone knows that active learning is an important component of teaching no matter what the format. But how does it change within the context of the framework (if at all)? Well, this is where you can think of your active learning as a bag of tricks to be used along the way. OK, so you've been doing this with all of your one-shots, and you have a really good handle on how to use each activity. But this framework will undoubtedly change the way in which you apply these activities. Let's take evaluation of sources as an example. One way you might have approached this element prior to the framework is to present a group of students with a website and based on criteria that they either generated themselves or that you gave them (author, domain name, and so on), they have to decide if it's a "credible" resource.

Let's try to break down this activity and see how that might change given the new context of the framework. First of all, this exercise is usually limited to websites, which, in the domain of research tools, are but a small subset. Similar criteria can be applied to articles and books, but seldom has this been done. Second, these criteria are often developed independently of the larger assignment and therefore present only a snapshot of the source's true value. On the one hand, if students have to find peer-reviewed journals for a topic, then yes, just about any website might not be considered suitable. If, on the other hand, students have to rely only on websites for their project, then of course deeper scrutiny would be required.

But there are other issues still. Criteria such as author, domain name, and so on only tell part of the story. Nowhere does CRAAP address the concept of relevance, answering the "so what" aspect of the resource in relation to the assignment at hand. If you use a website from the CDC that provides reliable statistics on teenage accidents related to texting, that's great—but what does that have to do with your paper? There is a void in making the next connection, taking that next step and going through the critical thinking process of synthesis. Discussion around the IL standards typically left the application of skills and knowledge into the hands of the faculty member so that once students left the library, it was very difficult to determine to what extent that final piece of the puzzle was completed, and students were often left with a lovely, yet meaningless, list of sources that they could point to as being somehow relevant to their paper simply because they were "reliable."

Finally, this approach does not take into account the myriad of resources that students might use to complete an assignment depending on what is required of them. Sure, a peer-reviewed article might be wonderful for that first-year paper on global warming. But would it be enough for an upper-level division project that tasks a class to create a new process for reducing greenhouse gasses? Most likely not.

So what's the point of all of this discussion other than to annoy you and make you feel like a terrible librarian for having used CRAAP in all of your classes (the authors included)? Perhaps it points out the obvious: the new framework will change your in-class activities by the very nature of what it presents. Gone are the website evaluations, gone are the rote criteria that may or may not be useful for the assignment, and in their place is a far more abstract and daunting task—how to teach students to think critically about the entire universe of information and help them make the connections to their assignments and ultimately to their majors and subject disciplines?

You Don't Have to Do All of This in a One-Shot Class!

Nor can you! While evaluating a website might very well be doable in 10 minutes or less, thinking about information as part of your discipline is not. You can help begin or continue this conversation depending on the level of the class and your working relationship with the faculty member. As said before in this book, the framework assumes a steady and scaffolded approach to its various concepts that are worked on throughout the entire career of the student, not once for 50 minutes.

This requires you as the librarian to understand where the students were in the continuum before they saw you and where they are going.

This also requires you to have that conversation with faculty members to determine how else they will continue to cover these ideas in class to reinforce and build upon what you're doing—perhaps this means that the class will come in for additional instruction, or you can see the final assignment or simply that the faculty member will go over the material after instruction. In other words, you are essentially talking about becoming a liaison that is involved with students beyond the traditional role of the one-shot. Finally, this requires a broader discussion at the campus level to make sure that the entire framework is embedded into students' academic work from their first year to graduation. This last item is nothing new, and it requires a high degree of discussions with various units on campus that might or might not be receptive to this idea. If your IL program is already part of your campus's general education program, this conversation might not be as difficult as you think given that it's been accepted into the fold, so to speak, and all you're really asking is for some changes to be made.

If, however, your program is not part of this framework, it might be very difficult to begin the conversation in the middle of everything else. A better approach might be to test out your new program and work on smaller pilots that can yield great results that you can take to administration as an indicator that if it were to be scaled up, the same results would apply. Connecting any data you have with student learning and retention at the institutional level will become the key to your success. Working with institutional research or a similar department and including IL outcomes into online courses or via software such as Taskstream (a tool to collect and organize student assessment data) might be your best bet. Then you can take all of this information to the appropriate administrators and talk to them about why it's important that your program be included alongside the other general education pathways and how it will sustain itself. These discussions will not be easy, and you might have to have them on multiple occasions and with several different people and committees. But now is the time to make these changes and to demonstrate that IL is more than just a one-time activity students engage in, it should become part of their academic lifestyle.

When to Do Active Learning and When Not To

Simply because active learning is a good pedagogical methodology doesn't mean it should be employed all the time or in every session. As mentioned before, this is something that is already part of your programs, and you've perfected the art of active learning versus lecture over the years. We're not asking you to abandon these practices. However, this new model will require you to think beyond the think-pair-share approach, even within the realm of active learning.

Not every part of every threshold concept will lend itself to active learning, especially as students will work on some applications outside of class time. This is where you will have to decide how to structure your instruction so that it makes the most sense given the type of class and assignment that is being provided. For example, you may want to make sure that all first-year classes are being taught in a similar manner because you are covering the same portions of the threshold concepts. You may decide that topic selection can best be made into an activity that students can walk through, and a (really) short demo of Google Scholar is fine as long as students get to explore it on their own and you move on to examining a blog for its level of authority on a given subject.

But you might also decide that in subject-specific instruction or upper-level classes it would be more effective to talk about something and have the assignment itself serve as that "active" learning portion, which might happen outside your session While in many ways one of the goals in teaching a class about research is about making sure that students aren't bored, if a brief, well-designed lecture is what is needed, then that engagement can occur elsewhere. You don't have to feel like a standup comedian trying to impress them with ever-growing levels of activity simply because the framework makes it seem as though keeping students talking the entire time is the best way to go (although it may very well be!).

As frustrating as it seems, there is no perfect answer for what should be made into active learning and what shouldn't. But you are encouraged to look at the educational literature, especially in instructional design and technology, to see how to make the most use of this type of instruction so that it does have an impact and you are balancing the talking with the doing in a way that makes sense for your program.

When You Should Consider Face to Face versus Online

Enter the art of the flipped classroom. Everyone has been writing and presenting on how they've flipped their instruction so that they cover the "how to" elements via videos or online tutorials and save the hands-on activities for the face-to-face sessions. As with active learning, there is an art to determining what can be covered online effectively and what needs to be saved for class. This sounds like a great concept in theory, but there are several things to keep in mind.

Simply throwing a bunch of videos online and asking students to watch them ahead of time is not really achieving the point of flipping the content. Sure, you can dispense with the lecture on Boolean operators, but if the students are not engaged, it won't help them understand how they can use them later on. Some programs add quizzes at the end of the videos to ensure that students have at least watched them. Great, but do they understand them, especially when taken out of the context of the overall purpose of the class? Probably not. Instead, create a tailored mix of online and in-person elements. And remember, they don't all have to come at the beginning or prior to an instruction session. So what might that look like?

Think through everything that you hope to cover—better yet, talk with the faculty member about the entire course to see where to introduce the various research elements that need to be covered. Remember that this framework will really need to be stretched out across the entire semester, and the online content can help you maintain a presence and still deliver the needed information. Then you can begin to discern what can be placed online or not and at what point in the semester it can be introduced. It doesn't make sense for citation information to be presented up front before a student has even had a chance to find sources because it won't mean anything and it will be long forgotten by the time the paper or project is due. Modular tutorials work well for this reason, and if they can be integrated into the course management system or other component of the course itself, that will get you the biggest bang for your buck. Also asking the faculty member to offer extra credit for any quizzes or assessments you add along the way will be very helpful in making sure that students do actually complete the rest of the components after you've seen them.

Assessment Redux

Finally, think about the assessment for these various pieces as your overall picture of how students are doing. Again, breaking various areas into smaller parts might be the better way to go, and whatever work students have to complete can double as your assessment so that you don't have to go back and give them yet another survey or rubric-based test to get that data.

Work with your instructional technologist and designer colleagues; they can be your biggest assets in this arena. They can assist you with the creation of truly engaging online tools and identification of appropriate technologies for both your online and face-to-face elements. Once you have your blueprint for what you want to cover online and in person, talk with them to see what your options are. Lately, our tendency is to make everything into a video, as if that magically transforms a lecture into something more interesting—but a talking head is still just that. There are some easy ways to weave more interactivity into a tutorial without necessarily having a multimedia designer on hand. This is where knowing what tools can accomplish certain goals comes in very handy, and there are many different instructional design websites that can assist with this process. The point is, get help from others so that you don't feel like you have to learn an entirely new set of tools in addition to creating all of the other components of your program. Too many times using tools such as Camtasia, while useful in pointing out the various elements of a database, are so time consuming to edit (and have to be reshot when an interface changes) that it really doesn't make much sense to spend your time on them. Try not to choose resources that are too complicated for your needs when there might be something even better out there. Same goes for Libguides—they appeal because of their easy-to-use interface, but the time it takes to create a guide that is not too text heavy and is interactive enough might simply not be worth it.

What online learning materials should you create from scratch, and what can you outsource? Knowing when to ask others for their product and when to create your own is also important. If someone created a great tutorial on citing resources in MLA style, you might not need to do the same thing because it's generic enough to repurpose. But if you want to demonstrate a specific way to narrow down a topic, it might make more sense to go ahead and create something on your own. Ask yourself if it's worth putting together a particular tutorial in the first place and how easy it will be to maintain and update. If the answer is that it will be too difficult, save yourself the headache and ask to use someone else's tool.

TRAINING, SUPPORT, AND OTHER LOGISTICS

Now that you have a better idea of how to approach the framework from a pedagogical perspective, let's turn our attention to other elements that will contribute to your program's success. Not much is written about what librarians can do to train themselves or support each other during the process of implementing something new, yet it is of vital importance.

First and foremost, you need to create a training program that will not only cover the basics such as how to teach using the new framework but also provide opportunities for students to discuss and share experiences and materials. This can be done in several ways, but the easiest is to incorporate these activities into regular departmental meetings or a set training time each month. One way to approach this is to have an initial workshop to introduce the framework and address any questions that arise. Then follow up each month with a different learning outcome that your (new) program contains until you've covered everything. Use this time to introduce new concepts, teaching, and assessment methods, and provide time for feedback and open discussion about how everyone is doing.

Think about what things need to be covered regularly, what specific topics might need to be addressed as they arise, and what order and format they need to occur in. An introduction to the framework would probably be best served by face-to-face meetings at first, but videos or webinars might do the trick later on. Similarly, if you are having a showcase of active learning exercises, introducing those in person would probably work best with follow-up materials online. Do you want a program that spans an entire year or just a few workshops interspersed with online resources? Will there be reading materials or other sources that need to be made available? Will you want to award attendees a certificate? Will you want to create an assessable program? These things will also drive how everything is structured, as you will have to decide how to assess that learning has taken place or that all the elements required for the certification have been met—will you ask participants to take quizzes, or is attendance enough? Who will recognize this certificate? Will it become part of library-wide awards or something similar?

Teaching observations and co-teaching are great tools for this purpose. They serve as support networks and as experimentation modes that are "safe" in the sense that your colleagues are there to help you either by sharing the load or simply providing constructive feedback. A few words of advice for those wishing to embark upon these two activities, because even the most well-meaning colleagues can end up hurting feelings:

- Work with someone you trust, especially if you are planning to co-teach. Your teaching styles and goals have to mesh, and you have to feel totally comfortable with the other person if this is going to work. Knowing what your lesson plan is ahead of time and working through your respective parts will help alleviate any stress on the front end. Both sides have to feel as though they have contributed equally to the effort at the end of the day, and if something goes wrong, you need to know that the other person has your back and will not criticize you.

- If a coworker is going to observe your teaching, make sure that you specify what exactly you want feedback on. This will help prevent a laundry list of things you could've done better, and it will keep the focus on improving your teaching. Again, trust is vital, and if you can't hear anyone say anything negative about your instruction, then this might not be the best approach for you, as there is bound to be something the other person will comment on.

- If you are the observer, try to put yourself in the other person's shoes, and think very carefully about how you word things. Saying something like "I loved that last activity, but have you thought about trying it this way?" is much better than "Here's what you need to change." Remember, you are both in this to improve and grow as instructors, and even if you think someone is truly horrible, helping the person instead of berating him or her will go a lot further.

- Make sure that all of these discussions also occur at a group level and as part of your instruction program so that you can effectively share feedback among yourselves. The purpose of letting others into your instructional world is not so that they can point out all of its flaws, but so that they can assist you in becoming better, and they will want you to return the favor. This is about group growth and moving forward as a team, not showing everyone that you're better than them (even if that's the case).

- In terms of materials, create a repository that everyone can access and share freely. You will have to decide as a group how to ensure that you give credit to the people whose content you adapt; having a set handout template or format might help. In addition, clean out your folders periodically, removing old or multiple versions of handouts and activities, to avoid having an unwieldy collection of items that never gets used because it's too difficult to find things. Decide on what you're going to collect, how often it will be updated, and what the criteria for inclusion are as a group so that there are no misunderstandings.

- You will also have to think about what platform to use. A database might be ideal but very difficult to set up and maintain. Likewise, formats such as websites and Libguides will have to be kept current in order to maximize their efficacy. You can always start small and see what works best for your group—some prefer wikis that are easily adaptable while others would view that as an added chore. Will there be a group responsible for updating these items or just one person? Whatever format you choose, make sure that it will actually be used, as that's the most important issue.

Teaching Junkies versus Teaching Stingies

Let's talk logistics. As with any new or growing program, you will want to streamline incoming requests as much as possible and have clear processes for how classes are assigned.

Make sure that you don't take on too much—50 classes a semester, even if they are repeats of what you've already done, seems to be about as much as anyone can handle. Realistically, 30 is probably an optimal number depending on the size of your department and the number of requests. While not necessarily advocating for quotas, you will have to monitor teaching loads to make sure they are distributed as evenly as possible.

This is much more easily done at the first-year level because the curriculum is the same as opposed to at the subject or upper levels where different disciplines have different patterns of instruction. Adding your courses onto an existing liaison instruction program can be difficult to manage as there will be competing needs for attention and the librarians may give their subject areas (however light in terms of number of sessions) full priority.

Depending on your role, you can try to negotiate this in several ways. This means having a frank conversation with all those involved in instruction at your institution. In some, liaisons are expected to contribute fully to first-year instruction, in others they are not. If liaisons are expected to participate, you will have to decide as a group what classes need to be covered in person and what content be put online. This will drastically alter how people spend their time—preparing for a face-to-face session can take more time than directing students to a tutorial link. Alternatively, teaching online is far more time consuming than doing a 50-minute one-shot you could cover in your sleep.

Where do you think having that personal contact will have the most impact? First-year classes are often the first introduction students have to research, and you want to make sure they not only see a real live librarian whom they can go to with questions but that the material you cover has those active elements and opportunities for feedback. Alternatively, if you know that SOC 230 class typically has students that have been to the library before, perhaps a well-timed, well-developed tutorial will do the trick for their assignment, therefore freeing that librarian to teach those first-year courses.

If, liaisons are not part of your program but you still need them to help, you can try several approaches. See who is interested in assisting you, and work with just those folks; it will be nearly impossible to convince the others if they don't see the benefit or they don't feel they have enough time. Talking with their supervisor might also give you a good idea of their priorities to see where yours fit. If you absolutely need every liaison to pitch in, you might need something more formal like a committee to oversee the process and perhaps even draft a Memorandum of Understanding so that everyone is clear on expectations. If that supervisor is not willing to help, appealing to administration is your only option. You need to make sure that your program needs are made clear, and you need to know where they are in terms of supporting those directions.

But what about the pesky colleague who either always wants to take another class or never does, regardless of these other issues? Sorry to disappoint, but the answer again depends on your situation, and there is no magical correct way to proceed. It could be that a private conversation is all you need to help the person understand that his or her actions are not contributing positively to the overall program. If having the person teach a ton of sessions is not a problem, then great, perhaps having someone who is willing to do all that work is not the worst thing, and you can concentrate your efforts on making sure that the quality of the instruction matches the quantity. If that quality is not there, and you are not the person's supervisor, having him or her participate in your training program might do the trick without necessarily having to come out and tell the person that his or her instruction is not up to par. Having the person observe what others are doing and co-teaching would be perfect ways to help him or her get up to speed.

If you really need the person to help more, a discussion with his or her supervisor (assuming it's not you) might be warranted to get a sense of why that person is resistant to the idea. Is he or she too busy with other stuff? You cannot be captain of everyone's instructional world; at some point it might simply be easier to move on rather than coerce someone who does not believe in your program as much as you do.

FINAL TAKEAWAYS

1. The ACRL *Framework for Information Literacy* is not ideal for the one-shot approach to instruction.
2. Training is the key to success, especially if you're relying on colleagues or graduate students to share the teaching workload. You need to have various support structures in place to facilitate training in different ways and provide access to materials that can be shared and repurposed.
3. New curricula will require different decisions about your content in terms of formats, activities, and collaborations with faculty.
4. Come up with a plan for how you will collaborate and organize your workflow with your colleagues, especially if they don't report directly to you.

Case Study: Designing a User-Centered Instruction Program

Elizabeth German, Texas A&M University
Stephanie Graves, Texas A&M University

Brief Abstract: Texas A&M University Libraries provides library instruction through a distributed network of subject librarians working independently with university departments. With the release of the new ACRL *Framework for Information Literacy*, the libraries have taken this opportunity to revisit their instruction model and develop a strategic approach to information literacy instruction. This case study describes a training program developed at Texas A&M Libraries as part of a strategic approach to library instruction. The Library Instruction Training program is a professional development program based on the *ACRL Standards for Proficiencies for Instruction Librarians,* designed to create a culture of teaching excellence within the University Libraries.

INSTITUTIONAL BACKGROUND

Founded in 1876 as a land-grant institution, Texas A&M University is the sixth-largest university in the nation. Serving a student population of over 63,000 students, the university has nationally renowned programs in engineering, business, and agriculture. The institution is a tier-one research university and on track to becoming ranked among the top 10 public universities nationwide by 2020.

The University Libraries at Texas A&M University is a large, comprehensive research library system encompassing five locations on the College Station, Texas campus. With access to over 5 million volumes and millions of e-resources, the Association of Research Libraries ranks Texas A&M University Libraries as ninth among academic libraries in U.S. public institutions. The University Libraries employs approximately 75 faculty librarians, over 200 paraprofessionals, and hundreds of students. The libraries offer a wide variety of services to meet the teaching and research needs of the A&M community. Consistent with large university libraries, issues of scope and scale can complicate library service and programming efforts, including library instruction. This case study describes the establishment of a professional development program designed to create a culture of teaching excellence within the University Libraries.

DESCRIPTION OF PROGRAM, PROJECT, OR SPACE

Similar to many large university library systems, Texas A&M University Libraries provides library instruction through a distributed network of subject librarians. These librarians work independently with university departments to address the library instruction requests from their assigned departments. Efforts to embed library instruction into curricula have varied widely across subject librarians and disciplinary areas. In addition, the university curriculum lacks a natural point of entry for information literacy instruction. Discussions around library instruction have historically centered on tips for teaching library tools and dealing with instruction to large class sizes.

With the release of the new ACRL *Framework for Information Literacy*, the libraries have taken this opportunity to revisit their instruction model and develop a strategic approach to information literacy instruction. As part of this process, the authors undertook a SWOT analysis of current library instruction practices. One of the results indicated that librarians needed and had a deep desire for professional development programming in the areas of information literacy, instructional assessment, learning theory, and pedagogy. Many librarians did not receive formal teacher training in library school and reported some discomfort with classroom instruction. As a response to this articulated need, members of the Learning and Outreach Unit of the University Libraries formed a team to develop the Library Instruction Training (LIT) program.

Launched in January of 2015, the LIT program has hosted monthly teaching workshops, numerous webinars on library instruction topics, and developed a peer-to-peer coaching program for library instructors. Workshops and webinars are posted on our LIT intranet page hosted by the library. A biweekly announcement of upcoming events is emailed out to library instructors to invite participation. As a voluntary participation program, librarians are free to attend based on interests and availability. Registration and attendance for workshops are recorded for programmatic assessment purposes.

TACKLING THE LENS

A multistage approach was taken for the development of the LIT program. This was an attempt to create a sustainable program that was relevant to our library. Additionally, there was a need to grow the program cautiously so that it was within our capacity to develop and administer. Our stages can be broadly defined as:

1. Planning
2. Incremental implementation
3. Iterative design

Planning

Benjamin Franklin once said, "If you fail to plan, you are planning to fail." As with the start of any new initiative, good planning can help prevent problems down the line. For the LIT program, the planning focused on vision, scope, and program elements to lay the foundation of the program.

The original vision and scope of the program was defined by the *ACRL Standards for Proficiencies for Instruction Librarians*. All programming needed to be related to one of the 11 skills areas as defined by the standards. In order to choose specific focus areas, a survey was sent to the libraries, asking individuals with teaching responsibilities to rate themselves on the particular proficiencies. However, the results of the survey were relatively inconclusive. The majority of the responses fell in the neither effective nor ineffective range. These results led to the reexamination of how programing would be developed. The program is intended to create a culture of teaching excellence within the Texas A&M University Libraries. Following the survey, the program's scope was refocused. The emphasis on the culture of teaching was chosen in order to drive the focus of the program to be about people. This gives agency and a sense of ownership about the teaching culture to the entire library. Focusing on the culture aspect also drives the programing to be based on enabling and empowering librarians rather than on skill deficits.

In order to narrow the scope, it was determined that all programming needed to be event based (such as webinars, workshops, or brown bags). This was done in order to keep the LIT program from morphing into a policy or best-practice documentation program.

In the planning stage, the following program elements were identified:

- Create an online calendar and registration system for centralizing instructional workshops, conferences, webinars, and training events.
- Schedule and host existing instructional webinars and on-campus training events on behalf of the University Libraries.
- Develop and conduct an in-house instructional training series.
- Provide financial support for librarians to attend professional development opportunities related to teaching.
- Create a Community of Practice program for peer engagement.
- Develop assessment methodology to measure the success of the LIT program.

Incremental Implementation

One of the values in the design of the LIT program was incremental implementation. It was vital that the LIT program not overextend the capacity of the Learning and Outreach unit with new procedures and added responsibilities before those initiatives could be sustainable. Therefore, the program was developed and released in increments. The elements were prioritized based on the perceived time and resources needed to complete the task and the needed political influence within the library (this was important when asking administration for funding). First, a program document was drafted and presented to library administration. Next, an Internet page was created for hosting information and the event calendar. The intranet site provides a gathering place for LIT programming materials such as PowerPoint presentations, handouts, activity sheets, and rubrics. Once the communication mechanism was set, the next logical step was hosting webinars readily available through professional organizations such as ALA and ACRL. After several successful events, the LIT team began developing locally hosted workshops. Using the incremental model also allowed for the compartmentalization of the elements of the program into separate projects, which made the planning and implementation process more manageable.

Iterative Design

In addition to the incremental implementation of the LIT program, the LIT team has also taken an iterative design approach to our programming. The team meets every other week to discuss what is going well and what could change. This works for the various elements of the program. For example, the list of professional development opportunities was not being updated as frequently as intended. Our iterative design approach allowed us to discover the issue and develop a new workflow quickly. Another example includes a feedback loop from training events. Event feedback is discussed at the biweekly meeting, and new opportunities for training can be quickly identified.

Where We Are Now

In its first year, the LIT program has sponsored at least one in-house workshop each month, either through leveraging existing expertise or the development of new content. Additionally, the LIT team funded and hosted numerous webinars offered from professional organizations. During the summer, a peer-to-peer teaching observation pilot program was launched. Six librarians have participated in the peer-to-peer observation pilot, learning from each other throughout the fall semester. All programming is hosted on our LIT program intranet along with a calendar of events. The program has been embraced by library administration and funded generously as a strategic initiative.

A sample of the topics of in-person training sessions include:

- Active learning techniques
- Reflective teaching practices
- "Teach and Tell" (peer examples of teaching activities)
- Developing learning outcomes
- Web accessibility

Next Steps

Through incremental implementation, iterative design, and programmatic assessment of the LIT program, the LIT team are continually looking for new ways to deliver library instruction training. The LIT team strives to create quality programming within the confines of the time and resources available in the Learning and Outreach unit. Future ideas for LIT include an online toolbox for library instructors, a public-facing web presence with library activities for instructors, an incentives program for participation within LIT, and a library-wide instruction retreat. The possibilities are endless, but through the process of planning, incremental implementation, and iterative design, smart choices can be made to create a sustainable culture of teaching excellence at the University Libraries.

LESSONS LEARNED

The LIT program is still within its foundational year, and reception from the library has been primarily positive. As the different elements of the program have been implemented, lessons have been learned to make the program even better.

Think about Participation and Recruitment

As with most libraries, our subject librarians have many demands on their time and attention. The LIT program was designed to be a voluntary participation program. Librarians are encouraged to engage with instructional professional development at a pace that is comfortable for them. This allows librarians to engage as their schedules permit, when topics are of direct interest to them, and avoids any appearance that instructional development is a punitive process. There are a few librarians who have attended almost every LIT workshop and webinar. They are highly engaged and active participants. However, a few librarians have chosen not to engage with the LIT program. It is unknown if their lack of attendance is due to time constraints or a lack of interest. Assessing reasons for attendance and nonengagement will be important for the future of the program. The LIT team may consider several approaches to programmatic improvement, including surveys, focus groups, and individual needs assessment meetings. The programmatic assessment plan will be drafted once the first year of programming is complete.

Organizational issues may also affect buy-in and attendance in this type of programming. Librarians at Texas A&M University carry tenure status, which adds additional pressure to make sure that every activity can be codified for the promotion and tenure process. The LIT program did not attempt to tie into the requirements for promotion and tenure. As such, some librarians may be reticent to devote time to an activity that doesn't add direct impact to their dossier. While the LIT program may be unable to tie directly to promotion and tenure, we can make better correlations to the yearly evaluation process that assesses librarianship. This will take considerable buy-in from library administration and is fraught with political implications. Future discussions with key administrators will determine if this approach is plausible in our organizational context.

Library administration has been very generous with financial support for the program. In order to encourage participation, the LIT team is investigating ways to incentivize attendance. Several ideas are under consideration, including stipends for travel funding, monies for educational technology, and/or teaching awards. The LIT team is in the process of drafting documentation that will be given to library administration for funding consideration. Creating monetary incentives that are funded administratively provides several advantages. Receiving enumeration for extra effort provides a tangible reason to participate. Librarians also may interpret the financial support as buy-in from administration and be more likely to engage with the program.

Balance Theory and Practice

The initial instruction SWOT analysis indicated a desire for workshops on learning theory, but when provided, this programming sometimes fell flat as many of our library instructors are looking for solutions to current problems. Fortunately, the LIT team included assessment as part of the programmatic elements, so the mismatch was discovered early in our first year of programming. Each LIT workshop includes a post-event assessment survey. The LIT team reviews the feedback during meetings, using the comments to plan which topics to present in upcoming workshops. Results thus far have indicated that librarians enjoy the sessions that include hands-on activities and practical applications for their everyday instructional situations.

Based on the feedback, the LIT team has tried to readjust programming to create a balance between theory and practice. If theory is presented, it's essential that the implications for application of that theory be explicitly discussed as part of the LIT program. Each workshop now lists a brief description and least two learning outcomes on the registration form.

This helps librarians understand what will be covered and what they should be able to do or know as a result of attending. LIT workshop instructors are encouraged to use active learning and keep the style of presentation informal. Experimenting with a variety of workshop formats has also been successful. The topic of teaching movements in academic libraries, a very theoretical discussion, was made more interactive by hosting an article discussion group. A workshop on active learning included hands-on experimentation with online polling technology. The need to inform librarians on how to create accessible learning objects was made more interactive by listening to screen reader software read a typical LibGuide.

Feedback forms still indicate a desire for more content on learning styles and theory. In the second year of programming, the LIT team will investigate ways to offer this content in an interactive format that demonstrates impact on library instruction practices. It may be necessary to explore formats outside of the one-to-two-hour workshop model. Daylong retreats or immersive deep dive experiences may be more effective approaches to meet this need.

Be Adaptable

As aforementioned, it was the original intent that the content for the library training program be driven by a self-assessment sent to library instructors based on the ACRL proficiencies. The large variants between individual survey results highlighted the individual nature of teaching as well as the inconsistent nature of pedagogy training in librarianship. Some librarians felt proficient in areas while their colleagues felt unprepared. The survey results did not help the LIT team have a holistic understanding of librarians' needs, as everyone needed a little bit of everything, but not the same things.

In order to get the program started, the LIT team decided to develop training based on in-house expertise. A group of librarians who had instructional expertise were identified. They met and brainstormed what topics each of them felt comfortable teaching. The first six months of programming was gleaned from that list. This was an easy way to provide training while more authentic measures can be created on the needs for instructional development. Additionally, at the time that the LIT program was being developed, the libraries were also making the transition to a new website and the new version of LibGuides 2.0. These large-scale web projects highlighted the need for training on topics such as universal design, accessible design for learning objects, and instructional design principals. The LIT team reached out to on-campus partners such as Instructional Technology Services to provide workshops with on-campus experts. The ability to adapt LIT programming to the current needs of librarians makes the program more nimble and relevant. Any libraries considering similar programs should keep adaptability in mind.

Leverage Existing Resources

Many opportunities for professional development are available from organizations such as LOEX, ACRL, and ALA. The LIT program has leveraged existing resources by hosting webinars from these resources on behalf of the libraries. While some of these resources have associated costs, they are often less than the cost of dedicating in-house staff to develop similar curriculum. Librarians also receive the benefit of hearing about instructional programs from a variety of institutions. This provided an easy entrée into programming.

Additionally, we have reached out to strategic campus partners like the Center for Teaching Excellence and Instruction Technology Services to host local workshops. This has been a successful model. Outside experts often carry more authority than in-house personnel, which has added depth and legitimacy to our program. There are some considerations to working with partners outside of libraries. Our LIT team has found it necessary to meet with workshop presenters prior to their visit in order to make sure that the content is applicable to the library's unique context. For example, a LIT team member collaborated with a campus IT presenter to alter her typical web accessibility presentation to include a discussion of LibGuides accessibility. As another example, the Center for Teaching Excellence allowed the LIT team to revise their peer-observations teaching rubric to meet the unique needs of a one-shot library instruction session. Collaborating with these campus partners on professional development workshops not only helps the librarians learn but also helps campus units have a better understanding of the library's instructional environment.

Table 3.2.
Survey and Program Components

Title of Document/Material	Description
LIT Proficiencies Survey	*See survey below.*
Library Instruction Training Program Presentation	www.slideshare.net/elizabethgerman /library-instruction-training-program

LIT Proficiencies Survey

Welcome!

This survey is to help inform the programming for the Library Instruction Training (LIT) Program. The LIT Program is a professional development program designed to create a culture of teaching excellence in the University Libraries and we need your help to guide us in choosing programming that can be the most impactful at the libraries.

About the Survey

- The survey is going to ask you to rate your personal effectiveness at set of instructional skills.
- The instructional skills are from the ACRL Standards for Proficiencies for Instruction Librarians and Coordinators (adopted 2007).
- Participation is voluntary.
- This survey is anonymous and no identifying information will be gathered.
- The survey is a little long so please allow for about 15 minutes to take it. Your response is extremely important!

This is not a test :)

- It's O.K. if you don't feel proficient at one or more of these skills.
- Being honest is more important than trying to make the libraries "look good".
- Don't worry if you feel there are areas that you need to work on. That's the point of the whole program.

Please rate your personal effectiveness at the following set of instructional skills

Your ASSESSMENT AND EVALUATION skills

	Very Ineffective	Ineffective	Somewhat Ineffective	Neither Effective nor Ineffective	Somewhat Effective	Effective	Very Effective
Designs effective assessments of student learning and uses the data collected to guide personal teaching and professional development.	○	○	○	○	○	○	○

Your CURRICULUM KNOWLEDGE

	Very Ineffective	Ineffective	Somewhat Ineffective	Neither Effective nor Ineffective	Somewhat Effective	Effective	Very Effective
Analyzes the curriculum in assigned subject area(s) to identify courses and programs appropriate for instruction.	○	○	○	○	○	○	○
Keeps aware of student assignments and the role of the library in completing these assignments.	○	○	○	○	○	○	○

Please rate your personal effectiveness at the following set of instructional skills

Your COMMUNICATION skills

	Very Ineffective	Ineffective	Somewhat Ineffective	Neither Effective nor Ineffective	Somewhat Effective	Effective	Very Effective
Maintains awareness of communication needs of different learning styles, and adjusts own communication style and methods accordingly.	○	○	○	○	○	○	○
Leads or facilitates discussion of controversial or unexpected issues in a skillful, nonjudgmental manner that helps students to learn	○	○	○	○	○	○	○
Uses common communication technologies to provide assistance to students in and outside the classroom.	○	○	○	○	○	○	○

91

Your **INFORMATION LITERACY INTEGRATION skills**

	Very Ineffective	Ineffective	Somewhat Ineffective	Neither Effective nor Ineffective	Somewhat Effective	Effective	Very Effective
Collaborates with classroom faculty to integrate appropriate information literacy competencies, concepts, and skills into library instruction sessions, assignments, and course content.	○	○	○	○	○	○	○
Communicates with classroom faculty and administrators to collaboratively plan and implement the incremental integration of information literacy competencies and concepts within a subject discipline curriculum.	○	○	○	○	○	○	○

Please rate your personal effectiveness at the following set of instructional skills:

Your INSTRUCTIONAL DESIGN skills

	Very Ineffective	Ineffective	Somewhat Ineffective	Neither Effective nor Ineffective	Somewhat Effective	Effective	Very Effective
Collaborates with classroom faculty by defining expectations and desired learning outcomes in order to determine appropriate information literacy proficiencies and resources to be introduced in library instruction.	○	○	○	○	○	○	○
Sequences information in a lesson plan to guide the instruction session, course, workshop, or other instructional material.	○	○	○	○	○	○	○
Creates learner-centered course content and incorporates activities directly tied to learning outcomes.	○	○	○	○	○	○	○

(continued)

Your INSTRUCTIONAL DESIGN skills *(continued)*

	Very Ineffective	Ineffective	Somewhat Ineffective	Neither Effective nor Ineffective	Somewhat Effective	Effective	Very Effective
Assists learners to assess their own information needs, differentiate among sources of information and help them to develop skills to effectively identify, locate, and evaluate sources.	○	○	○	○	○	○	○
Scales presentation content to the amount of time and space available.	○	○	○	○	○	○	○
Designs instruction to best meet the common learning characteristics of learners, including prior knowledge and experience, motivation to learn, cognitive abilities, and circumstances under which they will be learning.	○	○	○	○	○	○	○

	Very Ineffective	Ineffective	Somewhat Ineffective	Neither Effective nor Ineffective	Somewhat Effective	Effective	Very Effective
Integrates appropriate technology into instruction to support experiential and collaborative learning as well as to improve student receptiveness, comprehension, and retention of information.	○	○	○	○	○	○	○

Please rate your personal effectiveness at the following set of instructional skills:

Your PRESENTATION skills

	Very Ineffective	Ineffective	Somewhat Ineffective	Neither Effective nor Ineffective	Somewhat Effective	Effective	Very Effective
Makes the best possible use of voice, eye contact, and gestures to keep class lively and students engaged.	○	○	○	○	○	○	○
Presents instructional content in diverse ways (written, oral, visual, online, or using presentation software) and selects appropriate delivery methods according to class needs.	○	○	○	○	○	○	○
Uses classroom instructional technologies and makes smooth transitions between technological tools.	○	○	○	○	○	○	○

96

| Seeks to clarify confusing terminology, avoids excessive jargon, and uses vocabulary appropriate for level of students. | ○ | ○ | ○ | ○ | ○ | ○ |
| Practices or refines instruction content as necessary in order to achieve familiarity and confidence with planned presentation. | ○ | ○ | ○ | ○ | ○ | ○ |

Your PROMOTION skills

	Very Ineffective	Ineffective	Somewhat Ineffective	Neither Effective nor Ineffective	Somewhat Effective	Effective	Very Effective
Promotes library instruction opportunities and services to new faculty, underserved departments and programs, and elsewhere on campus, as relevant to instruction responsibilities and subject areas served.	○	○	○	○	○	○	○

Your TEACHING skills

	Very Ineffective	Ineffective	Somewhat Ineffective	Neither Effective nor Ineffective	Somewhat Effective	Effective	Very Effective
Creates a learner-centered teaching environment by using active, collaborative, and other appropriate learning activities.	○	○	○	○	○	○	○
Modifies teaching methods and delivery to address different learning styles, language abilities, developmental skills, age groups, and the diverse needs of student learners.	○	○	○	○	○	○	○
Participates in constructive student-teacher exchanges by encouraging students to ask and answer questions by allowing adequate time, rephrasing questions, and asking probing or engaging questions.	○	○	○	○	○	○	○

Modifies teaching methods to match the class style and setting.	○	○	○	○	○	○
Reflects on practice in order to improve teaching skills and acquires new knowledge of teaching methods and learning theories.	○	○	○	○	○	○

Are there specific topics in instructional training that you would like to see offered in calendar year 2015?

99

Case Study: Technology Tools, Tips, and Tricks: Implementing a Staff Training Program at the University of North Carolina-Chapel Hill Libraries

Doug Diesenhaus, University of North Carolina-Chapel Hill

Brief Abstract: In 2013, the University of North Carolina at Chapel Hill Libraries established a library staff technology training program as part of an effort to increase staff technological core competencies and comfort with digital tools. The program, which was implemented with no additional allocation of resources, was effective in offering library staff training on using familiar tools more effectively, providing insight on productive possibilities for using new tools, and spurring interest in future training opportunities with additional tools and technologies.

INSTITUTIONAL BACKGROUND

This training program took place at the University of North Carolina-Chapel Hill University Libraries, a Carnegie Classification RU/VH: Research University.

The libraries, which include a main library, undergraduate library, special collections library, health sciences library, and a number of branches, serve over 29,000 undergraduate and graduate students in more than 70 programs and professional schools.

The libraries employ over 125 professional librarians and over 170 paraprofessional staff, as well as over 300 undergraduate and graduate student workers.

DESCRIPTION OF PROGRAM, PROJECT, OR SPACE

In 2013, the University of North Carolina at Chapel Hill Libraries established a library staff technology training program called Technology Tools, Tips, and Tricks as part of an effort to increase staff technological core competencies and comfort with digital tools.

As library staff work to adapt to a changing information environment, this program, which originated in the Library Human Resources office, sought to develop staff technological information literacy and build comfort with existing programs and software as well as cultivate skills for adapting to future needs.

Eight instruction sessions were offered over the course of one year, including:

- Web 2.0 tools (such as Dropbox, Evernote, WordPress, and social media tools)
- Microsoft Office products including Word, Excel, and Access
- Data tools, including ASAP Utilities and Open Refine

The program had an additional requirement: it needed to be accomplished without the allocation of any additional expenditures beyond the portion of the coordinator's FTE directly dedicated to the training (estimated at about .2 FTE, or around 400 hours).

The primary strategy for keeping costs low was to seek graduate student research assistants already working in the library to serve as the instructors for the majority of the classes. Each of these instructors spent approximately six to eight hours of time on each class.

Aside from this staff time, no additional costs were incurred for the program.

TACKLING THE LENS

The program took an approach to building staff technological information literacy that prioritized teaching and training staff so that they can do their jobs effectively and productively, now and in the future.

The training emphasized a flexible and adaptive approach, looking to support staff members' comfort with a range of tools so that they could ease into learning when the inevitable next new thing comes along.

An additional goal of the program was to further enable staff to teach and provide access to library resources and tools to students, faculty, and the university community. In this manner the program used a "train the trainer" philosophy, seeking to provide staff with additional skills with which they can work with their patron groups.

In developing the program, one question that emerged was whether there was value in creating a new curriculum when a number of excellent training resources already exist both virtually and physically through the library, on campus, and through the North Carolina State Library. These include:

- Online training tools including Lynda.com and the Microsoft IT Academy, available through university subscription to all staff members and students
- In-person and online training from OCLC WebJunction
- In-person and virtual programs and curriculum offered by the university and the library

While each of these other programs offers valuable opportunities for training, the UNC libraries' staff training program under discussion provided some unique opportunities for a large academic library staff. Additionally, the program made an effort to circumvent some of the common training obstacles identified by Donna Chan and Ethel Auster, who cite Deborah Sussman's 1998 survey of Canadian workers in their own study of the professional development of reference librarians, including lack of time, expense, inconvenient location, and lack of support (269):

- Classes were in-person, physical sessions scheduled locally in the library at defined times. With instruction happening at a specific time and place, the decision to attend and to pay attention was hopefully more structured and intentional, whereas online resources, even excellent ones in bountiful supply, can go unused for lack of time or mental space.
- Participants completed these trainings during compensated work time. This distinction, while seemingly small, may have had a substantive impact on encouraging participants to see the training as worthwhile (or at least worth their time). This may have allowed participants to view their involvement in the trainings as more of a purposeful choice, rather than something they *should* be doing with their valuable free time during "lunch-and-learn" professional development sessions.
  The value of being granted the use of work time for the session is confirmed in Long and Applegate's 2008 study of continuing education for digital libraries, where they note that "although librarians generally are self-motivated in their professional development, organizational support is a key factor in creating a culture to encourage participation in [continuing education] activities" (180).
- The multiple instructors available during each training allowed for tailored, customized instruction and individualized attention. Additionally, most instructors were library science graduate students, which may have added an additional level of comfort (and some familiarity) in accepting instruction from a non-colleague.

At the same time, however, the primary challenge that this program faced was the process of finding a sustainable supply of instructors for the classes. While this worked in this iteration of the trainings, a future program might face challenges in finding enough trainers willing to engage in the work without additional compensation.

Additionally, as the classes progressed, there was a desire for instruction on more topics and at a more complex level. This would put further strain on the sustainability of the instructor pool, requiring those with a high level of specialized knowledge. Ultimately, it might be necessary to look outside the library in order to provide this level of instruction.

LESSONS LEARNED

While 97.5 percent of the 55 people who attended the instruction sessions provided feedback that indicated that they were "more comfortable with these tools/technologies after the session they attended," it was clear that the most successful classes in the training program were those that focused most directly on tools and skills that participants could directly apply to their work and personal lives. Trainings that focused on less directly applicable topics, such as social media tools, were less successful.

An effort was also made to follow up with program participants several months after the completion of the trainings to learn whether they were still using skills learned in the training.

One participant from the library's Research and Instructional Services department said that she has used Google Forms for scheduling and has even trained someone outside the library. This staff member also pursued further Excel and macros training using the Lynda.com subscription available through the library.

Two participants from the Digital Research Services department also noted how they used the ASAP Utilities tool after taking the data manipulation class.

The first participant installed ASAP Utilities (as well as Open Refine) on library lab computers, incorporated training on the tools into his own data cleanup instruction sessions for students and staff, and used Open Refine to complete some data cleanup for report statistics.

Additionally, after the data gathering course, this employee implemented Google Forms in several different ways: for feedback following workshops, for data entry for collection accessioning, with distribution of access codes for an online course, as well as more informal use for a departmental party signup sheet.

The second Digital Research Services employee noted that he had used ASAP Utilities in Excel with undergraduates and staff members because they found the tool to be less intimidating than formulas.

This staff member also expressed a desire to attend a full-day fee-based Excel workshop offered at nearby North Carolina State University.

As some of this feedback suggests, the trainings toe a somewhat precarious line. By design, they were created to offer library staff a general introduction to technology tools, to spur a desire to learn more at higher levels, or to suggest other training needs. However, the training curriculum was not comprehensive enough to provide advanced instruction to participants looking for higher-level training or for those who quickly moved beyond basic introductions.

While feedback suggests that the program was successful in encouraging participants to pursue additional and more complex training on various tools and skills, a coordinator of future trainings would need to take into account the wide variety of skill levels and needs of such a large user base in the library.

WORKS CITED

Chan, Donna C., and Ethel Auster. "Factors Contributing to the Professional Development of Reference Librarians." *Library & Information Science Research* 25, no. 3 (2003): 265–286.

Long, Chris Evin, and Rachel Applegate. "Bridging the Gap in Digital Library Continuing Education: How Librarians Who Were Not "Born Digital" Are Keeping Up." *Library Leadership & Management* 22, no. 4 (2008): 172–182.

Sussman, D. "Barriers to Job-Related Training. *Perspectives on Labour and Income* 14, no. 2 (2002): 25–32.

Flier Advertising Technology Training Session

TECHNOLOGY
Tools, Tips & Tricks

Library employees are invited to participate in a new program focused on technology training. The program will offer task-based, hands-on instruction in a variety of software programs and online tools, seeking to increase staff members' technological core competencies and overall technology savviness.

The program will continue with three sessions in April and May. Registration will be limited to approximately 23 seats per session, and attendance at class sessions will count as work time. Participants will need to register using the "Schedule Me" tool on the Library's Intranet page. Specific information (topic, date, time, meeting room and registration information) will be sent to the AllStaff email list.

Three themes will be explored in this training: Web 2.0 tools, Microsoft Office tools, and Data tools. If participants complete all three courses offered in a theme, a Certificate of Completion will be awarded.

Coming Soon:

April / May 2013	THEME: MS Office Tools	Word Tips & Tricks
April / May 2013	THEME: MS Office Tools	Excel Tips & Tricks
April / May 2013	THEME: MS Office Tools	Intro to Access

This series is being organized by the Library Personnel Office. If you have questions, please contact us at the Library HR email address.

Feedback Form Used for Class Assessment
Feedback: Microsoft Word Tips & Tricks

Please take a moment to offer your anonymous feedback on today's session. Your thoughts will help us improve our instruction in the future.

After today's session, are you more comfortable with this tool/technology?

Do you see ways to apply this tool to your work in the library? To your personal needs?

Are there ways that this session could be improved?

Are there other tools or programs that you would like to see taught in the future?

Case Study: No-Shot Instruction Alternatives to "Library Day" for First-Year Composition Students

Don LaPlant, SUNY Cobleskill

Brief Abstract: This case study describes the development and assessment of an initiative by the University of Tennessee Libraries to reach First-Year Composition students not being served by traditional one-shot instruction sessions. The library's liaison for First-Year Composition recruited librarians to staff shifts at the Writing Center, offering research assistance to students at the point of need. Further, the librarian used Adobe Captivate to develop a series of interactive tutorials on information literacy topics. Students were enrolled in a library instruction module on Blackboard where they could complete the tutorials asynchronously and have their progress monitored and assessed by the program's coordinators.

INSTITUTIONAL BACKGROUND

The University of Tennessee's flagship campus in Knoxville is an R-1 Carnegie class public institution serving approximately 27,000 graduate and undergraduate students. Of the four academic libraries on the Knoxville campus, the largest is the John C. Hodges Library, a 350,000-square-foot facility providing access to nearly 3 million volumes. Over a dozen librarians teach library skills to students, representing the full range of academic levels and subject areas, yet one-shot instruction sessions offered to first-year students in required English Composition courses account for a significant portion of the library's information literacy instruction efforts. In the four academic semesters between fall 2013 and spring 2015, for instance, over 250 one-shot instructional sessions were offered to First-Year English Composition classes alone.

DESCRIPTION OF PROGRAM, PROJECT, OR SPACE

While the Hodges instruction librarians are justifiably pleased to reach as many students as they do, they are nonetheless aware that only 20 to 30 percent of our university's English Composition instructors typically schedule sessions for their students in any given semester. Perhaps the most challenging students to reach are those enrolled in ENGL 103 and 104, one-credit courses that supplement the basic Composition One and Two courses for students needing additional development of writing and research skills. All students enrolled in 103 and 104 are registered in a large section led by a single instructor. Rather than meeting two or three times a week in a traditional classroom setting, these students—typically numbering over 400 per semester—are required to attend weekly tutoring sessions in the university's Writing Center. They earn weekly "writing credits" by presenting written work at self-scheduled sessions and consulting with tutors to improve it.

The self-scheduling model makes the course convenient for students but also means there is no single, specific time when all the ENGL 103/104 students are available to attend a traditional library one-shot. Previous efforts to reach these students by offering voluntary drop-in sessions proved ineffective—despite scheduling sessions at a variety of times—and attendance was limited and inconsistent. Recognizing the need for an alternative means of reaching these students in a more structured way, Rachel Radom, the librarian coordinating library instruction for the First-Year Composition program, developed two related initiatives to provide information literacy instruction outside the library.

TACKLING THE LENS

For the first of these initiatives, Ms. Radom developed and managed a program where librarians volunteered to staff weekly shifts at the Writing Center, located in another academic building in the center of the campus. During these shifts, students could request one-on-one consultations with librarians for help with finding, evaluating, using, and citing sources. Next, Ms. Radom and a graduate teaching assistant from the university's School of Information Sciences developed a series of interactive, self-grading tutorials made available through the Blackboard learning management system. Arrangements with faculty and staff in the English Department and the Writing Center enabled ENGL 103/104 students to earn some of their required weekly credits by working one-on-one with a librarian in the Writing Center and/or by successfully completing the tutorials.

The first set of tutorials offered to ENGL 103/104 students was produced using Adobe Captivate and focused on quoting, paraphrasing, summarizing, and citing source materials in both MLA and APA style. The series included two instructional presentations, each comprised of 20 to 25 slides featuring user-initiated interactions and formative assessment features. These two presentations were followed by a quiz requiring students to discern instances of plagiarism and demonstrate mastery of citation formatting. The Captivate platform allowed each presentation to be uploaded as a SCORM-enabled zip file to a Library Instruction course on Blackboard, making it possible to gather summative assessment data to be shared by the library and the ENGL 103/104 coordinator.

Ms. Radom worked with the ENGL 103/104 coordinator to market the tutorials through a series of targeted emails and publicity materials posted in the Writing Center. Because participation in this new program was completely voluntary, students were required to individually request enrollment in the Library Instruction course on Blackboard in order to access the tutorials. Facilitating this enrollment was one of the more challenging aspects of the project.

The ENGL 103/104 coordinator announced the program on the course Blackboard page and sent three emails to enrolled students describing the tutorial program, articulating how participation could earn extra writing credits, and explaining how to enroll in the program. Students interested in participating were instructed to email their request to a library email address monitored by Ms. Radom's graduate teaching assistant. This assistant then manually enrolled the students in the Library Instruction course on Blackboard.

Students were given a full week to register for the program and a strict deadline for completing the tutorials. A total of 113 students submitted requests, which accounted for 26 percent of the students enrolled in ENGL 103/104. Approximately 72 percent of students granted access (n=81) went on to successfully complete the tutorials by the deadline. Ms. Radom, her graduate teaching assistant, and the ENGL 103/104 coordinator were all given instructor status in the relevant Blackboard course, so all three were able to access completion data and assessment scores.

LESSONS LEARNED

Nearly 60 percent of students who completed the tutorials responded to a follow-up survey, providing useful (and almost unanimously positive) feedback about the tutorials. Representatives from the library, the English Department, and the Writing Center expressed interest in continuing the program, and work has begun on the development of a second round of tutorials to be used in future semesters.

Hodges Library already offered an array of screencast tutorials on YouTube and through its website, but interactive tutorials offered via a learning management system have some distinct advantages. Not only do they allow customization of these tutorials to specific courses, they also enable librarians and instructors to actively engage and assess students with built-in, auto-graded quiz features, yielding helpful data about which concepts are particularly challenging. More importantly, however, the asynchronous nature of these tutorials makes it easier for faculty to provide access to librarian-developed instructional content for their students. While not all faculty are willing to schedule an in-library one-shot for their students, custom-designed, LMS-embedded tutorials like the ones developed in this program have the potential to introduce important information literacy concepts to student who might otherwise not encounter them in their courses.

CASE STUDY REFLECTION QUESTION

Based on the experiences you've read about in these case studies, how can you leverage the existing resources at your institution to develop materials to supplement or replace face-to-face instruction, collaborate more strongly with colleagues, or provide more support for those who are teaching?

FURTHER READING

Alfino, Mark, Michele Pajer, Linda Pierce, and Kelly O'Brien Jenks. "Advancing Critical Thinking and Information Literacy Skills in First Year College Students." *College & Undergraduate Libraries* 15, no. 1–2 (2008): 81–98.

De Boer, Ann-Louise, Theo Bothma, and Pieter du Toit. "Enhancing Information Literacy through the Application of Whole Brain Strategies." *Libri* 61, no. 1 (2011): 67–75.

Locknar, Angela, Rudolph Mitchell, Janet Rankin, and Donald R. Sadoway. "Integration of Information Literacy Components into a Large First-Year Lecture-Based Chemistry Course." *Journal of Chemical Education* 89, no. 4 (2012): 487–491.

Maitaouthong, Therdsak, Kulthida Tuamsuk, and Yupin Tachamanee. "Factors Affecting the Integration of Information Literacy in the Teaching and Learning Processes of General Education Courses." *Journal of Educational Media & Library Sciences* 49, no. 2 (2011).

Mestre, Lori S. "Matching Up Learning Styles with Learning Objects: What's Effective?" *Journal of Library Administration* 50, no. 7–8 (2010): 808–829.

Chapter 4

OUTREACH

CHAPTER OBJECTIVES

- Explore strategies for approaching outreach with various groups (faculty, other campus personnel, library colleagues) ranging from setting up the all-important first meeting to achieving meaningful partnerships.
- Develop methods to assess the effectiveness of your outreach strategies; this is where learner-centered tools come into play because they apply just as effectively to assessment *of* your program as to what is *in* your program. You can plan your outreach activities using a backwards design model (Wiggins and McTighe, 2005) to get at those broader goals and instill a stakeholder-centered approach:
  - What action do you want stakeholders (faculty, campus, library, etc.) to take as a result of your meeting? *(goals and objectives)*
  - What activities/projects/events do you need to put in place to make sure stakeholders actually do those things? *(learning activities)*
  - How will you measure the success of the partnerships? *(assessment)*
- Create a plan for determining the impact of the collaborations that result from your outreach activities.

INTRODUCTION

Outreach and instruction may seem like opposite ends of the spectrum. In an ideal world, faculty would reach out to librarians and beg them to collaborate in designing the entire information literacy curriculum for their course, or better yet, ask to team teach it!

The harsh reality, more often than not, is that it is up to instructional librarians to make connections and get faculty on our side. Is that unfortunate? Perhaps. Is it unfair? Definitely! However, instead of bemoaning the state of affairs and relying on the old "I tried to email that person and never heard back from him," let's look at what you can do to change things, or at least try something different.

Outreach is an area where assumptions are made that are not necessarily accurate. For example, that:

1. Everyone in the library knows what is meant by "outreach"
2. Everyone in the instructional department actually knows *how* to do outreach.

Both these assumptions can lead to confusion, disappointment, or worse, failure to get anywhere with your program. What can you do to help combat and alleviate some of these issues? More importantly, what do any of these activities have to do with instruction?

The second question is easier to answer, because the truth is, outreach and instruction are inextricably linked. Especially for smaller departments, where outreach and collaboration may equal success or failure of an instruction program. In these situations, guerilla-type tactics may well be your bread and butter; without perseverance and the ability to convince program directors and faculty alike that they should pay attention, not much can be accomplished.

TYPES OF OUTREACH

Outreach to Faculty and Program Directors

Before launching into the details, it should be noted that there are differences between working with faculty at small versus large institutions. There are also several variations of the term "faculty," which can mean anyone who is a full-time permanent employee, a part-time permanent employee, an adjunct who only comes to campus to teach his or her classes, and even a graduate (GA) or teaching assistant (TA). Knowing who your audience is will obviously influence your approach.

Adjunct and part-time faculty can be difficult to track down, and they might not have much availability to meet or participate in pilot programs. If you feel like they are the best partners to collaborate with, you might have to meet them when it's convenient for them, not you; call them; or simply wait until they attend a required departmental meeting. If possible, offer a stipend for their help with the pilot as an added incentive Short of that, stalking them in the hallway after class might be the best way to get their attention.

Graduate students or teaching assistants can be an even more challenging audience than adjunct instructors. Meeting demands on their time to study, research, teach, and have a semblance of a social life is a tall order, even for the most seasoned scholars.

Full-time faculty members are often the most difficult to convince; although they may have the most time and should, in theory, be best positioned to collaborate with you, that is often not the case. They are frequently overloaded with their teaching, research, and committee work and might view any partnership with you as added work that they don't need. This is where the "what's in it for me" can be of service. Offering to grade or score assessment results and assuring the faculty member that no additional effort on his or her part is required will (hopefully) go a long way.

But that's not really an ideal situation; you certainly don't want to be the add-on to an already jam-packed course. So a subtler tactic might be better. What do students typically have problems with, and how can you save the faculty member from having to grade poor-quality research papers? Simple, you say! You can offer to help the faculty member design the assignment from the get-go and embed the information literacy component into the course in such a way (flipped and consultation models are discussed later) so that even though you only see the students face to face one time, you are actually providing them with an entire network of support!

But there's a long way between meeting with a faculty member for the first time and having him or her team teach a course with you, so what are the steps in between those two endpoints?

Phase 1: Reaching Out

This is often the most difficult part of outreach, because chances are you don't already have a rapport established with the chair, faculty member, or program director you're trying to woo. And that's OK. But you need to be able to get your foot in the door one way or another. So what can you do? There are a couple of permutations of this. You could be new to your position, which gives you a great excuse to reach out to that person and introduce yourself. You will often find he or she appreciates simply knowing that the contact person has changed! If the faculty member is new in his or her position, get in there and wow 'em before they know what hit 'em.

But what happens if that person doesn't respond to your painstakingly crafted email? You will find that email is no longer your trusty friend, and relying on a passive method of communication is no longer an option. If the person is a director or chair, chances are he or she has an assistant who is much more willing to communicate with you. Ask if you can attend a departmental meeting or if the assistant can help you set up a meeting with the person who can best help you work with the faculty in that particular department. Almost every faculty member has office hours, which is a good way to capture them (simply because they have nowhere else to be!). Face-to-face communication is always best for a follow-up, especially if you don't hear back from someone in a timely manner. Informally "dropping by" or the ever-popular "pop-in" does have its benefits. Picking up the phone doesn't hurt either—if the person is in his or her office, he or she might, just might, be inclined to talk with you as opposed to ignoring the email you sent days ago, which is by now buried under an avalanche of other emails and will be duly ignored. That brings us to the topic of deadlines. Being able to politely ask for someone to get back to you by a particular date often has a powerful effect; it communicates that you are also on a timetable and gives a sense of urgency that will enable people to prioritize within their department. This does not mean that if people miss the deadline you have the right to pester them until they give in, but gently reminding them that you need an answer might not hurt.

Phase 2: Building Partnerships

Let's assume (and it's a good assumption) that you actually *do* get to talk with the director, faculty member, or chair, and you have a meeting all set up—now what? Or worse yet, what happens if that person *loved* your predecessor and any changes you want to make are viewed as nothing short of anarchy? Always try to send potential allies an agenda ahead of time so they know what you're thinking. That additional time might just be the thing they need to be able to consider your ideas instead of having to come up with something on the spot. Plus, if you're nervous, that will serve as your discussion blueprint and can prevent you from rambling or going off on tangents. Remember, the person in front of you has many other things to think about, and like it or not, you have to make good use of his or her time!

After the meeting, thank the person and be sure to remind him or her of the action items that were discussed. That way, when you contact others within the department or move forward with your initiative, he or she will not be wondering what's going on and you can (usually) avoid stepping on toes. Additionally, asking who might be the best person to help with identified action items will help you to avoid pestering the director later. There's nothing worse than getting the green light and then having to backtrack or delay because you forgot to ask who to work with!

From there, creating a system for communicating regularly with all those involved in moving forward is your priority. Make sure everyone who needs to be at the table receives an invitation and understands why they are there, and clarify who is in charge and the expectations of the work. Assume limited prior knowledge and that the only thing the director has communicated is that he or she will be working with the library on an instruction project.

Phase 3: True Collaboration

This is the stage where you get to actually do the work that you want to do! The same rules apply here as in any collaboration.

Set up regular meetings and establish roles as early as possible to minimize confusion and set expectations. If this is your project, own it no matter who is at the table, be it a division chair, a GA, or a dean!

Come up with a timetable and goals. This will be heavily dependent on the type of program on which you are collaborating. Pilot programs are easier to develop because they are smaller in scope and more discrete. Having an outline of the entire program or the set of goals will help you chart where you're headed and can assist you as you examine each step individually.

Make sure you build in enough time to get everything set up and discuss logistics for homework, communication with students and faculty members, and any grades or extra credit involved. If you are setting up a new course in your management system or developing quizzes or other learning objects from scratch, this will obviously take much longer than if you are simply updating existing learning objects. You might have to bring in an instructional designer or ask for assistance from the assessment coordinator within the library or on campus. If the position is outside the library, it might not even have the word "assessment" in the title, so you will have to figure out who can assist you. Getting folks outside the library on board might take time if they are very busy. They might not feel the same urgency you do, so make sure you talk with them as early in the process as possible to give them a sense of your time line.

If you have never worked with a particular faculty member or group before, there may be an initial period of adjustment. You will have to proceed with caution and find a balance between asserting your vision while integrating their suggestions. Again, this will depend on the type of collaboration. If you're talking about a one-shot session, the stakes are much lower and you can find more room to compromise than if you're trying to design an entire program together. This may also influence your decision about the scale on which you'd like to collaborate. While it may be great to work with a person on a limited basis, you may not wish to have his or her influence the overall structure of the program. Or the reverse may be true and you find that you and the group are in sync and you can allow for more input where you might not otherwise think to do so. You will have to know ahead of time where you are in this process and what exactly you expect your collaborators to assist you with, as it will definitely shape the direction of the project.

Outreach to Other Campus Units

Some of your strongest allies can be colleagues in departments who have nothing to do with the library. The centers for teaching excellence or campus IT departments who help faculty with their courses can often be a source of great assistance. You can work with them to help create the resources needed for your own program, whether it's advising on what technology to incorporate or helping you make videos. They can also help work through decisions such as how to flip a class and what content to put online or cover in person, or provide training for other librarians or students in your area who are part of the program. Rather than feeling as if you have to do everything yourself, these partners can also be integrated into the fabric of your planning. How do you know who you need to talk to? Start with the basics and work your way out—make a stakeholder map of everyone on campus who could be a potential partner and prioritize. That center for teaching excellence might be higher on your list than the lone instructional designer in a department. Keep track of whom you talk to and what the outcomes are so that you don't work at cross purposes or duplicate efforts.

So how do you begin the collaboration process? That is more or less the same as working with departments. Meet with the director or head and explain to him or her what you are doing. Again, half of the battle is simply getting your foot in the door. Ask to be included on committees or boards or simply attend a departmental meeting to discuss ways you can collaborate. You will be surprised how many departments would welcome your assistance. In many cases they simply do not have the needed staffing to work on projects that might benefit greatly from the library's input and involvement. After that, make sure you follow through and set up meetings with the folks who are going to be doing the work, continuing to be involved and collaborating as much as possible.

As with everything, it's worth it to take some time to do things the right way, which means creating a programmatic approach to your outreach efforts. You want to make sure that you have all of the elements in place to support what you are doing from the start. Training is still an important component of outreach.

- Conduct outreach. Many people have no idea how to actually do outreach. Some of the ideas outlined in this chapter will help, but if you are hoping to build a small army of supporters, you need to give them all the tools possible to succeed. How you structure your program will, of course, depend on your context. You may want to conduct a formal needs assessment to find out exactly what people need the most to help with outreach. You will also have to determine how to prioritize content. If you talking outreach, the three levels discussed here might provide a good blueprint for structuring a yearlong look at the various issues involved with outreach. Or it could be that you really just need a quick refresher.

- Offer workshops. If you are not sure how to do outreach, chances are your colleagues aren't either. Working with your communications department within the library or the institution will provide you with the best tools for this program. After all, that's what they do! Workshops are always great to offer, but again it will largely depend on how your library works. It could be that a series of workshops for your department works well, or perhaps online tools would be more effective, or a combination of both. Don't think that just because your program does not contain a "typical" approach that it's not good or useful. One of the most important elements to think about, no matter what form your training program takes, is to build in check-in sessions to make sure that folks are actually applying what they learn and using it and that they have a support structure to turn to in case things don't go as expected.

- Behave like a subject liaison. Don't think of liaison work as unconnected to instruction, or at least to the program you are running. There is sometimes a feeling that subject specialists are some sort of secret group working on things that have nothing to do with your program. Instead of viewing their work as separate or different, think like a liaison. English composition, first-year or similar programs, exist at almost every institution, so think about engaging with them in the same way. Make sure the department knows who you are, and attend regular meetings, events, and so on. Contact new and stay in touch with existing faculty to keep them updated about your programs. Encourage students to schedule consultations with you (or those in your program), and offer to provide assistance with other things like the use of your instruction labs (even if they have nothing to do with instruction) as a way to become integrated into the department, to help you with future efforts, and to become more engaged overall. In addition, most of the outreach literature is directed at library liaisons. You may want to refer to that body of information for some ideas about how to approach dealing with your own "regular" departments or programs that fall outside of the subject-specific boundaries.

- Assess the effectiveness of your outreach program. Again, this will depend on how your program is structured and what its priorities are—if "numbers" are important to your administration, then connecting outreach to quantitative data is the way to go. You may feel the need to have some type of metrics built in from the beginning, such as how many people attend workshops, access online materials, and so on. Or perhaps a more indirect method might be to determine if the training actually made a difference in terms of the impact of your program on librarians' activities.

Were you able to talk to more faculty? Were you able to present information to them in a different way than before? Did you use new methods or tools to do so? For example, instead of relying an email, were you able to attend a departmental meeting that resulted in new projects or collaborations? Did more of them bring their classes in? More importantly, did you conduct deeper-level assessment or instruction as a result of your activities? And did the students themselves benefit more? Some of these questions are much easier to answer than others.

- See how those correlational and causational relationships develop, especially if you are talking about making a change in student learning? This will take some time, but you could try tracking what you do and recording either anecdotal information, measured impacts, or both. For example, if you were able to finally get that difficult faculty member on board to let you teach his or her class and you assessed student learning outcomes, how did the students do? Did you communicate with the faculty to let them know, and what changes will you make based on this information? In addition, were you able to tie in your collective efforts to your unit's or library's or institution's strategic goals or areas of focus for the year?

- At each level of communication, mark your progress to determine just how broadly your outreach efforts extend. It could be that you have great results at the unit level but not at the other two. So you will have to think about what constitutes "success" at each step and then decide how you will know you've reached it and what you can do if you haven't. One way to do this is by conducting student and faculty interviews. This goes beyond your typical survey knee-jerk reaction and seeks to broaden your understanding of what these groups actually got as a result of your increased efforts in reaching out to them. You can earn bonus points if these are the same faculty members who came back into the fold after not having had library instruction for a while. These are the people you need to talk to most! You really don't need a bunch of "N/A" or "Nothing to improve" on your surveys; you need honest-to-goodness real-life feedback, even if you don't like everything you hear! This, by the way, is also considered outreach, but it's pretty much the best kind—where you get to learn *and* share information at the same time. Asking the librarians themselves is also a sure bet for determining how the program has made *them* feel and how they are conducting their work differently as a result.

- Realize that you will need to think about all of these types of feedback in order to get a cohesive picture of how an outreach program is impacting populations. It's not enough to simply ask librarians to document how many faculty they spoke to. Finding out if those faculty saw a measurable improvement in student assignments suddenly adds another layer of information that will help you decide how to best shape and develop your program or where you need to focus your attention. Think holistically: don't be afraid to solicit input, even if it means hearing about things that might be uncomfortable.

Outreach within the Library Itself: Getting Colleagues on Your Team or Making Do with a Table Set for One

Sometimes convincing colleagues is harder than working with departments on these types of initiatives. Why? That really depends on your environment and how a program is structured. If first-year programming has nothing to do with subject-specific or upper-division instruction, it might be very difficult to get them on board simply because they don't see how the two programs connect. If you have a more harmonious arrangement and the programs are more integrated, even that might cause confusion regarding responsibilities, roles, and expectations simply because there are more people paying attention to your part of the spectrum. So either way, there are potential pitfalls to avoid.

This problem can also be compounded if you do not supervise any of these librarians. Working with colleagues in a lateral structure makes management of outreach all the more precarious because you cannot "make" anyone participate, even if you are desperately in need. In these situations, there are a few tactics that come in handy. (It is worth keeping in mind that, in some instances, it really is better to go at it alone and try to build up your own department either with graduate assistants, interns, or over the longer term, librarians you hire yourself.)

Communicate! If your colleagues have no idea what your program is all about, now is the time to change that. Getting information out there is half the battle and can often prevent much misunderstanding and conflict. Don't assume other librarians know what you're doing; it's your job, as the program coordinator, to let them know. Let them observe some classes to get a firsthand experience, or share the lesson templates and outcomes with them. If you work at a large institution, make departmental visits and talk about your program as often as you can and in any context that makes sense. Of course, by doing so, you open yourself up to unwanted feedback and perhaps even criticism. You also have the power to (try to) control this. Let's face it, your colleagues will always offer their opinions whether you want them or not. That's life. But when meeting with them, you have every right to indicate the type and level of feedback you expect. If they don't know that you don't want to hear their ideas on how you can improve your active learning techniques, say so! Or if you're having some issues with assessment and need some feedback, let them know! And if they still don't respect your wishes, you can always ignore them. Avoid falling into the trap of long-winded email exchanges with those whom you know will be critical no matter what. As long as they don't actively try to thwart your efforts, you can take their suggestions for what they are and move on; it will cost you nothing to be nice, and it will only reinforce your confidence in what you are doing.

You can approach colleagues very similarly to faculty partners. Find out if any of them are willing or interested in assisting, and just work with those folks. Having a small group of energetic colleagues can often be the best advantage in the world and will give you a safe way to try out new activities or simply run your ideas past others. If you want to get more formal, having an established instructional taskforce or council can also be a way to go. That will lend some support behind your efforts and give you the opportunity to think more strategically about how the program fits in with broader library goals and directions. This might also be the place where that dreaded curriculum mapping discussion takes place and you do look at the entire suite of instructional offerings as a comprehensive program as opposed to breaking it up piecemeal. You will have to think about the structure and leadership of the group and basic logistics, such as membership, length of term, purpose, and if you plan to use this group as a way to ask for resources and build some leverage or simply as a sounding board.

Make it clear that you do not expect the same level of involvement as you would from a librarian who would be working within the department. Most librarians cringe when we ask them to do "more stuff" on top of their already busy schedules. And for some that might be a justified response. But you can also show them that being part of your project does not mean they have to do it all or that they will have no support. Using your colleagues' expertise where it will be of most use will give you reinforcements where you need them and lessen headaches where you don't. Don't be afraid to bring in people at the point of need and tell them you only want their input at a certain stage. It's far better to do that than to find yourself saddled with a well-meaning but ineffective colleague who, frankly, is just getting in the way.

All of this may sound wonderful, but what if you *are* the instruction department, and there really isn't anyone available to help you? While none of these solutions is perfect, there is still something you can do. First, look into hiring and training students. This may sound like a large investment of resources for very little return, but there is a growing reliance on graduate and even undergraduate assistants and peer coaches as a way to help with large-scale programs. Peer coaching and instruction is often more effective than librarian-delivered instruction simply because students can identify more with someone who is going through the same thing they are. Training will be a huge component of the program, especially if students have never taught before, but it might be a great opportunity for graduate students to put their skills to the test and gain some classroom experience.

If your institution has a library school, you're in luck. Most library programs don't offer hands-on instructional experience for students, so working with someone in the program to set up some type of internship would be a great way to give students that experience and provide support for your efforts. You might be able to coordinate receiving extra credit or some other type of incentive if funding is a problem, and who knows where the partnership will lead as it grows and develops.

Setting up the program is discussed in the staffing chapter, but the idea is that you don't have to do this all by yourself. So what happens if you don't have any funding to do this? You can try to use temporary funding—most libraries have a pool of money used for student assistants that you can tap into. You will then have to use every piece of data about the effectiveness of the student assistants to help you make a case for future and ongoing funding. Alternatively, you can try to obtain a grant or some similar type of funding through either your institution or a larger organization. This is where you might be able to partner with your campus's first-year experience program or receive a faculty innovation grant to help get your program off the ground and assist you in collecting the data you need to make your case to administration.

You Got the Faculty's Attention! Now What?

The difference between outreach and collaboration is really about the depth of the partnership. Outreach is the means to get faculty and departments to pay attention to you and your programs, but you still have to deliver the goods and continue to impress them once they have agreed to partner. In fact, this can be the most critical stage because talking about a great program will only get you so far; eventually, you will have to actually implement it.

So what can you do to make sure that the collaboration is as successful as possible?

Pilot with those who are interested. There's no point in trying to convince those who do not see the value in what you're trying to do. As difficult as it is to admit it, sometimes it takes faculty hearing it from their colleagues before they are willing to give you a chance. Early adopters can be your biggest allies, and involving them in helping you spread the word can make your job a lot easier. At this point you may be wondering just how many allies is enough? Sometimes two or three influential people is better than a bunch of lukewarm supporters who don't really care one way or the other what happens to your program. Really all you need is one to get a pilot going and have enough data to help scale your future efforts.

Approach basic programs first, then build on success. Start small; that way you can make adjustments as you go, and if something goes terribly wrong (it won't!), you have the ability to fix the issues before trying to scale up. Additionally, focus on the programs that will have the most impact and potential to reach more students. Creating the curriculum for a specialized research methods course is great, but if you have an entire first-year program to build, that might be the better place to start as it provides the building blocks to just about every other instruction program you have.

Appeal to administration to help, but know when to start from the bottom and build up. Let's face it, once in a while you really need the help of your department head, director, or dean if things just aren't moving in the right direction. And that's OK; they're there to help! Make sure you are fully prepared before talking with them so that they understand what you're trying to do and why you need their assistance; this will ultimately help them to be your strongest advocates. They might be able to help set up a meeting with that elusive faculty or director, smooth over ruffled feathers, or simply introduce you to the right person and make that initial contact.

Involve your faculty partners in curriculum design, and make your component part of the class, not simply an add-on. Collaboration is about integration, not competition. So the more you can integrate your content with that of the course or program you are working with, the better. But what does that really mean? It could be as complex as weaving research and information literacy throughout the entire syllabus, grading assignments, and having part of the grade reflect that research component. OK, that's a best-case scenario and may be difficult to achieve given that faculty tend to get touchy about sharing their courses and the perpetual lack of time to devote this level of attention to every class. If you cannot achieve "best practices" levels of involvement, see if you can have one assignment out of the entire course that is yours to create, assess, and so on, based on the research component for the class. If that won't work, try to get the faculty member to provide extra credit for an assessment that you can administer that might also double as an instructional tool. How might that work? Again, the assumption is that at this stage there is at least *some* level of interest on the faculty member's part to let you weave in element(s) of your program; otherwise you are really just talking about the one-shot model, which is technically not collaborative in the same sense and is much more removed from the class.

But even a one-shot class is better than none. So how can you turn that into an opportunity for collaboration? Begin by asking which concepts students are struggling with the most. Instead of asking what the professor would like you to cover, focus on demonstrating *your* expertise. How many of us have fallen into the trap of being presented with a laundry list of "to cover" items and a missive to show students how to search the databases? But with the restructuring of the standards for information literacy into a new framework that strives to create a much more cohesive and holistic approach to teaching students how to research and situating their work in the broader context of scholarly engagement, it would be doing them a great disservice to approach our work with faculty in the same way as in the past. Interview the faculty member to determine what he or she really after; searching the databases is a means to an end, not the end goal in itself. Remember that design thinking approach discussed in the curriculum section? Now is the time to act on it! Here is how:

Ask the faculty member to walk you through the basics of the assignment and take note of things you find interesting or surprising. Take time to listen and take notes, and don't interrupt no matter what brilliant idea pops into your head. Take five minutes to collect your thoughts and reflect on what you've learned about the assignment. Synthesize your learning into a few "needs" that you have discovered and a few "insights" that you find interesting. Needs should be verbs describing what faculty want the students to be able to do as a result of your instruction, and insights are discoveries (or aha moments) that you might be able to leverage when creating solutions. Sound familiar? That's because these are the building blocks of creating your learning outcomes. See how easy that is? From here on out, the "solutions" you generate should be the various activities, online tools, handouts, and so on, that you provide to students in order to help them do whatever it is the faculty member needs them to accomplish as part of your session.

By doing something pretty simple, you've now turned your involvement in the instructional process on its head and taken control as well as given (hopefully) the faculty member *and* the students the help they need. Couple that with some well-planned opportunities for feedback for the students either in the form of consultations, follow-up group sessions, or additional materials, and you've turned your one-shot session into an instructional experience that students will truly benefit from.

Offer a stipend if you can. Money is always a welcome addition to any collaboration, and frankly it might be the only thing that sways some faculty to work with you when intrinsic motivation is lacking. Calling something a pilot can go a long way and will help you start small. Instead of asking for $10,000, giving a faculty member $500 for a summer project can probably be justified much more easily. Use donor funds, a small learning grant, or even temporary funds to help get your efforts under way, and don't worry about the longer term if you can demonstrate the success of your collaboration. Usually (and there are exceptions) if the project is successful, library administration will be more likely to help you get it funded on a more permanent basis and on a larger scale, especially if they get positive feedback from the faculty and the department and you have shown an improvement in student learning in whatever way makes sense for your environment.

Report, report, report. It's no surprise that once you have collected the data, you need to do something with it. Where do you begin? Start internally with a report or presentation to library administration and colleagues. You can have a formal meeting or a brown bag, whatever works for you, but make sure that those with whom you work most closely are well aware of what you've been doing. Why? Besides showing them your awesome program, you want to ensure that they can help spread the word to the faculty they work with, which might inspire some of them to actually help you. By discussing the impact of your collaboration, you can also make the case to library administration to help fund your program on a broader scale and perhaps bring in additional partners and resources. You will also want to co-present something within the department of your faculty partners. The reasons are much the same and will once again demonstrate the benefits of the collaboration. Again, this might inspire other faculty to want to do the same; you may find yourself with more partners than you know what to do with!

Present at any and all appropriate campus events. Do you have an assessment group? Faculty council? A local conference? Take the show on the road! Talk about it to anyone who will listen. Make sure you hone your elevator speech, as not everyone will have time to listen to your perfectly crafted one-hour presentation complete with an interpretive dance. Tell them who you are, what you did (and with whom you worked), and what happened as a result. Write it down, practice it, and be ready to deliver it to the provost, campus president, board of regents, chancellor, or anyone else who wants the abridged version. Talk to your dean or director to see if you can get a five-minute slot at the meeting. The most important thing to keep in mind is demonstrating impact or being able to effectively answer the "who cares?" question. If you nail that aspect, the rest will fall into place. (OK, not really, but you have a much better shot!)

Communicate the Value of Your Program to the University

Our information for this section borrows heavily from the work of Megan Oakleaf, who is nationally recognized for her work with assessment and library value. Megan's *Academic Library Value: Impact Starter Kit* is cited in our list of further readings. We recommend you go through the entire workbook.

Our focus here, however, will be on how you can adapt some of the same principles to demonstrate the value of your instructional program on your campus. Whereas our "Report, report, report" section provided a more informal look at disseminating the results of any pilot projects you undertake, this section will help you develop a more formalized approach.

Understand your institution's strategic directions. How does student participation in your instructional program connect to the learning outcomes of the program (and ultimately your institution's strategic directions) as evidenced by the assessment? In other words, does your instruction program help students do the work they have to do? Does it help them achieve their academic and professional goals? Does it help the institution support them in those goals? If the answer is no or I don't know, you have some homework to do.

So many times this is viewed as an exercise in futility. Sure, it's pretty easy to *say* your program contributes to student learning and throw some numbers to back it up. Student outcomes in evaluating information went up 20 percent this semester. Great! So what? Does this mean that students are now 20 percent better at evaluating information? Does this make them better scholars or critical thinkers? If your institution's strategic plan, mission, or vision does not include critical thinking (as an example), this would be kind of useless data to highlight.

Being able to connect the "what" to the "so what" is a crucial step in demonstrating the impact of your program. Oakleaf's formula for this is relatively simple. First, you must know your institutional goals, mission, vision, and so on. Then you know what you are connecting your information to. Next, define the nature of that relationship. Is it causal—do students who participate in your program do better in their classes overall than those who don't? Or are the two more loosely related—for example, students who participate in the program tend to stay enrolled longer? These are all decision factors that will influence how you approach this connection.

Here is where you will have to first define your terms and decide if you need additional information. What does "doing better" mean? Are you looking at grade point average? Are you looking at grades in a particular course? Or some type of test or exam? All of these things will affect how you answer that ever-important "so what" question. Based on this information, decide if you need to talk to an office on your campus that collects some of this information. Obviously, you will not have access to student grades or retention data, but someone on campus does. Even community colleges and smaller institutions are paying more attention to learning analytics, and this focus is likely to grow. Working with those types of units will be vital to your continued success.

Keeping these concepts in mind will impact program design. If demonstrating that students receive better grades is one of your top priorities, you might structure your assessment differently than if you were just collecting anecdotal or qualitative information. These types of decisions were discussed in the assessment chapter, but this is yet another facet to be aware of as you think about your program's ultimate goals.

Develop stakeholder maps and partnerships. Guess what? This means you will have to get out of your office and start talking with people! Knowing who the key players are on your campus is critical so that you can determine if they are potential partners, decision-makers, or roadblocks. Don't assume that everyone is on the same page. Most of the time you will find that other campus units are more than happy to work with you in whatever capacity you need. But you have to be able to articulate that need if you want assistance, and even more so if they don't see the value in spending their time and perhaps resources on your efforts. In other words, you need to determine who the players are, what they care about, and how much power they wield.

Test to see who is willing to help you and who is not. You don't always have to have 100 percent buy-in from every area on campus, but you do need to know what is the minimum coalition needed for success. Do you need the entire faculty council behind you, or is it OK if the VP for Academic Affairs (or equivalent) is your supporter because that position can pretty much set policy for the entire campus? Even if past relationships have prevented efforts from moving forward, now is the time to make changes. Perhaps a new person has taken over the role, or you yourself are new to the position, but there's no better time than to try again given all of the broader conversations that are happening in higher education at the moment. Even if you just take a new colleague with you and talk about the changes to the Information Literacy Framework, that alone might be enough of a catalyst for change. Remember, sometimes you have to create your own sense of urgency to get your voice heard and be able to talk about how your program is providing value and engagement for students, because no one else will.

Details of how to create an effective communication plan can be found in the sources listed at the end of this chapter. Only a few are included to get you started. Once you have established your story of success, you will need a strategic way to communicate that story to all parties in your library, on campus, and beyond, as appropriate. As mentioned in the "Report, report, report" section, your impact story becomes effective only when others hear about it. You can have the most wonderful program, but if no one else is aware of it, there's little value in that information.

At this point you may be asking yourself why you need to share this information. There are several reasons:

- Leverage your work to ask for resources. It's as simple as that. Administrators are going to want to know why your program is worthy of support when there are so many pressing needs. If you can make a data-driven and compelling case, you have a much stronger chance of actually receiving what you're asking for.

- Use your story to save you from having cuts made to your program. As everyone knows, budget crises are not going away, and no one is going to suddenly hand you money and staffing out of the blue. So you have to work hard to not only retain what you have but try to grow it. And this is where your impact story can help.

- Use this information to help garner resources from other methods of funding, whether it's grants or donors or corporate partners. Being able to prove that you are successful might sway them so that you can continue to capitalize on that success.

- Increase your colleagues' and administrators' understanding of what you do. This can open the gates to additional partnerships and calls from administration to have you participate on other projects or initiatives and increase the visibility of your efforts. No one will think, "Boy, they are doing such wonderful things with instruction in the library. I wonder why." Instead, they might be surprised to know how much you're doing and how you're helping students in their academic and professional careers.

- Work this information into accreditation and recruitment efforts. The library has often been cited as a factor in students wanting to attend a particular institution, most recently in the "Documented Library Contributions to Student Learning and Success: Building Evidence with Team-Based Assessment in Action Campus Projects" report, so being able to blend quantitative data with anecdotal evidence for a holistic picture of how your program furthers the academic mission of the organization can only help boost your institution's profile.

FINAL TAKEAWAYS

1. Be patient and persevere. Outreach is difficult, and it takes time. If email doesn't work, try making a phone call. Follow up and follow through on your action items and, most importantly, don't give up.

2. Come up with a plan of who you want to talk to, what you want to talk about, and what you need to do if they agree to work with you as well as if they don't.

3. Find alternative ways to communicate. Colleagues can be more difficult to get on your side than faculty or other folks on campus, especially if you are not in a supervisory position. Don't be afraid to call on library administration if necessary; management is there to serve as an advocate for you and your programs.

4. Sell what you are doing. You cannot oversell yourself, your program, and your results. The more people know about what you're doing, the better.

5. Connect your results to broad campus-wide initiatives, programs, and goals for maximum impact.

Case Study: Bridging the Gap from Non-credit to Credit: Outreach to ESL Students at a California Community College

Nancy A. Persons, Santa Rosa Junior College

Brief Abstract: This case study describes the first effort to provide targeted outreach to students enrolled in an off-site non-credit English as a Second Language program, with the intent to promote persistence and matriculation into credit-bearing degree programs at a California community college. At their instructional location, students were given presentations explaining learning support available at the library on the main campus and remotely. Emphasis was placed on introduction of English-language vocabulary specifically related to academic library services and resources. Follow-up sessions offered opportunities for hands-on engagement. Unanticipated challenges and their resolution are described.

INSTITUTIONAL BACKGROUND

Santa Rosa Junior College (SRJC) is a public two-year community college with campuses in Santa Rosa and Petaluma, California, serving the Sonoma County region. The college has an unduplicated headcount of 26,735. SRJC has three additional sites: the Public Safety Training Center in Windsor, Shone Farm in Forestville, and the Southwest Santa Rosa Center in Santa Rosa. The student body is increasingly ethnically diverse. Whites comprise 51.8 percent of the student population, Latino/Hispanic students 31.3 percent, Asian students 4.5 percent, multiple 4.0 percent, and African American 2.3 percent. The college was designated a Hispanic Serving Institution (HSI) in 2013 and in 2014 was awarded a $2.65 million grant from the U.S. Department of Education under Title V. In 2013, 42 percent of Sonoma County 12th-graders were Latino.

The Frank P. Doyle Library on the Santa Rosa campus, completed in 2006, is a four-story building of 145,000 total square feet, 1,045 student seats in varying configurations, including 27 group study rooms. The library occupies the upper three stories of the building and houses 280 public computer workstations and a laptop checkout program. Over 40 pieces of artwork from past SRJC Art faculty are permanently installed throughout the building, which has a very open floor plan with abundant natural lighting. The library's primary patrons are SRJC staff, faculty, and currently enrolled SRJC students. The Santa Rosa campus is over 100 acres in size with more than 25 separate buildings, many of them multiple story, found on winding paths graced by centuries-old heritage oak trees throughout the campus. Parking can be challenging.

The Southwest Center, located five miles west of the Santa Rosa campus, is a 10-classroom single building leased from a local public school district. Other buildings on the property are condemned. There is free and ample parking. The Southwest Center is located in the western region of the city of Santa Rosa known as Roseland, home to many of the city's Latino population with many shops and businesses culturally relevant and welcoming to the surrounding demographic. This center is the location for all of SRJC's non-credit ESL instruction, or lowest level of ESL ability. Adjunct instructors teach all courses.

DESCRIPTION OF PROGRAM, PROJECT, OR SPACE

This program was a response to problems of decreasing enrollment, the challenges of English language learners (ELLs) and first-generation students, and the differences in the size and complexity of campuses and sites. Libraries are known to be anxiety producing. The seemingly slight distance between the Southwest Center in the Roseland area of Santa Rosa and the Santa Rosa campus represents a huge divide for many students. Distance, language, a circuitous bus route, and lack of familiarity with the complex United States academic system, coupled with a lack of outreach, left students at the Southwest Center unaware of all that the SRJC Libraries have to offer students to help them bridge the gap from non-credit course enrollment to degree completion.

During the recent economic downturn, SRJC reduced the size of its instructional program 25 percent. In the spring 2013 to summer 2014 terms, the college was trying to grow back the schedule of classes, but overall enrollment continued to decline during this time, while non-credit enrollment increased. The rate of student matriculation from non-credit into credit programs and associate degree completion is poor. The Southwest Center enrollment grew so much during this period that the facility was at maximum capacity at the same time that credit classes were being canceled for lack of enrollment at the Santa Rosa and Petaluma campuses.

Prior to the fall of 2014, no library outreach to the Southwest Center population existed. Libraries are known to prompt anxiety due to the unfamiliar systems students must learn to navigate in order to use them. Library systems use specialized vocabulary that is unfamiliar to many. California ranks last of all the United States in terms of teacher-librarian to student ratio in the K–12 system. Students entering the college's highly digitized information ecosystem come poorly prepared for the challenges of conducting research and knowledge acquisition in such an environment (*Statistics about California School*, 2015). Students at the Southwest Center, isolated from the general population and facilities available at the Santa Rosa campus, receive limited exposure to the broad array of services and resources available there.

What I sought through this project was a way to introduce library concepts into the ESL classroom at the earliest stage of English language learning with the hope that this will facilitate deeper learning at the more advanced levels.

TACKLING THE LENS

Librarians at SRJC have a strong record of outreach to credit instruction programs and routinely collaborate with instructional faculty. I built the program to provide outreach to the Southwest Center ESL non-credit program with the intent to introduce basic library vocabulary to the specific student population at the center, to introduce a friendly and empathetic face, to make connections with the adjunct faculty teaching there, and to extend information regarding the wealth of resources and services available to students remotely and on-site in Santa Rosa. My intent was to employ some techniques of language instruction to reinforce acquisition of library-related terminology and concepts.

Making connections with adjunct faculty is a constant challenge—this sector of the teaching faculty often hold assignments at multiple colleges and are not compensated for work beyond that directly associated with their student contact obligation. They do not have offices one can drop by. Communication is a challenge. Prior to contacting instructors, I met with the manager of the center to gain an understanding of the culture there and become familiar with the facilities, and I reviewed the Course Outline of Record for each class offered there. I confirmed that the center has computer projection and Internet connections in each classroom and a 28-seat instructional computer lab. I sent group email messages to the instructors based on date range of classes, introducing myself and explaining the broad range of course-integrated instruction services available to their classes. This ranges from general introductions to what SRJC libraries offer through in-depth and hands-on instruction in the use of various databases and our EBSCO Discover Service (EDS). I offered to visit the center multiple times for each class, explaining that presentations could last anywhere from a half hour to the full two to three hours of the class period and that bringing students to the Santa Rosa campus was also an option.

Initial efforts to contact faculty yielded six invitations, roughly 30 percent of the classes scheduled there in fall 2014. The intent was to make two visits per class. The goal of the first visit would be to introduce myself as a friendly and accessible library faculty member and to introduce images of library services and resources reinforced with library vocabulary. The second visit would entail either using the center's computer lab to teach students how to access magazine articles online relevant to their interests and curriculum or having classes come to the Santa Rosa campus for a tour of the facility and hands-on instruction in our lab. I was fortunate in that several instructors who initially declined visits opted to have their students join in presentations given to other classes upon my arrival at the center.

In each initial presentation I introduced myself, explaining my own experiences as a university student in a foreign country and language. I used the library's online virtual tour, selectively displaying images showing the services desks that included the large signs identifying these locations while explaining them. I spoke slowly, used multiple synonyms, giving time for students to read words on slides on classroom projection screens, pausing periodically to ask for questions. Services and resources emphasized during presentations included circulation, reference, periodicals and reserve desks, group study rooms, workstations, including what resources were available at each point and what was required in order to access them. I included slides showing book stacks and close-up photographs I'd taken of call numbers appearing on spine labels. After showing slides of the various services and explaining types of resources, I concluded by performing a search on a topic of relevance to the class, limiting the search to magazines, and demonstrating the system's ability to read HTML text aloud while highlighting words.

The take-away I hoped for as a result of these visits was that the libraries have friendly and helpful staff ready to provide a welcome array of services and resources. In addition to print books, our libraries offer many group study rooms with whiteboards, and we check out dry-erase markers, laptop computers, headphones, calculators, and many textbooks. In essence, I demonstrated that we could help remove some barriers preventing students from persisting in their education.

Several of the classes I visited in the fall and spring semesters invited me back for a second visit in the center's computer lab or opted to bring students to the Santa Rosa campus. For follow-up visits at the center, classes met in the computer lab there, where I showed students how get from the college's homepage to the library's website, and then enter a topic, retrieve a list of results, limit to magazine articles, access HTML full text, and have articles read aloud while words were highlighted. For classes that came to the Santa Rosa campus, I gave a tour of the physical facility, reinforcing service points and resources, how to access these, and followed up with hands-on instruction to access magazine articles. For classes, we also demonstrated how to locate high-content low-vocabulary "easy readers" in our collections and to retrieve these from the shelves using call numbers.

LESSONS LEARNED

This project revealed problems with access to the full range of resources and services for students and staff at this location, the limitations of early ELLs, the lack of comfort and familiarity with technology on the part of this population, and the unfamiliarity on the part of the faculty there of the range of resources available. While I took the time to visit the facility, understand the types of classroom setups and computer lab facilities, it was not until my first presentation that we became aware that the center had a different type of Internet connection than that of other sites, and that the IP address range for the center had not been given to all our database and EDS vendors. This caused a disruption in the demonstration of accessing full text. Anticipating this problem in subsequent presentations the same day, I set up the remote connection in advance. We were able to correct the IP address omission before any further hands-on instruction occurred.

It was clear from some of the presentations that not all instructors were familiar with how to use the computer-projector arrays in their classrooms to access and display, and they were therefore less likely to follow up with instruction on their own in use of library resources. Many of the instructors were not aware of the types of materials and audiovisual features available and appropriate for their students. In addition, I learned that the delivery services running between the two campuses did not extend to the Southwest Center. Not only did mail not get delivered to the center via the college's delivery service (a staff member would routinely pick mail up at the Santa Rosa campus on his way to the Southwest Center), there was no extension of the library's book courier to this campus either. Mail delivery to the center has commenced, and we are exploring the feasibility of getting books delivered to and picked up from the center as well.

In initial presentations to classes at the Southwest Center, I used a virtual tour of the Doyle Library from the library's website, skipping past slides that were not highly useful. Due to the fortunate occurrence of a librarian colleague observing me at one session for the purpose of performing a routine evaluation, I learned that the use of the virtual tour had the adverse effect of nauseating visuals from scrolling sideways past slides I didn't want to use. Once I learned this, I selected individual images and created a PowerPoint slideshow instead. In the process of doing this, I was able to enhance the visual display of terminology and incorporate alternative wording to help reinforce language concepts. After learning that some classes were willing to come to Santa Rosa for additional sessions, I added a slide showing a map of the campus with parking and the way to the library highlighted.

Follow-up presentations with hands-on instruction in accessing online resources require multiple instructors or at least assistants who can walk around the room and troubleshoot. In these second sessions conducted at the center, ESL instructors were able to help out. For classes that came to the Santa Rosa campus for their second sessions, I was able to employ student assistants to help. Serendipitously, the primary student employee we engaged was fluent in Spanish. As the vast majority of students in these classes are heritage Spanish speakers, this was an unanticipated benefit. For the first of these sessions, our own computer lab was unavailable, so we set up in advance 40 laptop computers in a large and beautiful group presentation room on the main floor of the Doyle Library. This proved to be a hardship for most students, who were unaccustomed to using track pads (we had a limited supply of mice to offer), and the machines tended to go into sleep mode too quickly. Following this experience, I scheduled any sessions on the Santa Rosa campus only when our computer lab was available.

The final challenge was one of having adequate time for those classes that opted to visit the Santa Rosa campus. Though only five miles from the Southwest Center, the Santa Rosa campus is very large and parking exists only on the perimeters of campus and costs four dollars per vehicle. Students had to carpool, some got lost on the way there, and others got lost trying to find their way to the library. Because all activity related to these visits had to take place within the time frame of the class period, the amount of time for demonstration, discussion, and learning to find books using Library of Congress call numbers was woefully inadequate. Students needed basic instruction in library vocabulary, including elements of bibliographic records such as the words "title," "author," and "call number," and were challenged with using computer technology.

For future sessions we are currently applying for a grant to pay for bus transportation of entire classes to the Santa Rosa campus and back. Knowing the amount of time required for a worthwhile introduction to the library's ecosystem to an ELL population has helped me advise colleagues on how to plan workshops that avoid causing frustration and anxiety on the part of this student demographic.

During initial presentations at the Southwest Center, I explained the need to have an SRJC student ID card in order to borrow materials. Students were concerned about how to get the card. This must be done at the Santa Rosa campus and is mostly limited to business hours. Students voiced concern about handing over an ID card. Therefore, when students came to the Santa Rosa campus for follow-up sessions, we introduced staff (including pointing out student employees) at each service desk and demonstrated how ID cards are taken only to scan barcodes and that ID cards otherwise remain in the students' possession. To establish trust, I explained carefully in all sessions that librarians value the individual's right to privacy and that this is a core value. We showed students where to find the office that produces student ID cards, and for some sessions we were able to plan ahead so that students who wanted to could remain after class and obtain ID cards.

In planning future sessions, it will be effective to propose a plan of two sessions per class at the outset. It has proven very effective to limit the first session to an open discussion with students regarding what they are most interested in learning about and what questions they have, followed by a general presentation about services and resources available at the libraries. I will develop a small pamphlet to hand out that includes images of service desks and resources, complete with labels and definitions. Luly and Lenz suggest that a helpful resource to include for presentations is a list of the various service and resource vocabulary described, which students could be tasked to check off as they hear each term used (142). An additional page might provide images of services and resources with space for students to write in appropriate terms for these visuals. The authors also suggest (142) that having students work together using the target language to retrieve information may help with language production, so the second session will be scaled back to only include either instruction in finding magazine articles with HTML full-text (for sessions taught remotely at the Southwest Center) or how to locate "easy reader" books through the EDS and retrieve them from the book stacks, in both cases with students working in pairs using English.

Students and faculty engaged in this outreach over the course of the 2014–2015 academic year were enthused by the attention paid to them. It was clear from their reactions that students who came to the Santa Rosa campus were awed by the beauty of the Doyle Library and impressed with the facilities and services available to them. Many had not realized that even as non-credit students they were welcome to the same range of services and resources as credit students and that they had the same access to procurement of student ID cards for use in library transactions. Those participating in these sessions at either location expressed greater willingness to approach library staff for assistance, and many who came to the campus completed the process of finding and checkout of library materials. In the future, we hope to track the progress of these and future course-integrated instruction participants to assess if these students demonstrate a higher level of persistence than the general non-credit population.

REFERENCES

Bordonaro, Karen. *The Intersection of Library Learning and Second-Language Learning: Theory and Practice*. Lanham, MD: Rowman & Littlefield, 2013.

Bordonaro, Karen. "Language Learning in the Library: An Exploratory Study of ESL Students." *The Journal of Academic Librarianship* 32, no. 5 (2006): 518–526.

Conteh-Morgan, Miriam E. "Empowering ESL Students: A New Model for Information Literacy Instruction." *Research Strategies* 18, no. 1 (2001): 29–38.

Luly, S., & Lenz, H. "Language in Context: A Model of Language Oriented Library Instruction." *The Journal of Academic Librarianship*, no. 2 (2015), 140–148.

Santa Rosa Junior College ESL 714 course outline as of summer 2012. Accessed August 7, 2015. https://portal.santarosa.edu/SRweb/SR_CourseOutlines.aspx?CVID=22429&Semester=20125.

"Statistics about California School Libraries." School Libraries (California Department of Education). August 3, 2015. Accessed August 7, 2015. http://www.cde.ca.gov/ci/cr/lb/schoollibrstats08.asp.

Table 4.1.
ESL Course Outline

Title of Document/Material	Description
ESL 714 course outline as of summer 2012	https://portal.santarosa.edu/SRweb/SR_CourseOutlines.aspx?CVID=22429&Semester=20125

Case Study: Undergraduate Library Research Award Workshops

Matt Upson, Oklahoma State University
Tim O'Neil, Oklahoma State University

Brief Abstract: The Undergraduate Library Research Award at Oklahoma State University has provided a means for the library to collaborate with the university's undergraduate research office in order to promote the award, provide information literacy instruction, and connect freshmen to meaningful research experiences. Workshops have been offered to provide guidance and support for those interested in applying for the award but have failed to reach a significant number of students for a variety of reasons. In the future, the library will offer direct instruction to students participating in the Freshman Research Scholars program rather than offering independent workshops.

INSTITUTIONAL BACKGROUND

Oklahoma State University has been classified as a research university with high research activity. The total student population at OSU's primary campus in Stillwater, Oklahoma, is approximately 24,000, with an undergraduate population of approximately 20,000. Edmon Low Library is the primary library on campus and is used by undergraduates, graduates, and faculty. The Research and Learning Services division of the library includes an associate dean, nine subject specialists, and two instruction and outreach specialists for undergraduate and graduate students. This division handles most library instruction and library-faculty collaboration.

DESCRIPTION OF PROGRAM, PROJECT, OR SPACE

Undergraduate research has long been an institutional priority at Oklahoma State University, but programs have seldom coordinated efforts with the library—a crucial pathway to discovery in the development of original research proposals. Based on similar awards at the University of Washington and Kansas State University, the Undergraduate Library Research Award was established in 2014 to directly tie information literacy instruction to undergraduate research, promote library resources and services, encourage reflective research practices, and tap into the growing effort to connect undergraduates, especially freshmen, to meaningful research experiences. The award requires students to submit a research project completed for a course or research program at OSU under the supervision of a faculty member, a 750- to 1,000-word reflective essay describing their library research process, a bibliography, and a short faculty recommendation form. The evaluation criteria for the essay, which is the emphasis of the award, address topic development, research strategies, information resources, and finding and evaluating information. A panel of four library faculty, two non-library faculty, and two representatives from the Honors College and the Office of Scholar Development and Undergraduate Research evaluated the applications and determined award winners and honorable mentions in the two categories of upperclassmen and underclassmen. The winners receive $1,500, and the honorable mentions receive $750. Funding has been drawn from a chaired professorship in the library and from the Office of Scholar Development and Undergraduate

Research. More detailed information on the award can be found at http://info.library. okstate.edu/researchaward.

A workshop series was developed to provide support and guidance for students involved in research and interested in the award. The first of two workshops featured the following objectives:

- Review basic library research process: topic identification, research question creation, information gathering and narrowing, and evaluation.
- Create and narrow a research topic and question.
- Develop search statements.
- Successfully locate relevant background sources.
- Become familiar with the basics of various library tools (databases, catalog, discovery service, etc.).

The second workshop featured the following objectives:

- Become familiar with relevant library subject guides (info.library.okstate.edu).
- Identify and communicate with relevant liaison librarians.
- Demonstrate advanced searching techniques.
- Locate journals relevant to their research and use citation to track down additional articles.
- Demonstrate basic competence with citation.

TACKLING THE LENS

The natural partner in developing and promoting the award and workshops was The Henry Bellmon Office of Scholar Development and Undergraduate Research via the Freshman Research Scholars (FRS) program, which offers 60 students in any field of study $1,000 scholarships and the opportunity to pursue faculty-guided research in their first year. Some FRS, depending on their major, receive targeted instruction within program-specific freshmen orientation courses while others rely on a network of college-level coordinators to help them identify faculty research mentors and develop meaningful research experiences. All FRS participate in a series of supplemental seminars focusing on topics such as ethics, proposal development, and research poster design. Information literacy has not yet been included as a seminar topic, but partnership with the library promises to enrich the program by providing coverage of this critical topic. This collaborative effort was initiated with a simple email from the librarian to the Office of Scholar Development and Undergraduate Research, and continued collaboration between the library and the office has the potential to introduce additional undergraduates to research opportunities.

Offered twice since its inception, the Undergraduate Library Research Award has provided 10 workshops (independent of a specific course or program) but has failed to attract a large number of participants. Over the course of those workshops, only 13 have attended and of that small number, many attendees were international graduate students, visiting faculty, or were not actively interested in applying for the award. Despite promotional efforts to the FRS population, inclusion on university-wide events calendars, and promotion by liaison librarians to faculty, participation in the workshops was minimal and unfocused. Workshops were held on various days and times throughout the semester, which was intended to offer greater flexibility for students but may have contributed to the low attendance through inconsistency in scheduling. Workshops will no longer be scheduled in the run-up to the award deadline. Instead, there will be a greater push to inform faculty (who drive the research in their courses and programs) and increase marketing through social media, videos, flyers, sidewalk chalking, signage around campus, utilizing library student ambassadors, and conversations with academic student organizations. Additionally, as noted below, the library will bring the workshop to the FRS group, offering direct instruction and support.

LESSONS LEARNED

While requiring FRS participation in the workshops was briefly considered, a better option appears to be the inclusion of focused instruction offered to FRS students participating in for-credit orientation courses. The librarian will participate in a class session, replicating some of the workshop content during this time, and will support the completion of annotated bibliography and research proposal assignments. The lesson will cover the development of search terms and search statements, followed by an introduction to basic searches using WorldCat, databases, and the library discovery search. Students will also be made aware of online subject guides and subject librarians. The lesson will end with a group walkthrough of an academic article, focusing on general evaluation, identifying in-text citations, using the bibliography to locate other sources, and engaging in the scholarly conversation. Follow-up sessions may be scheduled, and the librarian will remain in contact with students and instructors. The greatest weakness of the award has been the lack of viable applications for the underclassmen category, with no awards being offered in that category since its inception. The primary goal is to increase underclassmen participation in the award to the point that awards can be offered in that category. Additional goals are to improve student success with freshman-level research and provide positive and meaningful interaction with the library at an early stage in the students' academic careers. As supporting evidence, past winners of the award have noted the value of reflecting on a project and process and the importance of various library spaces and services to their research, and they have offered encouragement to other students seeking assistance from the library. Videos featuring award winners can be found at http://info.library.okstate.edu/researchaward/winners.

Case Study: Library Instruction from Sage on the Stage to Guide on the Side

Matthew M. Bejune, Worcester State University
Sam O'Connell, Worcester State University

"I believe that the greatest opportunities for librarians lie in deeper connections to the curriculum, adapting to new modes of pedagogy, linking technology-rich and collaborative spaces in libraries to learning, and ensuring that individuals who enrich the library's role in teaching and learning are on staff. Overall, the trajectory is for the increasing integration of librarians and libraries into the teaching and learning program of the college or university" (Lippincott, 2015, p. 34).

Brief Abstract: This case study addresses the challenge of incorporating active learning techniques into information literacy sessions at the individual course level, a format that many faculty traditionally identify as prepackaged lectures delivered using the transmittal model. We instead argue for a constructivist approach based on facilitating active learning through pedagogical, innovative strategies and close faculty and librarian collaboration. Through our case study, we show how collaboration can transform information literacy education into a user-centered learning process for students while also being course specific and not just discipline specific in its approach. We presented our research at the 2015 annual conference of the Association of College and Research Libraries, New England Chapter. (See References for additional information, including a link to presentation slides.)

INSTITUTIONAL BACKGROUND

Worcester State University (WSU), founded and located in Worcester, Massachusetts, in 1874, is a medium-sized public university with over 5,000 students. The student body is primarily non-residential with approximately 60 percent commuter and 40 percent residential students. The undergraduate curriculum is balanced between liberal arts, sciences, and professional programs. WSU is part of the network of nearly 30 public institutions of higher education in Massachusetts.

The library, located in the campus Learning Resource Center, is the intellectual heart of campus, a place where members of the campus community converge, collaborate, learn, and discover. The library collections contain more than 200,000 items including over 80,000 eBooks and more than 125 databases. There are a variety of learning spaces, including carrels for independent study, collaborative areas with flat-screen displays, large tables with ample space to spread out, lounge chairs with built-in desks, as well as coffee-shop seating in the library café. Library staff assist users with their personal, professional, and scholarly pursuits at the research help desk and by phone, email, or online chat. Librarians work with faculty in the classroom, enhancing students' ability to navigate the complex information network of Google, Wikipedia, printed and electronic books, media, and databases.

DESCRIPTION OF PROGRAM, PROJECT, OR SPACE

At the beginning of the researchers' collaboration in fall 2013, our library instruction program was in the midst of a renaissance coinciding with the hiring of the author, Matt Bejune, at the time as the information literacy and instruction librarian. Prior to then, the library instruction program was small (30 to 40 sessions per year) and just scratching the surface of the potential demand for library instruction at a university of our size. There were unmet instructional needs; however, the library did not have the necessary infrastructure in place to serve faculty and students.

Throughout the 2013/2014 academic year, library staff made the following infrastructure changes, and in doing so, increased our capacity to meet the needs of the campus. First, we established a liaison program designating one librarian to be the point person for each campus academic department (History, Psychology, Visual and Performing Arts, etc.) or academic program, such as First-Year Seminar. Liaisons work with disciplinary faculty, assisting them with library instruction, collection development, research assistance, and other affiliated services. As a way to reach out to faculty, we created a top-level page on our library website highlighting faculty services. The page included a list of liaisons as well as information about our newly formed liaison program and library instruction program, including our information literacy mission statement, tips for successful sessions, and links to information literacy documents published by the American Library Association and the Association of College and Research Libraries. Second, we adopted a shared calendar for booking library instruction sessions. Third, we selected a piece of software to record library instruction data needed for assessment. Fourth, we created an instructional classroom located within the library, perhaps the most challenging addition to our infrastructure, a change that took the better part of a year to complete.

As a result of the infrastructural changes and the collected work of the librarians, at the end of the 2013/2014 academic year, we had dramatically increased our outputs, teaching 185 classes and reaching over 3,000 students, a pace we have continued.

As the new library instruction program got off the ground at WSU, it quickly became clear that a change in the philosophy of teaching and learning was afoot. Library instruction was moving from a transmittal model of teaching information about the library and its resources to a model of faculty-librarian collaboration focused on improving student learning by positioning information literacy as a tool of active learning. This new model addresses the question "If we are moving away from a sage on the stage model to a guide on the side model, how do we move toward active learning?" with multiple goals: get students to utilize the library, its resources, and its staff as an integral part of their learning; increase active collaboration between faculty and librarians; and integrate information literacy into the university at both a campus-wide and discipline-specific levels.

Our work is inspired by Alison King's article "From Sage on the Stage to Guide on the Side," in *College Teaching* (1993). In her influential article, King champions a constructivist approach to teaching and learning based on active rather than passive learning. It stands in marked contrast to the transmittal model based on the idea that the student's brain is like an empty container into which the teacher pours knowledge.

TACKLING THE LENS

Our collaboration, developed over two years, has been centered on integrating information literacy into Sam O'Connell's course, Critical Thinking in the Arts. The course, part of the Visual and Performing Arts Department's (V+PA) interdisciplinary core, is charged with introducing students to critical thinking, creative thinking, and information literacy. Critical Thinking in the Arts is the primary course in which V+PA majors learn how to conduct research in the arts prior to their senior capstone course. As such, a strong information literacy component is essential.

Our first in-class collaboration occurred in the fall of 2013 when Matt Bejune, information literacy and instruction librarian at the time, was designated as V+PA's liaison librarian in his first semester at WSU. After attending a V+PA department meeting to pitch his services and encourage V+PA faculty to integrate information literacy into their classrooms, Bejune scheduled a session with O'Connell in his Critical Thinking in the Arts course. Students for this class were working on an annotated bibliography assignment for a research project about an artist and his or her body of work. Prior to the session, though, we had little communication beyond O'Connell sending Bejune a brief description of the assignment for which students would be researching. O'Connell, based on his previous experience with information literacy sessions in the classroom, expected a generic, prepackaged session about the library and its resources. To that end, he had not prepared his students with an information need. In his mind, that would come later, after they had been introduced to the library's Visual and Performing Arts research resources.

Bejune, however, had planned a hands-on research activity for the students to do real-time, active research in class. In this first meeting, students wound up choosing an artist on the fly and researching their artists during Bejune's in-class visit. For many students, the artist they chose had no connection to the one they would wind up working on for their final project.

Reflecting on the outcome of our first collaboration, we both agree it failed to meet our desired outcome of improving student learning. We fell victim to the tension between the traditional trap of viewing information literacy sessions as prepackaged guides to the library and its resources and hands-on learning based on a real information need. Rather than have an explicit conversation about shared goals or outcomes for the session, we each had our own implicit, historically based expectation of how it would go. As a result, our failure in our first attempt at working together came from both sides of the faculty-librarian collaboration, in part because it was our least collaborative session. As the faculty member, O'Connell underprepared his students for the session by not providing them with a clear information need ahead of time. As the librarian, Bejune did not highlight the importance of students having an understanding of their information need for the assignment at hand. Aside from these pedagogical failures in the first collaboration, we also had technical difficulties as a result of insufficient Wi-Fi, which prevented all students from being able to search online. Following our first failed attempt, we began working collaboratively over the next two years, identifying strategies that would help students conduct their research for their final projects in a more targeted way than had been available prior to the new direction of the library's information literacy program.

Based on our ongoing collaborations over the past two years (Table 4.2), we have arrived at a method that benefits both the goals of the information literacy program at WSU and the course-specific needs and learning outcomes for Critical Thinking in the Arts. Now our collaborations are based on regular contact throughout the semester and include joint review of the syllabus and the information need for the research assignment, clear communication about what the students need to bring to class with them, what instructional technologies we will use during the class session, and what questions the students will be expected to answer at the conclusion of the sessions. Additionally, our collaboration has fostered a working relationship for students that models the importance of curriculum-library integration both in and out of the classroom. It is our ongoing, regular contact and communication with each other that continues to make the collaboration a productive one, which can now be seen to have a positive impact on student learning. Our ongoing collaboration throughout each new semester is important as the research assignments for the class change as O'Connell adapts his syllabi based on new pedagogical strategies focused on active learning. Additionally, Bejune is able to integrate new research tools and methods for the students. Working together, our purposefully evolving approach continues to be based on evidence-based research into improving student learning through active learning strategies.

LESSONS LEARNED

Through our collaboration, our lessons learned can be divided into three broad lessons: (1) communicate openly in the preparation stage as part of the ongoing partnership between faculty and librarians, (2) articulate a clear information need to students before the information literacy session, and (3) embrace pedagogical failures as a necessary outcome of the risk taking required for innovative instructional design. Of these, the first and most immediate lesson we learned was that regular communication was the most important aspect of developing a faculty-librarian partnership. We both had our own approach to active learning within our respective fields, but in sharing a classroom space, we had to work and communicate on how to engender active learning in a way that benefitted both the students and our learning outcomes. Part of this was accomplished through O'Connell learning how to better prepare his students with a clear information need before Bejune's class sessions so that in-class time became active working time. Another factor, though, was communicating our dual focus on integrating information literacy into the curriculum of the course in a way that both of our perspectives enhanced student learning. That communication has also allowed our iterative process to develop and grow organically and has allowed us to embrace our failures and celebrate our successes in the process. We both envision this collaboration as a long-term process and partnership of integrating information literacy and not the traditional transmittal model of one-off, canned sessions. More importantly, though, we learned that giving faculty and librarians equal status in the students' and institution's eyes is not enough. At Worcester State University the librarians are faculty members. A case could be made that close relationships between teaching faculty and librarians are dependent on librarians having faculty status. That argument, however, misses a key point in our research and reflection on our own process. It is not that WSU's librarians have faculty status; rather, it is that at WSU both faculty and librarians have a shared commitment to teaching and learning.

Table 4.2.
Session Reflection Summary

Semester	Pre-Assignment Preparation	Learning Outcome Result	Rationale
Fall 2013	Bring your laptops	Failure	Students were unaware of a specific information need *and* faculty had the expectation of a canned information session.
Spring 2014	Bring your laptops and think about topic for a literature review	Improvement, but ... "not yet"	Combination of faculty paternity leave, so information literacy librarian was flying solo *and* students not fully understanding information literacy need.
Fall 2015	Submit research question in advance on shared topic	Success	Students were on the same page, were able to find a source using the tools demonstrated by Bejune, and were able to evaluate a new source using the CRAAP test.
Spring 2015	Create an artistic response to a preselected work of art.	Success	Students were able to use Bejune's in-class demonstration on information literacy to see the connections between information literacy and creative work.

REFERENCES

Bejune, Matthew, and Sam O'Connell. "Library Instruction from Sage on the Stage to Guide on the Side." Presentation, Annual Conference of the New England Chapter of the Association of Research Libraries (ACRL/NEC), Worcester, Massachusetts, May 2015. Presentation slides available from http://www.slideshare.net/mattbejune/library-instruction-from-sage-on-the-stage-to-guide-on-the-side-bejune-oconnell.

King, Alison. "From Sage on the Stage to Guide on the Side." *College Teaching* 41, no. 1 (1993): 30–35.

Lippincott, Joan. "The Future for Teaching and Learning." *American Libraries* 46, no. 3–4 (2015): 34–37.

Case Study: Quest 4 the Best—Using Food to Bring Outreach Programming to Residence Halls

Emily P. Frank, Louisiana State University

Brief Abstract: A recent reaccreditation process at Louisiana State University led to an institutional focus on using programming to increase undergraduate research. Considering this, a collaboration developed between a librarian, a faculty member supporting residential life, and a communications studio coordinator. They drew upon shared elements in individual priorities, including information literacy, residence hall programming, and communication skills, to design a co-curricular program. The event, Quest 4 the Best, targeted students living in residence halls. Working in small groups, students developed a position on why one of three brands of a food was the best before eating all three brands. In the process, they exercised research and communications skills. The program represented a novel outreach strategy that engaged the librarian with campus partners.

INSTITUTIONAL BACKGROUND

Louisiana State University (LSU) in Baton Rouge is the state's flagship university. It is a land, sea, and space grant institution with a Carnegie Research Active/Very High classification. The Libraries is composed of the main library and a separate special collections library, collectively serving 30,000+ students. LSU is doctoral granting, but the majority of the outreach efforts target undergraduates. While many standard outreach events—information fairs and orientations—occur collaboratively with various campus units, outreach programming traditionally has centered almost exclusively on library resources and services, has been less inclusive of campus partners, and has occurred within library facilities. This programming has often been inter- and non-disciplinary, like a library-wide open house, a special collections open house focusing on STEM, and elementary and high school student visits. An outreach librarian spearheads these efforts with many librarians participating in this work.

LSU's on-campus housing offerings include a residence hall system. While there are options for all students and majors, the residence halls are distinct from other campus housing in that they primarily target first- and second-year students. The residence halls include residential colleges, exclusively open to first-year students and organized around a discipline (e.g., business) or theme (e.g., career discovery), and traditional residential halls, which include a mix of single-sex and co-ed buildings. First-year students are not required to live on campus, but those who elect to have resources specifically available for them. Two faculty members act as faculty-in-residence, living in apartments within residential halls. The purpose of the faculty-in-residence is to enable structured co-curricular activities with students. They receive funding to facilitate this.

The initial impetus for the outreach program described in this case study came from LSU's reaccreditation. An element of accreditation for the Southern Association of Colleges and Schools is the creation and execution of a campus-wide initiative in support of a specific goal. The current accreditation plan focuses on undergraduate research with the goal of using incremental programming to move undergraduates to the pinnacle project—mentored undergraduate research. A meeting occurred between the instructional technologies and engineering librarian, a College of Engineering faculty member, and the coordinator for the college's communications studio to discuss plans for the semester. The faculty member, also occupying the position of faculty-in-residence, was excited by promotional materials she had seen outlining the undergraduate research agenda. The group brainstormed programming that she could bring to the residence halls. Collectively, they envisioned a program that would support her work while integrating information literacy and communication skills, priorities of the librarian and coordinator, respectively.

DESCRIPTION OF PROGRAM, PROJECT, OR SPACE

Embracing the theme of undergraduate research, in initial brainstorming sessions the group discussed how to create a program that would encourage students to understand they were all researchers, expose them to the importance of questioning sources and considering credibility, and yet be fun and engaging. The group envisioned a co-curricular activity called Quest 4 the Best (Q4B) to introduce students to basic information literacy concepts. Targeting undergraduates living in dorms and in their first year at LSU, the program's goals were to engage students outside of the classroom and demonstrate how information literacy has relevancy in contexts beyond a research assignment. Through application of critical thinking and communication skills in a fun environment, students would improve transferable skills while having positive interactions with faculty, staff, and one another.

Specifically, the objectives of the event were that through participation students would be able to:

1. Recognize the importance of seeking information to support decision-making.
2. Identify first-hand testimony as primary source information.
3. Apply one element of information evaluation (purpose, authority, usefulness, or currency) to a resource.
4. Describe how credible information supports a reliable and persuasive argument.

The program was designed to be relatively brief in length—under 45 minutes—and be held within residence halls. The librarian, faculty-in-residence, and coordinator acted as facilitators. In advance, they purchased one type of food from three vendors. For example, one event occurring in the Engineering Residential College centered on chicken wings, while an event within the all-girls residence hall used frozen yogurt. A mix of local brands and national chains was used. All funds came from the faculty-in-residence budget.

The events opened with an introduction by the librarian. She outlined the students' and facilitators' roles. Students were responsible for preparing convincing arguments for why one brand of food was the best. These could center on the advantages of one brand or highlight the disadvantages of the others. The librarian emphasized the importance of documenting the decision-making process.

Students then broke into small groups and collectively developed an argument as to why one of the three brands of a food item was the best. They were given 15 minutes to research and formulate their position. To encourage them to consider what information supported a reliable and persuasive argument, they were given a worksheet that included basic elements of information evaluation. The worksheet outlined elements commonly seen in information evaluation—authority, currency, usefulness, and purpose—and students used it to track their supporting evidence.

The spaces where the event occurred had Wi-Fi but did not have computers. Students completed all research on their phones and by interviewing one another. Students approached this research with creativity. Some emphasized aspects of the brand—looking at the company's history, environmental and sustainability practices, or attitude on corporate responsibility. They weighed the value and role of bias in information coming from sources like company press releases versus newspaper articles. Other students considered health, looking at nutritional facts and ingredients. Yelp, blogs, and newspaper restaurant reviews were frequently referenced. The librarian also promoted use of the library's discovery service to find articles from newspapers and magazines, such as *Consumer Reports*. Many interviewed one another to see if any students had previous experience with the foods or had worked for the companies. The facilitators moved around the room to interact with students during this process.

Once arguments were formulated, the students presented on their selected brand, using information to support their choice and to detract from the others. Attribution was emphasized, and if credit was not given, the facilitators asked follow-up questions to address this. They also asked questions to determine how students evaluated information—what made the information credible and worthy of inclusion. When students used first-hand testimony, the facilitators underscored how this acted as primary source information and explained what this meant. Results were tallied and then participants were able to eat all three brands of food to see how the positions they heard matched with the personal experience of eating. At the end of the program, students were asked to complete a brief survey. Participation was tracked by a headcount.

Student surveys provided basic feedback. Students overwhelmingly identified that they enjoyed the workshop and would recommend it to a friend. They stated that information was presented in an understandable way and offered written comments sharing that they had fun and enjoyed the food. Few critical comments were received. They centered on the logistics of the event and included requests that the food be presented at the start of the workshop and that more time be allocated to complete the research component. This feedback did not change the structure of the event. The group intentionally designed the workshop to be brief and to provide the food at the end to incentivize participation. While additional time would have allowed for more thorough research, often students began to get restless and divert into off-topic conversations as they approached the 15-minute mark. The survey asked students to describe one way to determine if information is credible. Less than half of the students provided a response, but those who did identified aspects like currency, bias, reliability, and author credentials. Nearly all respondents (96 percent) correctly identified first-hand testimony as a primary source.

Q4B was promoted using posters in dorm common areas. While they were placed on activity boards, the group recognized that these marketing materials were easily lost in the sea of events being promoted. As a result, the faculty-in-residence worked closely with the resident assistants (RAs). Since RAs are charged with programming and must engage their residents in a certain number of events per year, they were invested in encouraging participation. Leading up to the event, the RAs helped get the word out by promoting it to their residents. During step-up immediately before the event, the RAs interacted with passing students. The RAs often knew these students by name and were able to target them in the moment to encourage participation. The vast majority of students attended the program as a result of this. Therefore, while print marketing was used and the RAs promoted the event in the days leading up to it, holding the program in a space with foot traffic and using the RAs to interact with passing students captured their interest just prior to the event and proved to be the most effective strategy. Following Q4B, the RAs often remarked that it was their best-attended event of the year.

TACKLING THE LENS

This initiative engaged in collaborative outreach by partnering the library with other campus entities. While the librarian, faculty-in-residence, and coordinator work to support education and research on a daily basis, the development of this program integrated these efforts and brought them out of their departmental silos. By identifying individual goals—information literacy, communication skills, and residential hall programming—and building on established relationships, these campus partners drew upon shared elements to design a mutually beneficial co-curricular program. For the librarian, the collaboration allowed her to pursue a novel outreach program at no cost to the library—an important consideration in an era of tight budgets.

LESSONS LEARNED

Outreach programming inside the library helps bring students into the space and supports positioning the library as not only an intellectual but also a social commons. Nonetheless, using the residence halls for programming allowed the librarian to interact in a student space and meet students in a comfortable and familiar environment. Since students returning to their dorm after a day of classes may not be in learning or research mode, the program was designed and marketed to be fun and not strictly educational. While the program did seek to orient students to college-level skills, it presented information literacy in an approachable way by communicating its relevancy in everyday life.

The location did present challenges. Keycard entry made participation difficult for students from other residence halls or those living off-campus since they were unable to enter the building. Because of this anticipated limitation, marketing for the event occurred only in the space.

Within the residence halls, Q4B took place in meeting rooms and atrium areas. Using the atrium area allowed the facilitators and RAs to encourage students walking by to participate. While the foot traffic acted as a benefit, the openness of the atrium enabled some students to skip the activity and stop by just for the food portion. The meeting room, on the other hand, provided poor visibility but ensured that the students enjoying the food had participated in the activity.

Food was central to the success of Q4B. The group was thoughtful and intentionally chose food based on what they believed would draw students in that residence hall. While the group envisioned applying the Q4B format to non-food focused events—such as a debate the candidate event during election season—food was seen as the primary driver of student participation.

Librarians engaging with other campus entities on outreach programming may risk diluting their message, but the collaboration seen with Q4B acts as an example of the positive potential. By identifying common ground within individual priorities, the three campus partners were able to design and implement a mutually beneficial program that students enjoyed.

Q4B Worksheet

Criteria	Source 1	Source 2	Source 3
PRIMARY RESEARCH Observation: Does anyone in your group have experience with these foods?			
SECONDARY RESEARCH Purpose: What is the resource trying to do: sell, explain, analyze? Does knowing the purpose affect your trust in it?			
Authority: Can you trust the author? Why or why not? Does the author cite evidence? Can you interact with the author?			
Usefulness: How useful is the information to you?			
Currency: How current is the information?			

Q4B Survey

---

1) Describe one thing you learned about how to determine
if information is credible:

2) I enjoyed this workshop.

☐	Strongly agree	☐	Agree	☐	Neutral	☐	Disagree	☐	Strongly disagree

3) I would recommend a *Quest 4 the Best* workshop to a
friend.

☐	Strongly agree	☐	Agree	☐	Neutral	☐	Disagree	☐	Strongly disagree

4) Information was presented in an understandable way.

☐	Strongly agree	☐	Agree	☐	Neutral	☐	Disagree	☐	Strongly disagree

5) First-hand testimony counts as a:

☐	Primary source	☐	Secondary source

6) Comments or suggestions to improve the workshop:

CASE STUDY REFLECTION QUESTION

Based on the experiences in these case studies, what is one new practice or activity you could initiate at your institution to change the way you approach outreach and create new, or rekindle existing, partnerships?

FURTHER READING

Anthony, Kristin. "Reconnecting the Disconnects: Library Outreach to Faculty as Addressed in the Literature." *College & Undergraduate Libraries* 17, no. 1 (2010): 79–92.

Brown, Karen, and Kara J. Malenfant. *Documented Library Contributions to Student Learning and Success: Building Evidence with Team-Based Assessment in Action Campus Projects.* n.p., 2016. http://www.ala.org/acrl/sites/ala.org.acrl/files/content/issues/value/contributions_y2.pdf.

Johnson, Corey M., Sarah K. McCord, and Scott Walter. "Instructional Outreach across the Curriculum: Enhancing the Liaison Role at a Research University." *The Reference Librarian* 39, no. 82 (2004): 19–37.

Neely, Teresa Y., Naomi Lederer, Awilda Reyes, Polly Thistlethwaite, Lindsey Wess, and Jean Winkler. "Instruction and Outreach at Colorado State University Libraries." *The Reference Librarian* 32, no. 67–68 (2000): 273–287.

Oakleaf, Megan. *The Value of Academic Libraries: A Comprehensive Research Review and Report.* Association of College & Research Libraries. 2010.

Oakleaf, Megan, Michelle S. Millet, and Leah Kraus. "All Together Now: Getting Faculty, Administrators, and Staff Engaged in Information Literacy Assessment." *Portal: Libraries and the Academy* 11, no. 3 (2011): 831–852.

Wiggins, Grant P., and Jay McTighe. *Understanding by Design.* Alexandria, VA: Association for Supervision and Curriculum Development, 2005.

Part III

ADMINISTRATION

The final part of this book explores the administrative responsibilities that often accompany an instruction program. While the first two parts discussed the "what" and "how" of a user-centered instruction program, this part concludes the discussion with the behind-the-scenes work.

Chapter 5

STAFFING

CHAPTER OBJECTIVES

- Analyze the impact of staffing on the current capacity of the instruction program as well any future development.
- Determine how an increase in staffing would affect the organizational structure, reporting lines, and positional responsibilities.

INTRODUCTION

Looking at an instructional program through the staffing lens is interesting because so much exists outside your realm of control. Even when the growth or expansion of an instruction program is dependent on additional staff members, the ability to reassign job responsibilities or push forward a new hire often rests with library and/or campus administration, who may or may not see your information literacy instruction program as a high priority. Staffing also has ripple effects with other areas; the lack of dedicated staff may prompt additional outreach or collaboration efforts, or the modification of instruction methods by transitioning from in-person to online modules. When discussing staffing, the topic is much bigger than just a one-out-one-in exchange: it is a complex system of institutional politics that bleed into curriculum design, outreach, and development and can fundamentally alter the direction of an instruction program. However, it can also be one of the strongest agents of change; overcoming a staffing shortage or budget crunch often motivates an instruction team to be their most creative.

Perhaps as a result of these conditions, instruction librarians tend to be innovative, student-centered, and forward thinking. With limited resources and staff, instruction librarians serve the most vulnerable and at-risk students on campus: first years, undeclared majors, transfers, first-generation, and non-traditional students. While the size and scope of a position can vary, instruction positions are universally challenging. They demand significant emotional labor, often carrying high levels of teaching, training, and reference. They also absorb the tasks that do not fit under a traditional subject liaison position, such as large general education courses, living-learning programs, orientation activities, residential life, or bridge programs. As a result, instruction positions suffer high levels of burnout and staff turnover.

For those who manage first-year instruction programs, these challenges are magnified. Though the head of an instruction department may have some hierarchy within the division, overseeing an instruction program involves negotiation and cooperation with colleagues. In some situations, first-year instruction may be absorbed by a single individual tasked with the herculean challenge of coordinating a team of library instructors; or even more disheartening, left to design, teach, and assess the program on his or her own. Even in the face of these, instruction coordinators tend to be creative and optimistic. They display resilience and grace in the face of enormous obstacles, building incredible programs with limited positional authority, resources, or time. Instruction positions necessitate a strong backbone and a soft heart, requiring a person to be approachable and caring, yet have the mental fortitude to teach dozens of instruction sessions over short periods of time.

Because staffing and workloads are unique to each institution, this chapter is dedicated to the threads that run between each organization. It covers advocacy, supervision, time management, and collaboration. To simplify the discussion, the conversation is grouped in two broad organizational structures: (1) the lone individual, and (2) a small team of people dedicated to instruction, which might include librarians, support staff, and/or graduate students.

WHEN YOU ARE THE INSTRUCTION DEPARTMENT

For many instruction librarians, the program begins and ends with a single individual. Working alone to design, deliver, and assess an instruction program offers unique benefits and challenges. Although maintaining autonomy over an instructional program can be exhilarating, working in isolation on a large and lengthy project can be, unsurprisingly, lonely. Solo instruction positions can also take on a sense of destitution by absorbing the least glamorous of the public services: reference scheduling, classroom management, first-year instruction, and assessment. Although the majority of creating and overseeing an instruction program takes place behind the scenes, the most visible aspect of the program is the in-person instruction, which, particularly for first-year students, can appear (at face value) as introductory or simplistic.

If you are new to one of these positions, the first thing to keep in mind is that the existence of your position shows a commitment on behalf of the library to teaching and learning. Although it can be tempting to view the lone-wolf position as a manifestation of the inattention of the library to first-year instruction, the glass-half-full interpretation is not only much more likely but also more beneficial to your mental health. The fact that your position exists means that there is a person within the library dedicated to student learning. As with many things, much of the work of an instruction librarian is in choosing how to respond to a situation. Viewing your position in a positive light can keep you grounded when you start to feel overwhelmed, or worse, taken for granted. It is something that you can do for yourself that costs the institution nothing.

The other challenge of the solo instruction librarian is in managing expectations—not only outward expectations put on us by colleagues or administrators but also the internal benchmarks that we set for ourselves. When you are working alone, you set your own levels of achievement: you decide what a program needs, how long it will take to implement, and what will demonstrate that it is successful. This type of power can be particularly difficult to handle when the only thing stopping you from snowballing into an overambitious program is you. In these situations, it is important to identify, understand, and honor your boundaries. While it may be entirely possible to design and implement a comprehensive instruction program in a year, it is probably not realistic or even necessary. Often, the academic timetable is longer and slower than we expect. Set reasonable expectations, and hold yourself accountable by not only meeting goals but also attempting *not* to routinely exceed or surpass your benchmarks. Sometimes, taking three months to do something is better than killing yourself trying to finish it in a month. Ultimately, an institution is better served when you attend to self-care and mitigating burnout than it is finishing a project slightly ahead of schedule.

The other side of managing expectations is negotiating the assumptions of colleagues and supervisors. From the outside, programmatic management can appear deceptively simple. When you are working alone, you are also the only person able to communicate the enormous work of designing a program to colleagues and administrators. If you are asked to complete a project in less time than it requires, you have a responsibility to yourself and your colleagues to articulate the invisible labor. Taking ownership over a program requires not only delivering a successful product but also advocating for the time, space, and resources needed to complete the project. Do this by communicating challenges and publicly celebrating achievements. Take the initiative to send out a monthly email update on the program, even if it is not requested. As your instruction program reaches critical mass, communicate the limitations of the current staffing model to administration. The hard truth of managing the solo instruction program is that a need for additional staffing is not best articulated by meeting all of the needs of the program. Although, especially at a smaller institution, it is unlikely that an instruction program would ever have two full-time librarians, it may be possible to have instruction added to work plans of other colleagues or to find funding for a part-time or hourly graduate student to help with the work.

Gaining Allies

When you do not have positional authority, it can be difficult to get people to readily join your team, especially if your team focuses on teaching first-year students how to navigate the library website. However, in the likely event that an instruction program surpasses your ability to provide the requisite teaching, research help, and so on, it is important to have a plan in place for soliciting support.

The ideal outcome is general education instruction added to the work plans or job descriptions of some (or all) of your public services colleagues. You can do this in small ways, by asking for a brief statement to be added to the list of position responsibilities, or be more ambitious, such as asking for a specific percentage of the workload. As a fair warning, attempting to alter job descriptions can incite defensive behavior. We recommend starting with your allies and having those individuals approach their supervisors one on one. If someone goes to an administrator and asks to have general education instruction added to their work plan, it will be taken more seriously than if you ask on behalf of others.

If you are low on allies, start the conversation with your supervisor by clearly articulating the number of students that are served through the program and which services you will not be able to continue without additional support. Offer specifics rather than general statements. "At our current staffing level, we will be unable to support composition instruction this fall. I am asking for all of the public services librarians to participate by teaching two English 101 sessions each semester." Be prepared to negotiate. Although it is possible to manage a program without explicit statements of accountability, including the responsibility in a job description demonstrates a commitment from administration that can be important for others to see and recognize, especially when you are asking colleagues to rise above and beyond their job responsibilities.

If altering job descriptions is not a viable option, consider "selling" general education as an opportunity for service. Instead of sending out a general call for volunteers, target individuals by sending personalized emails explaining why they are being asked to participate and the value they would bring to the program. You can also respect their time by making sure you have materials readily available, such as lesson plans and in-class activities. When all else fails, recognition and gratitude can be more effective at overcoming barriers than an administrative mandate. If you demonstrate respect for your colleagues' time, they will be more likely to participate. The best way to do this is by acknowledging a person as an individual and the workload involved with the act.

Finally, when you are a department of one, the most important thing you can do for yourself is to be an advocate. Rather than assuming someone does not want to participate, always give him or her a chance to say no. Even when you can do something yourself, making the effort to solicit buy-in and participation can strengthen a program, bolstering relationships that will support the program as it continues to develop. Working by yourself to create and manage a program can be draining, but if you make the effort to communicate the milestones to your community at large and request the resources you need to continue growing and thriving, you will be successful.

WHEN YOU ARE PART OF A TEAM

Although positional responsibilities for instruction librarians often display some consistencies, the distance between serving as the only instruction librarian at an institution to being a part of a team, even if it is just one additional person, is substantial. A department is often indicative of a larger-scale instruction program, reaching thousands, rather than hundreds, of students. It is more likely for a department, or unit, to have specialized positions without traditional subject responsibilities. It also introduces an intermediary manager, which brings a different dynamic to the instruction program. Things that were individual become collective. Rather than *your* instruction program, it becomes *ours*. It is also more likely for positions to be specialized. While an individual instruction librarian might participate in the programmatic process, a member of a department might focus on assessment, training, or online development.

As with instruction positions, instructional services, user education, teaching and learning, and first-year program departments also include an amalgamation of tasks that do not fit in other areas. In addition to large amounts of teaching and reference, these units are sometimes responsible for tangential tasks, such as website management, subject guides, professional development for staff, or space management. The role of the department within the academic structure can be complex. Because the core responsibilities require less emphasis on faculty relationships and upper-level undergraduate or graduate research, these units are often viewed as separate and apart from traditional public services, reference, or liaison positions. This is reinforced by the fact that while instruction departments might solicit volunteers to participate in instruction, they are less likely to involve outside staff in the development or assessment of a program. As a result, instructional units have a high level of control over their services, managing the entire process from design to implementation to assessment.

Although instruction units can be insular, they also offer high levels of support to those invited to serve in their ranks. Instruction librarians tend to have similar values and priorities. The departments are often student-centered and dedicated to creative projects. They are also likely to include a variety of professionals, including adjunct and graduate student positions. Working within a department offers a chance to collaborate with colleagues on collective projects on a scale rarely seen in public service areas. Instruction positions have high intensity and low downtime. They are unique positions that come with specialized challenges. However, this is perhaps most apparent within leadership for the unit.

Supervision and Management

Whether or not you are currently in a leadership position, spending time contemplating supervision can be useful. Managing an instruction program involves administration of staff and resources. While this may not be in an official supervisory capacity, issues of time, scale, authority, and prioritization are consistent from position to position and institution to institution. Put simply, program management is a lot of work. It involves coordination and long-term planning, but it also has a high degree of day-to-day oversight. It typically revolves around a fluid audience of first-year students, graduate student teachers, and adjunct faculty. It can be hard to get all of the stakeholders in a room to talk about programmatic goals and benchmarks, and even if you do, you could be dealing with an entirely different group of individuals the next academic year.

For some, there may be some time in between serving as the only person in an institution to becoming the head of a small department. This can involve partial supervision of a part-time staff member, graduate student, adjunct librarian, or the reallocation of a portion of one person's position to your department. This liminal period is essential to demonstrating your ability to provide effective leadership, particularly if the ad hoc staffing is a temporary solution in response to a request for full-time staff members. When you are transitioning from managing yourself to managing others, it can be helpful to write down tacit knowledge and procedures. While you may know exactly what the system is for communicating with adjunct faculty to schedule an instruction session, or why you decided not to include the brainstorming activity in the lesson plan, these "obvious" details will be less apparent to those not mired in the day-to-day oversight of the program. With a single part-time or graduate student worker, it can also be tempting to forgo some of the management staples, such as goal setting and reviews. Leaning into the labor of management will help not only bring clarity and consistency to your program but also speak to your ability to lead a larger team.

At some point in the life of every instruction program, it becomes too big for a single individual to handle. This results in recruiting additional staff to participate (in one way or another). In these moments, it can be easy to think that hiring a new librarian is the best and only way to really build a program. However, the additional labor that accompanies a new staff member can mitigate some of the benefits. Supervision is work. It limits the autonomy of your position and changes your relationship to the program and your colleagues. It involves a different level of planning and oversight and limits the flexibility of the instruction becoming more standardized, more systematized. It's an entirely different beast.

Recruiting Students and New Professionals

Instruction departments often appeal to new professionals and graduate students by requiring fewer years of experience and less requisite skills. They offer the ideal place to learn and grow, allowing new (or future) librarians to participate in many different levels of service: from instruction and reference to assessment and instructional design. For this reason, instructional positions can be viewed as something that you grow out of with time and experience. They are the places to cut your teeth in the profession before taking on the *real* work.

For those of us in these departments, we know that teaching first-year students is just as much work, and perhaps more, than upper-level undergraduate and graduate students. It is a different kind of work, but it is no less meaningful or important. It requires compassion and patience and a level of knowledge on par with any other position in the library. Rather than viewing it as a lesser calling, frame the hiring process as service to the profession: by hiring emerging professionals, we have a chance to change the trajectory of a person's career and instill values of student-centeredness and inclusivity.

If you are considering taking on an additional staff person, keep in mind not only the work of supervision but also the mentoring and support that goes along with new librarians and graduate students. At the onset, plan to put in as much as you get out. Particularly for graduate students, factor in career mentorship, from reviewing cover letters and CVs, to serving as a reference, conducting mock interviews, and sitting in the audience of practice presentations. For new librarians, you will need to provide support for professional development and career planning. Plan to provide input on service opportunities, grants, scholarships, and research projects. The best supervisors are advocates for their staff. Take on the burden of supervision as a way to not only reduce your workload but also to give back to the person you have the honor and responsibility of mentoring.

The best thing you can do for yourself, as a supervisor, is to hire individuals that you can trust. Look for candidates that have enthusiasm and an interest in learning over those with the perfect experience. Especially when it is an instruction program that you have spent time building, it can be hard to hand over the reins to someone else. If you are hiring staff, be prepared to give them ownership over a specific project. To do this, maintain a professional distance between you and your program. This is easier when you hire staff who are motivated by creating something that is unique and special. Encourage everyone, including yourself, to make mistakes. Be courageous and kind. Be the kind of supervisor you would like to have over you.

Case Study: "Rowing the Big Boat Together": Mixed Staffing Arrangements for Large Instruction Programs, a UNLV Case Study

Greg Carr, University of Nevada, Las Vegas

Brief Abstract: Large instruction programs have a variety of stakeholders. Librarians, faculty, and students all have different needs and desires. It can be difficult to coordinate in a sustainable and programmatic way. The University of Nevada, Las Vegas, encountered this situation. This is a description of the attempt to get everyone on the boat and rowing in the same direction.

INSTITUTIONAL BACKGROUND

The University of Nevada, Las Vegas, is a public research university located in southern Nevada. UNLV is a minority-serving institution and home to nearly 30,000 students. Undergraduate education is an important enterprise on campus. Additionally, UNLV has started an initiative to become a top-tier research university. This initiative has increased the focus on research for students and faculty alike.

First-year seminars (FYSs) at UNLV are a two-to-three-hour required course that is meant to help with the transition to university-level work. Seminars are organized by major, and the individual colleges administer the programs. Students learn general college-success skills (e.g., time management and study skills) as well as major specific content. The courses were developed according to the AAC&U high-impact practices and focus on experiences like critical thinking, information literacy, and collaborative learning. Classes vary in size across the different schools. Some are smaller (around 20 students) while a few are very large (90+ students).

DESCRIPTION OF PROGRAM, PROJECT, OR SPACE

Information literacy instruction is vertically integrated with general education. The general education program at UNLV is centered on University Undergraduate Learning Outcomes. One of the undergraduate learning outcomes that is vertically integrated through the program is critical thinking and inquiry, a natural fit for the instruction work of librarians. Ideally, students encounter library instruction several times as they advance through their major program. Instruction is intended to scaffold with each subsequent class.

Information literacy instruction is an evolving program at UNLV. Typically, it is handled by two separate departments, the Library Liaison Program (LLP) and Educational Initiatives (EI). The LLP consists of subject-specialist librarians who are responsible for collection development, upper-level instruction, and faculty/student research support. The two departments work collaboratively to meet library instruction needs.

UNLV recently experienced a concerted effort to reform general education across campus. The goal was to implement a pragmatic approach that would guide students through a series of integrated classes. First-year seminars and composition classes would be completed as undergraduates to set the foundation for milestone and culminating experience classes later on. This vertically integrated program has learning objectives, called University Undergraduate Learning Objectives (UULOs), that provide direction at both the programmatic and class levels.

One of the UULOs is "inquiry and critical thinking" and includes objectives like identifying problems and determining the need for information, which comfortably fit the responsibilities of the librarians at UNLV. This is the common language that faculty and librarians can use when it comes to curriculum. With increasing enrollment every semester, it has become important that instruction for undergraduates is approached in an organized and programmatic way to ensure that quality scales with size (for example, in 2015 Educational Initiatives taught 132 sections of English 102 composition, or 2,900 students). English 102 was an early programmatic success for the department, ensuring that learning objectives, lesson plans, and assessments were standard across all sections. We are hoping, as a department, to bring a similar standard to the FYS program, and staffing plays a very important part in achieving that goal.

TACKLING THE STAFFING LENS

Sustainability of quality instruction has been a key concern of this arrangement, especially with the campus initiative to achieve top-tier status. The LLP had handled a lot of the lower-division instruction, but the push to the top tier has increased emphasis on faculty and student research, which is the purview of the LLP. Additionally, large enrollments every year meant there was also a need to focus on undergraduate instruction. The major composition class, English 102, had already been put under the direction of one of the first undergraduate learning librarians (ULLs), with great success. Next it was time to handle the FYS classes.

To accomplish this, the ULLs were paired with liaison librarians to assist with curriculum development and instruction load. Since so much of the decision-making for the FYS program comes from the individual programs, there was a vast array of teaching styles, class requirements, relationships, and outcomes to navigate. The liaisons were very familiar with these programs and helped to guide the inclusion of the ULLs. They successfully worked in pairs for the first semester (fall 2015), and in some cases the ultimate responsibility for some FYS classes was passed to the ULLs. They delegated dealing with the program administrators, planning curriculum, booking classrooms, and teaching.

Though successful, the majority of liaisons elected to retain most of those responsibilities for the time being. As is common in any workplace, the issue of job duties and redesigning long-standing modalities can be difficult and time consuming. At times it was hard for the ULLs, who had all been in their positions for less than one year (except for one librarian who had two years), to integrate their ideas with those of the more tenured veteran librarians. Since the liaisons would be responsible for assisting the students later on in their academic careers, a lot of them felt that getting to the students as early as possible would make it easier for the students later on.

The integration of the ULLs, development of programmatic curriculum, and delegation of teaching responsibilities are ongoing. Some decisions have been made by choice and others by administrative fiat. The decision to transition to a model where the ULLs coordinate the instruction for FYS has been mostly left up to the desires of the liaisons. However, moving forward, it has been decided that as open liaison positions are filled, FYS instruction will not be included in their job descriptions or assigned duties. Ideally, this will allow the new faculty to spend more time on activities that support top-tier initiatives like graduate and faculty research support.

LESSONS LEARNED

Assessment has started for the universal learning outcome, the information life cycle, which was chosen at the end of 2014. The library recently produced a professionally animated video on the topic, and it is shown in almost every FYS session and has a follow-up activity that is examined by the librarian. So far the results have shown that students across the varied discipline of the FYS programs are still having some issues with applying the concept. However, just being able to assess the outcome across so many sections is a success, considering the piecemeal approach that was being used before. Being able to gather such data will ensure that we are able to make improvements across a wide range of programs.

One step at a time. Reformatting a program that has been in place for years and involves several librarians can be a delicate process. Reassigning and redefining job duties are not easy tasks. People identify deeply with the work they have been doing (sometimes for many years). It can be felt as a condemnation of performance when responsibilities are moved from one person to another. A combination of concerted on-boarding and dialogue makes everyone feel like their thoughts matter and that they have a hand in the new program.

There is no magic bullet. Rarely do single solutions for every situation present themselves. In an attempt to approach things programmatically, we attempted to have one universal learning outcome across all of FYS. In doing so, it was discovered that it fit some classes better than others. We had to rethink the learning objectives from many different angles for each class and choose the best fit from those (or let it go altogether in some cases). Flexibility and understanding are key.

It is good to give people choices when possible. The delegation of responsibilities could have been decided solely by administration. Rather, we chose to go a slower route but one that includes making decisions by consensus. The liaisons were given many different choices regarding teaching duties, curriculum, and relationship with the undergraduate students in their subject areas. Those choices helped make a plan for ULL integration that was the most agreeable to the LLP.

Case Study: "Where Is the Library?": Establishing Traditional Library Services with an Invisible (Virtual) Collection

Rebecca Rose, University of North Georgia

Brief Abstract: This case study describes a new library with digital-only holdings in a small academic setting. The sole librarian was challenged with offering library services in a space that does not appear to be a library. To meet this challenge, the librarian found ways to add library staff to assist her with providing and marketing library services to the campus. With the addition of a professional librarian one day a week, a graduate assistant, and a student library assistant, the library offered workshops and events to raise both faculty and student awareness of the availability of library services.

INSTITUTIONAL BACKGROUND

The Cumming campus of the University of North Georgia (UNG) first opened in fall of 2012. Since that time, enrollment has doubled to serve over 800 students. Course offerings ranged from core curriculum classes up to graduate programs. The campus library serves a broad student body that includes 144 dual enrolled high school students and 64 graduate students. Traditional students comprise the majority with the population of nontraditional students at 19 percent. The staff ratio is one per 75 students, which demands cross-departmental cooperation by all employees. The library's professional staff initially consisted of one full-time librarian promoting and implementing all library instruction efforts for the entire campus.

DESCRIPTION OF PROGRAM, PROJECT, OR SPACE

Since the school first opened, the campus librarian faced inherent challenges, some of which persist to this day. For example, the transitional nature of the school limits the librarian's ability to establish lasting faculty partnerships, with only six full-time faculty stationed at the Cumming campus. The majority of courses have been taught by faculty based elsewhere, and often they teach at the Cumming campus for a single semester. This transient atmosphere extends to the students. Student demand far exceeds the availability of classes, with only 40 percent of full-time students able to schedule all of their classes at the Cumming campus. This requires most students to drive to nearby campuses in order to carry a full load of credit hours. Additionally, the digital nature of the library's collection generated misperceptions about the availability of library services offered at this campus. People erroneously perceived the lack of visible books to mean an absence of traditional library services, such as reference, library instruction, and other classroom support. The labeling of the library as a Learning Commons and the absence of a circulation or reference counter reinforced misperceptions about available library services.

TACKLING THE STAFFING LENS

The librarian determined that increasing personnel in the library would allow her more time and resources to raise awareness of library services to faculty and students as well as enable her to host more workshops and instruction sessions. In addition, staffing the library while the librarian was away would contribute to the appearance of the space as a functional library. As a result, reviewing options for increasing both professional and paraprofessional library staff at the Cumming campus was a top priority.

When an opening for a part-time librarian position at another UNG campus became available, it was suggested it be extended into a .75 position to facilitate sharing the position between the two campuses. This suggestion appealed to the dean for several reasons. First, the location of the part-time position was further removed from the closest large population center, limiting the professional librarian applicant pool. Converting to a .75 position added benefits to the job, thereby greatly enhancing its appeal to potential applicants. Second, a .75 position was more budget friendly than a full-time position. University-wide staff shortages generated stiff competition for limited hiring dollars. Third, the two campuses were located within an easy half-hour drive from each other, increasing the viability of someone easily driving to either campus. The dean of libraries received frequent updates and monthly reporting from the Cumming librarian that kept her aware of the growing need on the campus. She approved and secured the additional funding in the library budget for this arrangement, which gave the Cumming campus a librarian one day a week. This part-time librarian assists with teaching workshops and providing reference assistance.

Also, the Graduate Studies department funds one part-time graduate assistantship for the UNG libraries, which the librarian sought for additional library personnel on the Cumming campus. Justifying the placement of the position at the Cumming campus required a written job description and the approval of the dean of libraries. The librarian designed interview questions to demonstrate the applicants' abilities to brainstorm, create signage, and assist with library instructional programs and promotional events, such as Weeks of Welcome and Banned Books Week events. Desirable candidates' work histories demonstrated maturity, ability to work independently, and dependability. A Federal Work Study student worker and a student library assistant rounded out the library staff. Fortunately, the student library assistants possessed excellent work habits and greatly contributed to the brainstorming and promotion efforts.

Managing the student workers required transparency of performance expectations coupled with a high level of communication. The student workers must communicate with the librarian anytime they encounter anything unfamiliar. Emails or texts to the librarian with questions that arise during their shift were strongly encouraged. The librarian's responsibility includes keeping the staff well informed of any issues that might affect library services. Student training was supplemented with a handbook detailing library procedures and policies and includes talking points for when tours walk through the library.

The addition of personnel facilitated hosting several library-related events with fliers and promotional materials created by library staff. For example, for the Weeks of Welcome event, library staff trained so they could assist students in crafting their own paracord bracelets. Library staff decorated the drawing entry box, stuffed goodie bags with library fliers and treats, created signage, and dispensed trail mix and other desirable items. Hosting events such as this one introduced students to the library and generated unique opportunities for them to interact with library staff.

Some of the other promotional materials that student library assistants created included a web page filled with comments gathered from a library open house, clever Bingo cards depicting banned books, and a slideshow describing library services used for campus open houses. The library workshops and related instruction programs demonstrated positive attendance numbers. The most highly attended events benefitted from faculty support, such as the citation workshops and the poetry reading event where students received extra credit for their participation. Other successful events occurred with giveaways of food, scantrons, and water bottles, which attracted interested students.

However, a few programs went unattended. Recent student and faculty focus groups also revealed a continued lack of awareness of the services offered by the library. Students stated they preferred a library that offers physical rather than virtual books. Some students were unaware that a library existed in the building. Likewise, faculty focus groups uncovered misunderstandings about the variety of library services offered. Additionally, a 2015 LibQual+ survey of faculty, undergraduate, and graduate students showed that 10 percent rarely or never use the Cumming library resources on the library premises, and 15 percent never access the library resources through the library web page.

LESSONS LEARNED

Attracting a quality library workforce who assists with the implementation of user-centered programs contributes to student success. However, the practice of hiring student workers (even students of excellent caliber) can be problematic in that they work minimal hours, their academics take priority, their position terminates at the close of the school year, and students often transfer to other campuses or institutions, graduate, or even lay out a semester. Another issue to consider when employing student workers is that their work schedules require flexibility so as to fit around their classes. Their class schedules shift each semester, sometimes dramatically. Also, the combination of low tuition rates and the location of our campus in an affluent area generates a lack of students who qualify for Federal Work Study, thus reducing the workforce pool. For example, in the fall 2015 semester only one student on the Cumming campus qualified for Federal Work Study. Typically, our Federal Work Study students attend other UNG campuses for classes, which also factors in their availability to work. Lastly, all hiring in recent years has been affected by changing federal regulations that continue to impact the workforce landscape in the library as well as the entire university. Specifically, recent changes that impact our workers have been the number of hours part-timers can work and the minimum pay scale for the graduate assistantship position.

The student's availability determined the part-time librarian's schedule. Changing the day the librarian was assigned to work at our campus helped to ensure consistent staff coverage throughout peak hours. However, changing the part-time librarian's schedule at the Cumming campus requires consultation with the head librarian at the Dahlonega campus, since the part-time position is shared across those two campuses. All of the librarians' schedules at the other campus must be considered, and schedule planning takes place weeks prior to the forthcoming semester.

As our campus continues to experience double-digit enrollment growth, planning for the addition of staffing hours makes sense. Options include adding a permanent position or increasing the hours that the part-time librarian works at the Cumming campus. Current library program offerings have risen to meet the demand, but the rate of increased requests for services suggests that additional staff will soon be necessary to maintain consistent levels of delivery. Employing additional permanent staff would be transformative for the Cumming campus library, in addition to maintaining our ability to provide quality library programming. For example, rather than training new staff at the beginning of each school year, permanent staff would continue their training beyond the basic skill set and facilitate the development of professional expertise and responsibilities. Increased staff retention means that library employees are better positioned to establish long-term rapport with students, staff, and faculty and acculturates them within the library's strategic mission within the university setting. Lastly, the addition of permanent staff will expand opportunities for additional partnerships and programming ideas with the final result enhancing the library overall within the institution.

Possible considerations for forthcoming full-time paraprofessional staff could include hiring a student accepted in the field of library and information science or a similar field. Hiring a budding librarian could develop into a mentor/mentee relationship that benefits both the library and its constituents. The library graduate student could be given opportunities to stretch his or her wings in library outreach and programming, with guidance provided by an experienced librarian who is willing to share years of expertise.

Consideration for the addition of a faculty position at the Cumming Library must take into account the number of library instructions and programs requested at the campus. As the demands for these types of services continue to grow, eventually another librarian presence will become critical.

Additionally, any future staffing options for the Cumming Library must factor in inherent space constraints. The current layout is problematic for staffing more than one person in the workroom at a time, since only one desk fits in the tight space. One option is to outfit a circulation desk in library space currently occupied by tutors. The growth in demand for tutoring services slated them to move into another area outside of the library before the end of the budget year. The tutoring area provides sufficient space for the installation of a circulation desk. The highly visible location from both inside and outside of the library is ideal for a library service desk. Another benefit is that the addition of another staff workstation facilitates scheduling overlapping shifts and will resolve the current space issue of only accommodating one student worker and one librarian working simultaneously.

In multicampus situations, often smaller campuses can get lost in the shuffle, especially in an atmosphere of intense competition for hiring dollars driven by continued growth at all of the University of North Georgia campuses. Fortunately, the dean of libraries is keenly aware that our campus needs additional staffing hours and is working toward this goal for the Cumming campus library for the upcoming budget year.

One final consideration is that smaller campuses typically receive allocations of new financial and staff resources only after the demonstration of need reaches critical levels. Unfortunately, this organizational model can encourage the adoption of a reactive rather than proactive management style. Even after a need is sufficiently demonstrated, often additional resources still lag in their delivery due to locked-in annual budget cycles.

In retrospect, communication and marketing efforts require creativity, time, and effort, and having additional library staff helps greatly. The more successful library instruction programs involved close coordination and involvement of the faculty. Cumming campus's lack of a permanent faculty base and the high number of students who split their sched-ules between campuses demand that the library continues its promotional efforts in order to build better awareness of its strong user-centered instruction program.

Table 5.1.
Handouts and Links

Title of Document/Material	Description
UNG Library	Promotional slide show created by a graduate assistant: https://drive.google.com/file/d /0B4OMsv1dt5OxT1psSUNIdXVQcm8/view ?usp=sharing
Tell Us What You Think Web Page	Created by a graduate assistant: https://trello.com/b/1Q6G14pw
Banned Book Bingo	Banned Book Week entry cards for raffle drawing created by a student library assistant: https://drive.google.com /file/d/0B4OMsv1dt5Oxek5GMm1PUnFzZHM /view?usp=sharing
Banned Book Week 2014 Slide	Slide advertising open mic session for Banned Book Week created by library assistant: https://docs.google.com /presentation/d/1bOsbuZCnBTLt7BIfxKVnLu Y2b_2Xvq8JmBp5ZdTHJYM/edit?usp=sharing

CASE STUDY REFLECTION QUESTION

How are instruction responsibilities divided among staff at your library? Based on the experiences you have read about in the case study, what is one creative way that you could either realign responsibilities to allow more room for innovation or develop a new facet of your program by bringing in additional staff?

REFERENCES

Belker, Loren, Jim McCormick, and Gary Topchick. *The First-Time Manager.* New York: Management Association, 2012.
Runion, Meryl. *Perfect Phrases for Managers and Supervisors.* New York: McGraw Hill, 2010.
Stewart, Andrea Wigbels, Carlette Washington-Hoagland, and Carol T. Szulya. *Staff Development: A Practical Guide.* Chicago: ALA Editions, 2013.

Chapter 6

SPACES

CHAPTER OBJECTIVES

- Evaluate the ways in which physical spaces impact curricular design and programmatic management.
- Develop strategies for mitigating the administrative burden of classroom management, including reservations, renovations, and general maintenance.

INTRODUCTION

Though classrooms receive the least attention during the instructional design process, they can wield enormous influence over an instruction program. An inflexible space could encourage a "sage on the stage" teaching approach, while a newly renovated classroom can breathe life into an outdated instruction program, encouraging users to explore new approaches to teaching. However, just as often, the process of working around a rigid teaching space can inspire users to explore new ideas, while the possibilities of an innovative classroom are wasted on the continuation of the same old routine. Physical classroom spaces can motivate teachers to improve their practice or they can undermine innovation and suppress ideas. They are both a gift and a burden, but they are almost always left to instruction librarians to manage, including everything from updating software, to organizing instruction schedules, to remodeling teaching labs. These tasks demand significant time and resources. If not managed carefully, they can drain your energy and take away valuable time for creativity. This chapter will discuss strategies to mitigate the emotional and intellectual burdens that come with serving as the "keeper of the room" and explore the role of the physical space in the development (or reinvigoration) of an instructional program. Although space issues impact first-year programming, they extend across the curriculum and impact all levels of teaching in the library. While Part I focused on pedagogy and outreach, this chapter focuses on management issues.

MANAGING TEACHING SPACES

When faced with the real-life challenges of classroom management, keep in mind that a teaching space is neither the beginning nor the end of an instruction program. Nor is it the arbiter of your pedagogy. It is possible to do great things in a windowless box with rows of forward-facing computer monitors, and it is equally possible to deliver a positivist and disengaged instruction session in a state-of-the-art instructional space. While physical spaces are important, if you let them, they can develop a power of their own—dictating the direction of the program, limiting creativity, and forcing you to adhere to a code of behavior that really only exists in your mind.

Imperfect Classroom Spaces

It is tempting to see creative programming as dependent on access to an innovative classroom. It can be hard to think outside of the box when your box consists of an instruction lab with forward-facing desktop computers, an overhead projector, and a single whiteboard. For some libraries, having any dedicated classroom space at all might be a luxury. In these situations, you might have limited (if any) control over the space in which your teaching takes place. If you find yourself bound to a classroom that is not ideal, whether that be living the life of a nomad, moving from computer lab to computer lab, or being a prisoner in your own outdated teaching space, it can be difficult to expand your instruction program beyond the visible limitations of the classroom.

Frustrations with spaces typically revolve around one of two issues: (1) outdated or insufficient technology and/or (2) inflexible furniture arrangements. If you happen to suffer from both of these, it can be easy to get trapped in a defeatist mentality. When this happens, remember that a classroom is just one of many tools available to you as a programmatic designer and instructor. Consider these questions: How can you modify a dysfunctional teaching space to reflect the values of your library? Where is the low-hanging fruit (or the small changes that will make the biggest impact)? What can you bring into the space to encourage creativity? What can you take away that is tying you (physically, emotionally, intellectually) to the past?

Outdated Technology

Let's call it what it is: the rows of forward-facing desktop computers. You want to connect to your students, but you find yourself staring at the backside of 25 monitors. The organization of the computers in the room limits the possibilities for group work. The computers might be slow or out of date. The overhead projector is attached to a stationary instructor computer that sits at the front or (even worse!) back of the room. You are isolated from your students, and students are separated from each other, making the learning process feel segmented and artificial.

These "traditional" spaces recall the transition within the profession from bibliographic instruction to information literacy. Though easy to forget, library instruction "labs" reflect an early dedication within the profession to user-centered learning and were built to encourage students to take an active role in the learning process. Although labs can be frustrating for today's teachers, it can be helpful to remember that these spaces are rooted in a genuine desire to promote student learning and reflect the socially minded values of our profession.

Despite the good intentions, if you let them, computer labs can become an instructional crutch, reinforcing the distance between teachers and learners and promoting an over-reliance on demonstrating instead of guidance. Rather than hiding behind the limitations of technology, create a curriculum that works with the space. Use the "front of the room" as an opportunity to encourage students to participate in the presentation process. Better yet, embrace the idea that there need not be a front of any room and let go of the projector all together, asking students to share a computer to promote peer-to-peer learning. If you are feeling bold, consider how dependent your teaching is on access to a computer. Are you really teaching, or are you spending your session demonstrating resources? Use this opportunity to distance yourself from the instructor computer station by creating flipped classroom materials and focusing in-person class time on community building by incorporating more conceptual or ethical discussions.

The inspiring thing about library instruction is that there is no standard practice. Your instruction program does not have to look like anything you have seen before. A computer lab can be isolating and limiting, but if you let it, the process of working around those challenges can be liberating. Rather than feeling defeated by the behemoth desktop computers, use this opportunity to build a community of practice with your colleagues and push the envelope of your teaching program.

Inflexible Layouts

The second frustration with a space often revolves around inflexible furniture. This comes in many forms: instruction labs with computers spread across the perimeter of the space, facing the wall, forcing the instructor to stand in the center of the space and speak to the backs of 25 learners; rows of forward-facing desks, in some cases literally affixed to the floor; irregular spaces with views obscured by poles and pillars; spaces with limited electrical outlets, grouping computers around the few available power sources, or crisscrossing the floor with conduits and cords covered in duct tape. These issues are challenging for teachers but even more so for those of us managing these spaces or developing instructional programming.

If you have access to funding, there are small improvements that can make a significant impact in the classroom space. Invest in inexpensive materials such as large sticky pads and small dry-erase boards to encourage group work, or explore IDEA paint, which turns a wall into a whiteboard writing space. If you have a more significant allowance and can afford to make a capital investment, spend money on low-profile moveable chairs to promote "huddling" around a computer rather than isolation in an individual work space. Another high-impact purchase is a wireless projection system, which can release instructors from the "instruction station" prison and open up the space in unexpected ways.

If the budget is strapped, cost-free changes can alter the dynamic of a space. Rearranging tables, with computers facing each other, can turn rows of workstations into smaller group stations. Reducing the number of desktop computers can free up open work space. Encouraging students to bring laptops or encouraging group work on a shared workstation can offset the lack of computers. Typically, the most significant holdup to these types of changes is failing to ask for what you want. If you approach your colleagues and administrators with a solution, they will be more likely to support your vision for the space. Do not be fooled into thinking the only way to change a space is to invest in a significant renovation. Keep moving toward the kind of classroom space you want by implementing small and steady changes.

Alternative Spaces

When you are feeling defeated by your classroom space, it can be helpful to remember that a classroom is just a concept. Any space that allows teaching to take place can be a classroom; it does not have to have walls or computers or identical chairs. It doesn't even need to be located in the library. Whether it is inadequate teaching space to meet the instructional demands, or a classroom space that has seen better days, sometimes exploring a new space can help you to think about teaching in a new way. For an example of repurposing a space, see the case study at the end of this chapter.

Renovations

While working with inflexible teaching spaces is frustrating, managing a renovation or remodel can be equally laborious. As with many nebulous and time-dependent tasks, instruction librarians often have the privilege of managing these classroom design projects. Whether you are in the midst of a renovation, or see the potential for one in the future, it is helpful to think through the design process as a linear progression. Although each renovation will be specific to the institution, there are four general stages to keep in mind: funding, design, implementation, and management of the new space IRL (in real life).

Funding

If you are interested in securing funding for a classroom renovation, the first battle is internal support. When resources are scarce, garnering support for projects can take on a sense of competition rather than collaboration. To gain support from colleagues, start by building a narrative that goes beyond you or your instruction program. Hold a workshop or brown-bag lunch for colleagues and share images of classroom renovations, showing examples of the kinds of technology and furnishings you could incorporate in a classroom renovation. Take suggestions from library instructors about the kinds of designs, technology, and tools they would like to see incorporated into a classroom. The best projects start as an idea that spreads into a movement. For a renovation proposal to be successful, it should be supported by the library as a whole.

To fuel inspiration, repeat, over and over again, that a classroom is a space that benefits not only the library staff but the campus as a whole. To better share these stories, gather testimonials from library instructors about specific projects, courses, or workshops that an updated classroom space would enable them to create. Collect statements from students about the kind of classroom spaces that promote learning. Foster an entrepreneurial spirit and be creative in your advocacy. If it is something that will genuinely impact the way your instruction program will be able to move forward, it is worth the work.

Next, start accumulating data to help make your case. To demonstrate a need for the space upgrade (rather than just a desire), compile the cold hard numbers. How many faculty and students do you currently impact through instruction? Will renovating the space increase these numbers or improve the quality of instruction for current users? How will you demonstrate this impact? How will you speak to the value of your teaching program, and how will investing in the space help to improve or secure that legacy? While numbers only tell part of a story, these quantitative details can be useful, especially if you are asking library administrators to lobby campus on your behalf. Build a case that makes sense to those outside of the library profession by including the details that resonate in your campus culture.

Submit a budget request that is backed by multiple departments, or if your library does not have departments, for a specific committee, working group, or ragtag group of library innovators. Whatever you do, make sure that the proposal does not come from you alone; it should be a group effort. Although librarians have a tendency to be conservative in their requests for budgetary resources, in the initial funding proposal, ask for a little more than you think you will need. While allocations for a project are often scaled back, it is unlikely that the project will be supplemented by additional funding as you move forward. Be realistic in your estimate, assuming that certain aspects of the project will cost more than you expect.

If funding is the only thing stopping you, remember that changes can happen in small increments. Another option is to check with vendors to test out new equipment, or seek grant opportunities, which are available through both commercial and public institutions.

Design

Although funding and design are separate processes, they are interrelated. To understand how much funding to request, you have to have an idea of what will be in the space and how much those items will cost. To know what you can afford to purchase, you have to know what resources can be allocated toward the project.

When crafting an accurate funding proposal, the first consideration should be whether your institution has contractual obligations for technology, furnishings, labor, or consultation. If you are restricted to a list of approved vendors, do not include a request for furniture that you will be unable to purchase. You should also find out if you are able to make technology purchases directly or if they should be routed through the IT department. Knowing what is available for purchase and how much autonomy you will have in the process will strengthen your case. If you can demonstrate that you understand the renovation process and can be trusted to manage the project, the proposal is more likely to be taken seriously by decision-makers.

A classroom renovation typically comes in one of three packages: (1) an aspect of a full library (or floor) renovation or construction, (2) an individual project directed at a single space or a small group of spaces, or (3) end-of-year funds that are directed at a classroom in the hopes of a quick turnover. Obviously, the dream is option one: designing a classroom as part of an entire library renovation or new construction. If this is the case, you are more likely to have the support of professional architects and designers who can help you make smart decisions. You are also in the rare position of being able to design a classroom space the way your library wants it to be, from the ground up. This is not to say that it is not work, and that the process will not be long and frustrating, but you will be well supported.

In the more likely event that you are undertaking a small-scale renovation project, now is the time to lean on your colleagues. Renovations of every size and scale are notoriously long and unpredictable. Do not burn yourself out in the early stages of the process by taking on more than you can handle. At larger institutions in particular, seek out colleagues who have participated in renovation projects in the past. If you are at a smaller institution, seek colleagues outside of the library to compare renovation projects on campus. Ask them what they would have done differently if they had a chance to do it again, and find out who they contacted in and out of the university for specific aspects of the process. This is also the moment to pull in stakeholders of the project. Facilitate buy-in and support by encouraging your partners in the renovation to contribute ideas and seek out information.

An additional component of the design should be an accounting of the full range of activities that take place in the space. For many libraries, a classroom doubles as a study space for students. It provides access to computers, printers, and valuable table space. While it can be tempting to view this as a secondary function of the space, keep in mind that a classroom should be owned by the learners it exists to serve. Preserving the ability of the space to support multiple types of learning is an important part of the design process and should be taken seriously. In some cases, this might alter or limit technology decisions. Moving from desktops to laptops, for example, can limit student access to workstations. Or it might be that students would benefit from additional electrical outlets, which need to be included in the budget proposal. One way to ensure that the interests of students are represented in the design process is to include students on the committee. To create an inclusive space, you have to have a diverse body of decision-makers. Including stakeholders early in the process will help guarantee that the classroom is transformed into a space that continues to serve users equally.

Technology

When considering the technology for a space, it is easy to be seduced by equipment, particularly in regards to instructor tools. While at the time, purchasing the SMART Board or the $15,000 annually billed software package to promote group work can seem like a great decision, think carefully about the needs of your library. Remember the guiding principle of the renovation process and be realistic in your purchases. If you are working with a team of librarians who have proven resistant to change, it is unlikely that they will suddenly hop on board with your great new plan to get rid of computers and switch to iPad-based instruction. Select technology that pushes boundaries but is not so unfamiliar that it incites defensive behavior from instructors. While you should always look forward to the instruction program you want to have, strike a balance between your current reality and the development of the program by selecting software and hardware that is flexible, intuitive, and necessary.

The largest technology purchase of a renovation is often the computer workstations. Equipment can be expensive, especially if being used by students, who are notoriously hard on computers (read: everything). Assume that the cost of equipment will include the purchase of warranties for the workstations, which can add several hundred dollars per unit to the purchase price. Second, carefully consider the type of computers to purchase. For basic library instruction, it is unlikely that learners will need access to the full capabilities of a MacBook Pro. While some instruction sessions might require Adobe Illustrator or specific GIS equipment, maybe five or 10 workstations with the necessary software could meet the needs, rather than purchasing a full classroom set of 35. This is also an opportunity to take the pulse of the campus. If your campus requires the purchase of a laptop by students, leverage that in your technology purchase by viewing your equipment as supplemental rather than essential. And always purchase the extra set of chargers.

Furniture

Furniture such as tables, chairs, and podiums can completely alter the feeling of an instruction space. When selecting furnishings, think about the message that it will send to users of the space. Will it promote playfulness? Flexibility? Conformity? Although it is important to select items that will hold up to the wear and tear of undergraduate students, it is equally important to create an environment that encourages radical learning. If you want the instruction program to be collaborative, make sure to purchase furniture that can accommodate co-teaching and group work. Leave space for movement and growth, and select items that can transition to the various needs of the space. If the classroom doubles as a study space, students might benefit from desks that can be sectioned off into individual workstations or joined together to promote group work. Think in advance about the placement of cords, location of outlets, and existence of structural barriers. This is also an opportunity to rethink the front of the room. Maybe the "natural" teaching space (opposite the door) is not the best location. Be bold in your choices and consider all the options, even the ones that are less obvious, before committing to specific pieces.

Above all, these decisions should not be made in isolation. In all likelihood, your library will have to live with this furniture for a very long time. If you do not have a committee or other supportive body sharing in the labor of the renovation, solicit buy-in in any way possible. Crash meetings, send out email polls, corner folks in elevators. Be aggressive in your desire to collaborate and make sure the responsibility of those choices does not begin and end with you.

Implementation

Once you arrive at the implementation phase, it is tempting to assume that the hard part is over and to start to lose your laser focus on the project. Do not allow this feeling to get the best of you. Speaking from experience, hiccups such as budget cuts, furniture lost in transit, incorrect technology purchased, and the inevitable discovery of asbestos have a tendency to emerge at the least opportune of moments. Assume it will take longer than you think to get everything in place and that it will all cost 15 percent more than you thought it would. You should also expect for things to look different in the space than they did in your mind. The coming together of a months- or years-long renovation project with the reality of the physical space can be both cathartic and unsettling. Once everything is in place, the rest of the work becomes more apparent: the colleagues that will need to be won over, lesson plans adjusted, moveable furniture that will somehow need to be defended against the late-night student.

The transitory period, after the last laptop is plugged in and carpet square adhered, but before the next instruction period begins, is an important time. Use these moments to be proud of yourself and show appreciation for the colleagues and administrators who supported the project. Spend time in the classroom admiring the pristine furniture. Encourage library staff to visit the space. If you can, try to schedule a few important meetings in the room to show off the new space. Be unashamedly self-promotional. Be joyful.

New Classroom in Real Life

Unfortunately, renovations do not end after the furniture is installed. Looking back, we wish we had been warned about this. While it is tempting to view a renovation project as temporary, keep in mind that the labor extends weeks, or sometimes months, after the last upgrades to the space have been made.

The most likely challenge you will encounter is colleagues who are not appreciative of the new instruction space. Hopefully you headed this off by creating a diverse and far-reaching renovation committee. But even so, this does not guarantee that you can win over every person. Instructional spaces are often representative of the teachers that use the space, and changes can be viewed as a rebuke on the instructors whose styles are reflective of a more traditional teaching approach. Here are a few things to keep in mind. First, librarians are a profession of deeply caring people, and at least one of them will find something to care loudly about regardless of what changes you make. Do not take it personally. Second, after the renovation, there is really very little that anyone can do to revert back to the previous layout. The new reality is that there is a new reality, and eventually everyone will get on board. Do not devote headspace to folks that just want to complain. This does not mean that you should not take seriously suggestions for improvement or take action on aspects of the redesign that are genuinely disruptive, but be selective. It is possible to demonstrate empathic listening without feeling the need to respond to every complaint about the new space. Be patient with your colleagues and kind to yourself. This phase is tough, but it will pass.

The other issues that might come to light are logistical. As the campus community discovers the space, there might be an increase in the number of requests to use the space for events or classes. The introduction of new technology or furniture might also change the use policies regarding the space. Although previously the rooms might have been open for study during nights and weekends, it could be that the new classroom requires more oversight, resulting in fewer open-study hours. The introduction of new technology often involves a learning curve for library instructors. When the new projection software fails to launch, laptop cart refuses to charge, or one of the iPads goes missing, who will respond to those issues? Will there be someone available to provide support for evening class sessions or student groups? Who will report technology issues to IT?

The best advice for a renovation is to assume that if it can happen, it will. Thinking about the issues in advance will help you to institute space management policies that are both responsive and considerate of your own time. If nothing else, remember that you are more than the classroom in which you teach, and your instruction program is bigger than the four walls in which it is delivered. Even when it takes up all of your time and energy, you are more than any room, renovated or otherwise.

INVISIBLE LABOR

While it is great to tell yourself that your value does not lie in the ability to manage a classroom, it is difficult to keep this perspective in the midst of a September meltdown over a double-booked room, or a projector that refuses to cooperate, or the Internet connection that has, yet again, crashed in the middle of an instruction session. Unfortunately, the burdens of policing a socially political space, such as a classroom, come in many forms: the emotional weight of managing an outward expression of many different teaching philosophies, the intellectual labor of balancing instruction schedules and room reservations, and the exhaustion that accompanies a long-reaching and often tedious task. When in the dark trenches of space management, it is helpful to enforce a healthy distance between your professional identity and the classroom(s) that you happen to manage as part of your positional responsibilities.

To begin this dissociation, remove the phrase "my classroom" from your vocabulary. It is not *your* classroom, because you are not *its* teacher. A classroom is owned by the collective. While you might manage the space, your job is not to keep people out or shut down ideas; it is to facilitate a space that promotes learning and growth. In some cases, that means that the best thing for the library is for you to not be in control of the space. If you look at your professional life and realize that classroom management is absorbing an inordinate amount of time, make a suggestion to administration that space management become a rotating responsibility. Believe us when we say that the small bit of peace you get from being the only person that is able to place software requests is not worth the burden of "owning" a cooperative space. Whether you are a veteran or new to the field, we encourage all managers of classroom spaces to facilitate balance in their professional life by maintaining firm boundaries.

Real Talk: All about Those Policies

The beginning to healthy boundaries is the establishment of clear, concise, and readily available policies. When you are in the process of developing an instruction program, which is by nature amorphous and evolutionary, non-instructional activities are easily absorbed under the programmatic umbrella. This comes in two ways: (1) the slow creep from overseeing aspects of an instruction schedule to managing the instructional activities for an entire department or library, and (2) the absorption of increased responsibilities under the guise of managing the physical space.

Head this off early by establishing internal and external policies to guide the use of the space. If there are no policies currently in place, create these as part of a team that includes both administrators and practitioners. Pro tip: Use this meeting as an opportunity to release yourself from as much managerial minutia as possible and bring to light the enormous invisible labor that can be associated with the management of a heavily used space. Following are some questions to consider.

Instruction Scheduling

- Who participates in first-year or general education instruction (e.g., freshman composition, first-year experience courses, living-learning, or honors programs)?
  - Is this written into job descriptions or work plans?
  - Are the sessions divided evenly among instructors? Does each instructor get a percentage? Are those percentages weighted?
  - Who is responsible for initiating requests (e.g., sending an email out to the departmental listserv)?
  - Who is responsible for scheduling the sessions? Rescheduling for weather delays?
- Who decides when a request for instruction cannot be accommodated due to scheduling issues, lack of available space, or other circumstances?
- Who prints and places materials (handouts) for specific sessions in the classroom? Who checks to make sure there are enough copies throughout the semester?
- Who creates a priority list for instruction? If a session falls during a faculty meeting, who will cover the session?

Room Reservations

- Who can reserve the space—anyone in the library? Who decides?
- Who will manage the reservation request process? Will this be listed on forward-facing communications from the library (e.g., the website)?

- Who will accept reservations (in a shared calendar, scheduling system, etc.?)
- Who will decide if and what specific pieces of information should be included with all reservations?
- Who will decide if the classroom is open for reservation by non-library staff, students, or community members?
- Who makes the decision about which or if certain reservations take precedence over others (e.g., teaching over meetings, or student groups over community)? Who is responsible for enforcement?
- Who will create a request form, or is one needed?
- Who is responsible for deciding how far in advance reservations should be requested? Will there be a limit on how long or how often users can request the space?
- Who will decide if non-library requesters will be able to use the technology in the space? If so, will non-campus affiliates need special logins for the computers or resources? And who is responsible for generating/requesting those logins?
- Who will honor evening and weekend requests? If the room is kept locked, who will be available to grant access?
- Who is responsible for software and hardware upgrades? If it is a specific department, who will reach out to the department and how often?
- Who will deal with the little things (e.g., ordering dry-erase markers, reporting broken fixtures and furnishings, reorganizing furniture)?

Thinking through these questions ahead of time will help you develop (and adhere to) policies that alleviate the burden of classroom management. At the least, it will bring to light the associated labor that is often forgotten when someone assumes the task of organizing a space. Use these opportunities to advocate for yourself with colleagues and administrators, and assert the need for recognition and reconciliation.

SUMMARY

Managing a classroom space is hard and messy. It takes time away from important tasks and is often mired in social and institutional politics. If you are in this situation, the best thing that you can do for yourself is to be open and honest about the challenges and associated workload. Creating policies can help, but only insofar as people follow them. Hold your colleagues, and yourself, accountable. Do not do the work for other people, even when it seems like it's easier to "just do it" than go back to people and ask them to follow the appropriate procedures.

Finally, remember to keep looking forward. The way you have always done things does not have to be the way that you do them forever. Policies can be changed, responsibilities shifted. Scheduling a room calendar does not have to be a librarian-level task. A well-trained student or graduate assistant can manage if you are willing to let go.

Case Study: No Walls? (Almost) No Problem: An Open Classroom Experiment

Lauren Goode, College of William and Mary
Paul Showalter, College of William and Mary

Brief Abstract: In response to building renovations that closed off two-thirds of teaching and event spaces during the fall of 2014, the Earl Gregg Swem Library created the open classroom as an experimental space to use for teaching, workshops, and community engagement. The open classroom was located in a highly visible and heavily trafficked area of the library. Many events and classes were held in the space. However, the overall consensus from both participants and presenters was that the space was too "open." The feedback was considered, and the open classroom model was moved to a new location in the library, where it remains well received.

INSTITUTIONAL BACKGROUND

The College of William and Mary is a residential public liberal arts university located in Williamsburg, Virginia. The college enrolls approximately 6,300 undergraduates and 2,100 graduate students and employees 609 full-time faculty engaged in teaching and research. The Earl Gregg Swem Library is William and Mary's primary academic library and is staffed by 25 professional and 29 operational staff. The library's 265,375-square-foot building holds 2 million volumes spread throughout four floors. The library has 1,500 seats, 28 group study rooms, three classrooms (one mediated with 20 PC workstations, two with flexible furniture and access to Apple MacBook and iPad carts), social/active spaces, quiet spaces, and a variety of furniture. Professional school and departmental libraries notwithstanding, Swem supports the bulk of the research needs of undergraduate and graduate students, faculty, and staff. The library is open to the public and serves local and regional communities.

DESCRIPTION OF PROGRAM

In the fall of 2014, major renovations to the library's media center closed off one of our classrooms. A heavy library instruction load (upward of 200 a semester), coupled with requests from campus partners to use library spaces for various events, created a need for development of alternative spaces. To avoid a reduction in the campus usage of library spaces and without the ability to undertake an additional construction project, Swem Library had to get creative. We were inspired by the successful implementation of alternative learning spaces at Grand Valley State University and Eastern Kentucky University and developed the concept for our open classroom. The intent of the open classroom was to create a space to use for highly visible drop-in workshops and to cultivate relationships with campus partners. It was also available as an alternative to a traditional classroom for library instruction.

Swem Library's main floor has a large 4,000-square-foot open area called Read & Relax, mostly used by students as a study, meeting, and social space all hours that the library is open. Because of its high visibility, Read & Relax was selected as the area to place our open classroom. To create the open classroom, some of the existing tables and chairs were moved to other areas of the library to clear a space for the open classroom furniture. The furniture used in the open classroom was repurposed from other areas of the library. One of the library's mobile 80-inch HD displays with laptop connectivity was devoted to the space. Brightly colored, cushioned, wheeled chairs with attached, collapsible desktops were pulled from study spaces. Whiteboards and a lectern were also moved into the space. The open classroom was made available for instruction and events beginning with the fall 2014 semester.

TACKLING THE SPACE

First, the open classroom itself is a space. It was designed to alleviate the perceived need for additional space and as an experiment in teaching and learning in nontraditional spaces. The open classroom was not delineated from its immediate surrounding area by walls or doors. The furniture in the space, which rendered the boundary somewhat fluid, essentially defined the boundary of the open classroom.

We had three primary objectives in the implementation of the space. We first sought to bring programming into the library in conjunction with our campus partners. We also encouraged teaching librarians and library staff to use the space for classes or other library events, such as drop-in workshops. Both of these efforts were intended to increase our users' exposure to our spaces and the many activities within. Lastly, we hoped that by holding classes and events basically out in the open that we would pique our users' interest and curiosity and motivate them to get more involved in those activities.

Throughout the fall semester, the open classroom was used frequently for lunchtime brown-bag sessions for faculty and led by faculty from the College of Arts and Sciences. Other campus partners offered workshops on academic advising and study abroad information sessions. However, attendance at library-sponsored events was low. Few teaching librarians used the space for instruction, and students were generally uninterested in "dropping in" on the drop-in workshops.

At times, there was some tension between participants in open classroom activities and students working nearby in the Read & Relax area. Noise, specifically, was a problem for both. Instructors and other speakers in the open classroom had difficulty being heard due to the acoustics of the space and the busy, popular, often-loud surrounding area. Participants were often distracted by happenings around them. Comments from the faculty indicate that the background noise level was problematic. One faculty member noted, "Often, students were using the nearby study tables, and those discussions going on made it hard for people in the open classroom to hear the speaker, especially in the back rows of seats, closest to the student groups."

Librarians had a mixed reaction to using the space for library instruction. Only eight of the nearly 200 library instruction sessions in fall 2014 were held in the open classroom. Three instruction librarians were responsible for the eight classes. One instruction librarian who used the space commented, "The space was great for things where you wanted to potentially have external interaction; for example, I used it for an art course where we were looking at our materials collection and then talking about online research. Having other students stop by in that situation was actually interesting and valuable for everyone. Unfortunately, even after orientation changes, the space was distracting for other kinds of instruction. I think we're already battling technology distractions and having noise and foot traffic on top of that made other kinds of teaching difficult."

Librarians who did not teach in the space made the choice to avoid the open classroom based on personal preferences and faculty pushback. When presented with the opportunity to host their class in the open classroom, some faculty members were hesitant because of the perception that students would not be focused in an alternative environment. Librarians were unsure of how to make the space work for a "traditional" library instruction session.

LESSONS LEARNED

After gathering feedback from participants and statistics from event attendance, we found that the open classroom was not working out as originally planned. However, we learned that setting up a space like the open classroom is a fairly low-stakes endeavor. Essentially, we just moved some furniture around and gave the space a name. When the "experiment" didn't work out like we had hoped, we were able to quickly move on to other ideas. Since we knew that we could create this type of space relatively quickly, we were motivated to try the same idea in a different space in the library.

One thing we might do differently is to perform some kind of space-use assessment to determine the best location for a space like the open classroom. On its face, the Read & Relax area seemed like an obvious choice: it's heavily trafficked; there is no expectation of a quiet, studious environment; and it's centrally located in the library. And while we were only able to collect a small number of comments from students, those few comments do indicate that the students liked the "alternative" nature of the space and did not feel that it detracted from their learning. For example, one student remarked, "I felt immersed in the library atmosphere, and I liked the different location from the traditional classroom setting." It would be irresponsible, however, to generalize about students' perception of learning in the open classroom based on the single-digit number of comments we received.

We learned that in order to create an excellent alternative space, we need to strike a balance between space that is visible but also comfortable for librarians and other speakers to work in. A space that is open and well lit but that isn't in a heavily trafficked area. We found such a space on the main floor of the library, near the Research desk, in a space recently reclaimed from the consolidation of a print reference collection and the removal of multiple rows of shelving. The space was tucked into a corner of the building with numerous floor-to-ceiling windows looking out toward our college woods. The layout provides a sense of privacy with the ability for people to move freely in and out of the space. Initially the reclaimed space was set aside as a student study area, but we found that it was easily adapted to dual purposes—as a study space and as a flexible, open meeting space. In late fall 2014, we moved the furnishings from the open classroom to the new space and named it the Research Room. Our campus partners were invited to use the space and responded favorably to our change.

The Research Room has been in use since spring 2015. It has been used for faculty lunches, presentations, and library instruction sessions. Our next step will be to assess student perceptions of the space on their learning and faculty and librarian perception of the effect of the space on their teaching.

CASE STUDY REFLECTION QUESTION

How might delivering instruction in a non-classroom space impact your teaching or the teaching of your colleagues? What doors might it open; what challenges might it exacerbate?

FURTHER READING

Bennet, Scott. "Learning Behaviors and Learning Spaces." *Portal: Libraries and the Academy* 11, no. 3 (2011): 765–789.

Julian, Suzanne. "Reinventing Classroom Space to Re-Energise Information Literacy Instruction." *Journal of Information Literacy* 7, no. 1 (2013). Accessed December 15, 2015. doi: 10.11645/7.1.1720.

Staley, Laura A. "Using Survey Sites for Information Literacy Scheduling and Teaching." *College and Undergraduate Libraries* 14, no. 3 (2007): 103–106.

Online Resources

Fizika Active Learning: www.fizikagroup.com/active-learning/funding.html

K-12 BluePrint: www.k12blueprint.com/toolkits/active-learning-spaces

Steelcase Active Learning Center Grant: www.steelcase.com/discover/information/education/active-learning-center-grant

CONCLUSION

SUMMARY

We've come to the end of our journey, and we hope that you've found some useful information in this book that will help you craft or at least rethink how you're approaching your Information Literacy program. These are our final reflections on the main areas that all of us have struggled with over time and have found some solutions that might be of assistance with your own efforts. Taking things one step at a time and being persistent are perhaps two of the biggest lessons we learned along the way. We tend to get overwhelmed by our own ideas, and we forget that often the best thing to do is just start somewhere. Anywhere. And see how it goes. And if one way doesn't work, try another, and another.

Think like an entrepreneur: start small, fail quickly, and plan for scalability. Creating too many committees and attempting to plan out too much in advance works against this innovative drive. Instead, developing pilot programs is a way to focus on the idea rather than the logistics. Finding a few people who are willing to help you get something started is often the most important part of the journey. And don't be afraid to fail. That's often when we learn the most. Being able to say this worked and this didn't is as important as proving that you are successful all the time.

PEDAGOGY AND CURRICULUM

We are all well aware of the new framework that is being discussed and implemented at most, if not all, academic libraries. Everyone is struggling with this new model and trying to figure out how to best adapt it within their own institutional contexts. This will likely continue for some time to come, and the best advice we can give you is to keep trying different things and see what works! Just as there isn't a clear-cut threshold concept, there isn't one way to implement and approach this very complex schematic.

Determining what to teach, how to teach it, and when to teach it is a mammoth task. Think about your overall program and what you really want to have students accomplish at the end of the day. Forget about what you think you should do, and focus on what you can do and what's best for your students. Then you can unpack the most important elements from each concept and design your program from there. Keep in mind those mapping assets and decide where each piece of your program fits into the larger world of the university's course offerings and time lines. Begin to think across time and curriculum with your approach as opposed to focusing on just your one-shot session. It's better to teach fewer classes that are well developed than squeeze in 100 lecture-based sessions simply to beef up your numbers. Think about quality over quantity and how you can tell the story behind the numbers.

In addition, think about those outside the library who can help you—instructional designers and IT colleagues can assist you in making decisions about what format to use and even make tutorials and videos to help extend the reach of your face-to-face sessions into the virtual environment. Use free instructional design tools to create small learning objects that can have a significant impact and can save you time, for example, you won't have to cover how to search a database when your wonderful two-minute thingamajig does just that.

FORMING PARTNERSHIPS BOTH INTERNAL AND EXTERNAL

You cannot do this alone, no matter how much you would like to! You will need to strengthen the relationships you already have with your allies and develop new ones even with folks who might not be all that willing!

Having a clarity of vision for what you want to accomplish can go a long way toward convincing others to help you. One of the authors recently had the experience of approaching an important director on campus about a possible collaboration only to be asked, "What can the library do for me that I cannot do myself?" When several possibilities were suggested and the meeting ended without any clear follow-up items, it seemed like the end of the road. Only a few months later, that same director contacted the author again to say he had thought more about it and was interested in pursuing one of the ideas discussed. That was the beginning of a brand-new partnership that is continuing to grow as we speak. Granted, there was a little bit of luck involved, but the director would've never come back to the author had that initial connection not been made.

If you're beginning to feel like a used-car salesperson, good! Talking with people face to face can be more effective than 1,000 emails, no matter how lovely they might be! And knowing how to toot your own horn is equally important. Let everyone know what you're doing even if you think they won't care or they haven't asked to see anything from you. In fact, seeing your assessment results and hearing about your success stories might prompt administrators to pay attention to what you're doing and get them to support your work.

LOGISTICAL ISSUES

Wouldn't it be lovely if we all had unlimited amounts of money and staffing and our classrooms were models of best-practice learning spaces? Right, and then we wake up. Staffing and funding is always going to be a challenge, so you will once again need to think through a ninja-style approach to how you will recruit assistance where you might not have any.

Fellowships, assistantships, internships, and even volunteer(ships) make great programs to funnel student support into your program if there is absolutely no way you can hire full-time staff or faculty. If you cannot get physical people to help, see about online options and what things can be covered virtually to free you up for face-to-face components. You can also train your faculty colleagues to cover these things themselves if there's really no one else to do it. And yes, it might not be as perfect as if you had a well-trained army of minions to do your bidding, but at least you won't have to say no, or worse, shut down your program because you lack staffing.

Learning spaces pose equally broad challenges. They can be inflexible, dark, uninspiring, and downright scary, and the mere thought of doing a remodel sends your boss into a fit, especially during these times of budgetary hardship. See if you can get donations from industry vendors to test out their equipment or seek grant opportunities for renovations. Talk to IT about reconfiguring the existing space without having to do any construction or move any power ports that always seems to be the sticking point.

If all else fails, teach somewhere else on campus or empty the room completely and ask students to bring or check out laptops. The bottom line is that you will have to change where the space cannot. Don't be so reliant on a specific configuration that without it you are completely lost; equally, don't let it detract so much from your activities that it becomes a barrier to engaging teaching methods, which should be about the activities and the content, not about the bells and whistles.

We find ourselves at a unique moment in the history of higher education; all of this work would not be possible without building communities of practice that can share knowledge and expertise to position libraries as catalysts for change. Nowhere is that shift more important than in our instructional work, and we leave you with one last thought: you are shaping and influencing students and their academic path, perhaps even their lives, and for that we thank you.

INDEX

About the Authors

CINTHYA M. IPPOLITI is associate dean for research and learning services at Oklahoma State University. She has over 15 years of experience in creating information literacy programs and teaching credit courses in institutions ranging from large universities to community colleges. In 2016 she participated in the Leading Change Institute. In addition, Ippoliti has led professional development workshops for librarians on design thinking, assessment, and incorporating technology into instruction.

RACHEL W. GAMMONS is head of teaching and learning services at University of Maryland Libraries, where she coordinates first-year programming, information literacy, and assessment efforts. In 2015, she participated in the American Library Association's Emerging Leader program. Gammons has published numerous works on teaching and assessment in the academic library. She earned both a master's degree in information systems and a bachelor's degree in art history and English literature from the University of Tennessee as well as a master's degree in English literature from West Chester University.